When Richard died Janet not only lost her husband, she lost her job, her position in the community, his income and their home.

We have been trying to help her put her life together again.

The Corporation of the Sons of the Clergy was established 300 years ago, in Cromwell's time, to give support to clergy and their families in times of crisis.

We give cash grants to clergy and their dependants for a variety of reasons – to elderly retired clergymen or widows, for instance, who find heating or repair bills more than they can manage, for school uniforms, to provide books for ordinands in training, to help divorced clergy and their wives at the painful period of separation.

It isn't enough, of course. No cash grant can take the place of a loving husband, a father to see the children through the difficult years of adolescence, a leader in the parish, a breadwinner, a priest. But it is something; among other things it is a reminder that people care.

With your help we could do more. Please help us – in whatever way you can – with a legacy, a covenant or a donation.

Corporation of the Sons of the Clergy

I Dean Trench Street, London SWIP 3HB.   Tel: 0171–799 3696.

Charity 207736

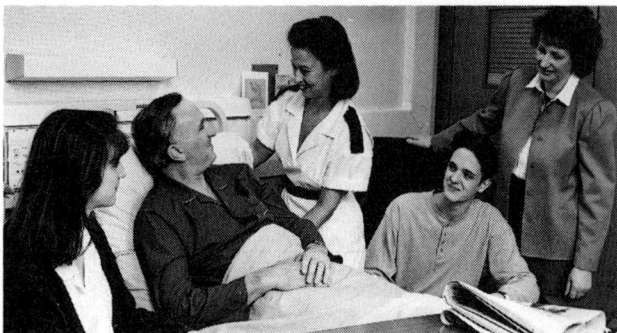

CHURCH PULPIT

YEAR BOOK

*A Complete set of Expository Outlines for
the Sundays of the Year, also for Saints' Days
& Special Occasions*

1996

CHANSITOR PUBLICATIONS

Published 1995 by Chansitor Publications,
a wholly owned imprint of Hymns
Ancient and Modern Limited, St Mary's
Works, St Mary's Plain, Norwich,
Norfolk, NR3 3BH

ISBN 1-85175-098-3

Photoset by Rowland Phototypesetting Limited,
Bury St Edmunds, Suffolk
Printed in Great Britain by
St Edmundsbury Press Limited, Bury St Edmunds, Suffolk

Preface

Shrines, not Museums

The Sherborne Abbey West Window affair has attracted considerable publicity in the national Press, with more informed reviewing in the excellent 'Church Building' magazine. The point is whether a decayed and washed-out Victorian window – albeit with the revered name of Pugin attached to the remains – should be retained, or replaced by a brilliant design by a leading stained-glass artist of today, John Hayward. The case is (at the time of writing) undecided, since the Victorian Society has appealed against the Chancellor's decision in favour of the Hayward design – solidly supported, incidentally, by the Parish.

What has really been going on behind the scenes is a conflict between those who want to conserve everything from the past, precisely because it *is* from the past, and those who believe that buildings are living things, and that works of are have life, and sometimes die. This was put tellingly by Lawrence Lee, doyen of our stained-glass artists, who wrote to the Chancellor:

'Over the years there has arisen an army of experts whose efforts in many fields I would commend; but now, growing ever more intrusive into the life of Diocese and Parish, tend to defend poor quality works simply because they have *historical* rather than *artistic* importance. Inevitably this has led to regarding our churches as museums rather than living communities. In a museum you are safe, you may display any work – good or bad – as having some place in historical development. But a church is a living organism, serving the people of its Parish. It takes risks, it may make mistakes, but this is how life proceeds!'

We parish clergy have a unique and important role in caring for our churches; may we continue to maintain them as living shrines, illustrating the story of the People of God and their encounter with Him, with all that art and craft can offer.

Francis Stephens
Editor

CHANSITOR PUBLICATIONS

Preliminary Note

For each Sunday of the year, two sermons are provided. The *first* is for the main Service, assumed to be the Eucharist and at which the Readings will be those from the ASB, simply because of the wider range over the Holy Scriptures compared with the older Book. Where possible links are provided with the BCP, and in any case the indexes of *Subjects* and *Texts* (at the back of the book) can be consulted to find an outline that suits or can be adapted.

The *second* outline is nominally for use at Evening Prayer and has a text usually from the ASB EP Readings; but freedom is taken to deal with other subjects from time to time. Included this year is a feature that has met with approval in previous editions – Material for sermons or discussions on half-a-dozen evenings each in Lent, Summer and Autumn (Prayer, The Faith, Beliefs).

For Saints' Days and special occasions *one* outline is provided, to be used at the Eucharist or Evensong as desired. In any case the Editor hopes that users will feel free to adapt and alter to suit the needs of particular churches or congregations.

A few alterations to the Calendar have been taken from 'The Promise of His Glory' (e.g. The Confession of St Peter, 18th January, as an introduction to Unity Week)

Comments and suggestions are always welcome and should be addressed to the Editor; as also material for possible use in future editions.

*Acknowledgements:*The Editor gratefully acknowledges permission from the Central Board of Finance of the Church of England to reproduce material from *The Alternative Service Book 1980; Lent, Holy Week and Easter; The Promise of His Glory;* and *Patterns for Worship.* Thanks also to many other sources, from individuals and schools of thought, for help with this publication. He trusts that the use of material will be forgivingly regarded as a small aid to the advancement of the Kingdom. Special thanks are due to the Revd Philip Buckler, the Revd Howard Hollis, the Revd Tom Devonshire Jones, the Revd Mark Oakley, the Revd John Ovenden, the Revd Canon Phillip Roberts, the Revd John Slater, the Revd Dr John Thewlis and the Revd Joanna Yates, for their contributions and help.

CONTENTS

For Indexes of Texts and Subjects, please see end of book. The ASB readings are for Year 2, changing to Year 1 on 27 October 1996.

SERMONS FOR SAINTS' DAYS
AND SPECIAL OCCASIONS

Advent Sunday *Fourth Sunday before Christmas*
3 December 1995 **The Day**

'It is far on in the night; day is near' Romans 13.12 (ASB NT Reading),
or, *'Now is our salvation nearer than when we believed. The night is
far spent, the day is at hand.' Romans 13.11,12 (BCP Epistle)*

A Note of Triumph

St Paul has a note of triumph in his writing to the Romans. He
looks ahead into the future with confidence and hope, unlike
some thinkers who dismiss history because they believe it moves
simply in cycle after cycle, each period repeating itself as time
moves inexorably onward. For St Paul, and for all of us who call
ourselves Christians, we look to the future; not back to some
hypothetical Golden Age of the past. Our religion is not a religion
of pessimism nor of fatalism, but a religion of hope.

Just as Lent looks forward to the gladness and joy of Easter,
so Advent looks forward to the wonderful and happy event of
Christmas. Through all this season we are being taught to remember the first coming of the Christ, that coming 'in great humility',
while at the same moment we look forward to the promise of the
Lord to come again at the end of Time. That end of the age is to be
the summing-up of all history in Christ himself; for he promises to
come again in glory as Redeemer and as Judge.

Double View

This double view gives Advent its particular flavour and meaning;
we are rejoicing in what is to come, the Birth of the Saviour, and
the joy and hope which that brings to our hearts – yet at the
same time there is the element of trepidation as we consider
Christ's coming as Judge. His coming as Saviour 'in great humility' and as the supreme revelation of God in the Person of the
Incarnate Son, the Christ who was born, grew, taught, ministered, died, rose from the grave, ascended to heaven, while leaving his Church to work his will for humanity – all this we know
and believe. His coming again is to complete the work of redemption in summing up its results; for us this must mean a mixture
of trepidation and hope. His promise is, to come at the end of
the age and claim his true followers to be with him, himself, in
the joy of the Father's presence.

The summing-up of all history will, we believe, be our vindication as believers in Jesus Christ, in his message, in his teachings, in his sufferings and in his death and resurrection.

Our Vindication
The Advent message, the Advent call, is as contemporary to our needs as ever it was. The faith that Christ will claim us as his own, and will present us before the Almighty Father, with much joy, is a belief that gives dignity, significance and point to our lives.

The fact that the final summing up of the history of this fragile planet of ours, will be our vindication as believers in Jesus, tells us that our human lives have both meaning and reward. Human life is not, after all, empty and at best a dream, but the gift of the God who made us and who will claim us for his own.

A PRAYER FOR THE COMING OF THE LORD

Come to your Church as Lord and Judge:
Help us to live in the light of your coming
and give us a longing for your rule.
Maranatha
Come, Lord Jesus.

Come to your world as King of the nations,
Before you all rulers will stand in silence.
Maranatha
Come, Lord Jesus.

Come to your people with the message of victory and peace.
Give us the victory over death, temptation and evil.
Maranatha
Come, Lord Jesus.

Come to us as Saviour and Comforter,
Break in to those areas of our life
where we live with failure and distress,
and set us free to serve you for ever.
Maranatha
Come, Lord Jesus.

Come to us from heaven with power and great glory
to lift us up to meet you,
with all your saints and angels,

2

to live with you for ever.
Maranatha
Come, Lord Jesus

(Patterns for Worship, p. 65)

Advent Sunday *Second Sermon* Santa Claus

'Jesus said, "Let the children come to me, do not hinder them; for to such belongs the Kingdom of God."' Mark 10.4 (Cloud of Witnesses: St Nicholas)

A Very Popular Saint

On Wednesday this week, December 6th, the Church commemorates St Nicholas, better known as 'Santa Claus', and one of the most popular saints both in the East and in the West. Although so popular, no more is known of him than that he was bishop of Myra in Lycia in Asia Minor during the first half of the fourth century AD. He is said to have been present at the Council of Nicaea (325 AD) which formulated the Creed after the teaching of St Athanasius, and set up the four Patriarchates (Jerusalem, Antioch, Alexandria, and Rome) on a level of spiritual equality. The emperor Justinian dedicated a church to St Nicholas at Constantinople about two centuries later; but historically Nicholas remains a shadowy figure.

His 'Life'

The 'Life' of St Nicholas consists mainly of a string of edifying acts of charity and some spectacular miracles, which testify rather to the creative imagination of the biographer, than to any historical accuracy.

Thus, he is said to have answered the prayers of some storm-tossed sailors and, joining them in their boat, to have quietened the fury of the waves; then appearing in a dream to the Emperor Constantine, he induced him to pardon three innocent 'princes' who were in prison awaiting execution; he provided wheat for his country during a famine, by persuading the crews of Alexandrian ships to unload some of their grain on the understanding that, when they reached their destination, they would find their cargoes undiminished: he restored to life three boys who – during another famine – had been killed, cut up (after the style of

3

Sweeney Todd) and thrown into a pickling tub, by an innkeeper who had no meat to set before his guests. These and other marvels made Nicholas a most popular patron, especially in sea ports.

His Churches

In England 372 churches are dedicated to St Nicholas, seven to SS Mary & Nicholas, and one to SS Nicholas & Swithin. In our churches mediaeval representations of him are rare, though there are eight of his miracles depicted in stained glass in Hillesden Church, Bucks., in a most attractive style; and in North Moreton, Berks., the east window includes some incidents in his life.

Nicholas is usually depicted as a bishop fully vested, in either Western or more rarely in Greek style, accompanied by the three boys in their tub; or he may be holding a ship. His best-known emblem is to be seen suspended over pawnbrokers' shops; St Nicholas is patron saint of pawnbrokers, who adopted for their sign three golden balls, these representing the three bags of gold which the saint left by stealth, one night after another, at the home of an impoverished father, to serve as dowries for his three daughters, and save them from being sold off into a life of sin.

On the Continent

Abroad, and especially in Holland, St Nicholas appears before Christmas as the rewarder of good children, riding through the streets on his horse, in full canonicals, with a bagful of presents. He is accompanied by his servant 'Die Schwartz', who with a large broom or whip deals out punishments to the badly-behaved or truant schoolchildren.

From this figure derives our more usual 'Santa Claus' (St Nicholas) so well-known in Christmas tales; and nowadays too often replaced by the entirely secular 'Father Christmas' who hands out gifts in our stores, or may be seen spreading Christmas cheer – sometimes more than a little alcoholical – with his hand-bell and 'Ho,ho,ho!' – in US streets.

A CHRISTMAS PRAYER

Almighty Father, lover of souls,
who chose your servant Nicholas
to be a bishop in the Church,
that he might give freely

out of the treasures of your grace;
make your people mindful
of the needs of others,
and as they have themselves received,
so teach them also to give;
through Jesus Christ our Lord.
('Cloud of Witnesses' & 'The Promise of His Glory')

Second Sunday of Advent *Third Sunday before Christmas*
10 December **The Scriptures**

'All the ancient scriptures were written for our own instruction, in order that through the encouragement they give us we may maintain our hope with fortitude.' Romans 15.4 (ASB NT Reading).

Authority

An academic teacher friend said that he thought we Christians spent too much time discussing rather academic questions – how we should behave, as Christians, in various imagined situations.

Jesus himself, you will remember, was often surrounded by people asking what we might consider as 'academic' questions – Who is my neighbour? Is it lawful to heal on the Sabbath? If seven brothers in turn married the same woman . . . ? Some of the questioners were maliciously trying to trap him, some wanted to test the credentials of this apparently unqualified rabbi – others just wanted a good solid theological discussion.

In our own time, many devout people would be happier if there were an authoritative answer to be found for all situations that might occur in life. It would certainly be convenient to have a Bible provided with an index for texts to solve all current problems; one could look up 'The Common Market', or 'National Lottery' and find an immediate answer! But the Bible does not work like that.

Yet, we are obliged constantly to consider how our faith works out in the real world in which we live, and we do believe that there is a Bible-based and Christ-centred way of dealing with our affairs and our living.

The essential thing is to be clear and honest about the difference between eternal values and temporal ones. As we try to avoid being dogmatic in the wrong way, let us not heed those who tell us that nothing is certain, that there are no abiding principles. Christians must know what they believe, and in Whom they believe; and what is expendable and what is irreducible.

Principles

The principle of love is eternal, the love that rests not on convenience nor on emotional liking, but on selfless, sacrificial concern. Our belief in this is different in kind from our belief, for example, in the secret ballot or in freedom of speech; these are rightly called good and are to be upheld – but not as principles by which the universe is governed. There could be circumstances in which they would no longer be good, for their goodness is dependent on their implementing the principle of total respect for individuals, as images of God. On the other hand, racialism – though in one sense a limited and localized problem – is to be condemned as an offence against that same respect; and the Christian cannot surely imagine any circumstances in which it would be admissible.

The other side of the picture is just as important.

Although the values of human society are not eternal and absolute, they are not necessarily contemptible. The Christian is certainly not to support the Establishment at all costs, but neither is he to be antagonistic simply for the sake of antagonism. We have been created to live in our country in this century – here is our time and our place – this is where we are to exercise our freewill. We have a duty towards society, to find and foster what is good in it, as well as opposing what is bad. If this is indeed God's world, as the Bible tells us and as we believe it is, we cannot set it and its values in contradiction to him. Yes, it is a fallen world, a corrupt world, but it is a world that still bears the stamp of his continuing creation. Its communities and institutions – any of them, not just the Church – can be channels of his enabling love.

Choice

Let us live, then, neither totally rejecting nor refusing to see and condemn that which is corrupt. Not to choose at all is the worst of choices; it is to be joined with those who made what Dante calls 'the great refusal', and who were fit for neither heaven nor hell. This world is the world which 'God so loved that he gave his only-begotten Son' and it is for the moment entrusted to us, to this generation.

It may be that in the light of eternity much about which we are now passionate will seem trivial. But that does not dispense us from being passionate according to the light by which we are now walking. Passionate, yes, but with charity towards those who differ from us. The tensions between eternal values and temporary commitment is resolved through our trust in God. Christian life, with its enormous corporate responsibilities, is still always in essence an individual encounter, and individual acceptance. What matters is not what the Bible might have said about the Common Market, but what it is saying to you and me, here and now.

The Christian Way

To know the eternal, to give due honour to the temporary to commit all to God – that is the way of the Christian. It was the world, the human society, that killed the Lord Jesus on Calvary. It was into the world, into human society, that he rose again. And it is into the world, the human society, that he sent and sends his Spirit, to be a bridge between this world and that which we call heaven, until the world itself shall end.

What is the Holy Spirit saying to you, what is he calling you to do, demanding of you as your loving duty? What is he showing you more deeply about yourself, as we begin another year of the Church's Life in this Advent season? That is not an academic question.

Advent 2 *Second Sermon* The Word of God and the Work of God

'All Scripture is inspired by God and is useful for teaching the faith and correcting errors, for re-setting the direction of our life and for training us in good living.' 2 Timothy 3.16 (ASB EP)

Witness

We should remember that these words were written about the Old Testament Scriptures, and if St Paul could witness to their truth in those days, what should the Bible be to us, who have also the whole New Testament Scriptures! The fact is that all these holy writings will unfold to our hearts and our souls and our minds, as we receive them and believe them, the will of God, as summed up in and by our Lord Jesus Christ. They will indeed prove to be the witness of the Father to the Son, in order to set forth our salvation in the Son, as mediated to our souls by the Holy Spirit.

Inspiration

The Bible is authoritative to us, because it is God's inspired word to us. By the term 'inspiration' we should understand that 'the Spirit of God has been at work in a writer; and just as the Bible as a whole is the record of God's revelation of himself in Israel and in Jesus, so we believe that as a whole it is inspired by God'. So said the Lambeth Report in the 1960s; and that statement still stands as a formal recognition of Bible truth and how we should regard it.

The messages of the Bible are the utterances of the mind of God, revealed to human beings: it was Gregory the Great who said 'The heart of God is in the words of God.' The Bible has a spiritual power and a moral power, properly understood; in it God speaks through human minds and brains, which have the various biases and outlooks of their times and places, and make the errors and accept the varied world-views of their periods and cultures. Without doubt the readers of our books in some distant future will smile or frown at what we have said about many events and thoughts of our small day! The ideas, the hatreds, the despairs and the prejudices of any author will show through what each has written: it is impossible to read some of the Psalms, for instance, without seeing exactly this. Yet we accept the Bible as inspired, because every book – some to a greater extent than others – reveals to us God's plan for this world, tells us things that God wants us to know, and shows us what he wants us to do for him.

The Work of God

Understanding, through study and prayer, of God's Word enables us to do God's work; by the use of holy Scripture the believer is continually being instructed more fully in holy living. So the gift of God's Word has as its aim the complete equipment of the believer, in life and in service, together with the inspiration from God to take up and shoulder the task, gladly and willingly. To quote the Lambeth Fathers again: 'All should read the Bible as nourishment for the soul, with prayer that the Holy Spirit may stir mind and heart and will, in response to it.'

In this way we shall be able to grow in grace and experience the power of the Holy Spirit in our souls.

> *Lord God, you feed us with living bread from heaven;*
> *you renew our faith,*
> *increase our hope,*
> *and strengthen our love.*
> *Teach us to hunger*
> *for Christ who is the true and living bread,*
> *and to live by every word*
> *that comes from your mouth,*
> *through Jesus Christ our Lord.*
> *(Patterns for Worship, p. 162)*

Third Sunday of Advent *Second Sunday before Christmas*
17 December   Joy in the Lord

'Rejoice in the Lord always; again I say, Rejoice!' Phil. 4.4 (ASB NT Reading)

Frivolity!

A clerical friend tells the story of how he once took an exchange with a priest of the Scottish Episcopal Church; that means the Episcopalian came to his parish for a few weeks, while our friend went up to a beautiful but rather remote part of the Highlands and looked after the Episcopalians there. It was something of a holiday for both clerics, and of course far from being expensive.

On his first Sunday there, our friend, making his way to the Church, saw a tall man dressed in solemn black, with a high clerical collar, bearing down on him. Our friend knew this must be the Minister of the Wee Frees, the Free Presbyterian Church; and he had been warned that the Minister was something of a severe and strict person. So our friend did his best, smiled and said 'Good Morning.' The Minister looked hard at him, and then said lugubriously, 'I have nae time for frivolity on the Sabbath.' And walked on.

Our friend thought later, when he read our passage from Philippians that morning, that the Minister's approach was something of a contrast to St Paul's writing 'Rejoice in the Lord, always; again I say, Rejoice!'

Rejoice!

We know that what the Apostle says is right; of course we should rejoice as Christians, filled with the joy of Christ, especially as we look forward in this season of Advent, to the commemoration of the Lord's birth at Christmas. Yet, sometimes, we do feel something of a Puritan streak in us – or most of us – a streak which holds us back and suggests that we should take Jesus so very seriously, so very soberly, that any lightness of heart seems out of place. Not so with Paul.

When he wrote – or dictated – these words, he was in prison, awaiting trial, most probably in Rome itself, in conditions that may have varied from very unpleasant to quite appalling. He was chained up; he was dependent on friends or the compassionate for food and the least of comforts, and had the knowledge that at any moment he might be taken out and faced with torture or execution. And yet – in these circumstance – he writes 'Rejoice!'

Uncertainties

Paul was writing to people who shared his uncertainties. The Philippians were also under stress and fear. Philippi was very Roman in its outlook, and the new Christian 'movement' was the object of thorough dislike. Philippi was 'more Roman than the Romans' – its lucrative trade had gained it the honour and dignity of a Roman 'Colony' and it was very possible that the Roman law might be invoked strictly against any sect that could be seen as undermining the Roman way of life and the Roman ideals.

In this stressful atmosphere, it was not only surprising that Paul could himself rejoice, but even more so that he should call on the Philippian Christians to rejoice. Can we explain this?

Perhaps the best analogy we can think of is this: Consider a little child enjoying himself. He does so without any care for the morrow, without a care in the world. He trusts his parents completely; they will care for him, they love him, so all will be well. With such abandonment he throws himself into the life of the moment. Let us translate this into adult life: We do have our moments of unconfined, unalloyed pleasure; perhaps connected with the family – a son or daughter is married, a grandchild is born. Perhaps when someone close to us achieves promotion, or the position he or she has looked for and worked for; or some unexpected joy or happiness suddenly comes into their life. We rejoice! And there are no strings, no worries any longer, no fears.

John the Baptist

Besides Paul, there is another very notable figure in our readings today, who is also in prison. John the Baptist – held in prison after the discreditable affair of King Herod's new wife (Mark 6.14–20). John is the example the Church holds before us for her ministers – not only the forerunner of Christ but a devoted preacher and teacher of much in the way of morality and faith, that was indeed to be confirmed and extended by the Lord himself. With all this, John yet placed himself far below the Saviour he proclaimed – 'I am not worthy to undo his sandal-strap' – a place of service, simplicity and devotion. The ideal for all clergy down the ages!

Jesus is clear in his answer to the critics – John is a prophet, and more; a herald who prepares the way for One greater, far greater than himself – and yet, John is the 'destined Elijah', the last figure in the old era of the Law and the Prophets.

Violence

The strange reference to 'violence' and 'violent men' is a mystery; it may refer to the vigour with which we should strive to reach the ideals and aims of the Lord – yet Jesus himself never used force. Some theologians have taken these words to mean that if it is not possible to persuade people into the Kingdom, then they should be bullied, forced into accepting the Gospel. Surely this is an echo of primitive times, the days of persecution of Catholics by Protestants, or of Protestants by Catholics, or the 'mass conversions' of Anglo-Saxon days, or of the Indians in South America, under the Spanish conquests. Such times have long gone; yet blunt and plain speaking, and warnings, cannot be omitted from the Gospel message. But in the end, it is mutual love and acceptance that makes the growth of the Kingdom; love is the letting go of fear, and it is through the sacrificial operation of love that fear, and the violence that comes from fear, can eventually be overcome. Rejoice!

Advent 3 *Second Sermon* **The Vision**

'Get you up to a high mountain, O Zion, herald of good tidings; lift up your voice with strength, O Jerusalem, herald of good tidings, lift it up, fear not: say to the cities of Judah, "Behold your God!"' Isaiah 40.9 (ASB ET)

Looking Ahead

Our thoughts about our country and our government are influenced strongly by the conception of a progressive society, in which everyone will have their rights to such things as a fair wage, employment, retirement pensions, decent treatment all round, decent living conditions and so on. How is this to be achieved? There should be better education, more science and more scientific ways of doing things, less taxes, proper 'cradle to grave' provision for the care of the disabled, the sick, the elderly, and of course full rights for all. Little is said about duties! Yet, here we are, having just remembered the devastation of World War II, and with the reports and pictures of war and brutality, cruelty and distress, all too clearly displayed day by day on our TV screens and in our papers. We see all round us a more violent society, a snatch and grab ideology, cruelty and bloodshed which would have seemed unbearable to our grandparents. There is an unwillingness to accept authority – of whatever kind – a feeling of dissatisfaction in general, and the desire for more money and more material satisfactions.

Failure . . .

The truth is that because of sin and selfishness, greed and love of power, there is in all human plans and efforts the seeds of failure, however well-meaning the attempts may be. Does this mean we should give up, drop all our ideals, 'take arms against a sea of troubles', adopt some apparently promising political party line as the cure of all human troubles? Politics can never be the answer, as a brief glimpse into the past will show all too clearly.

What can be done?

Let us go back to the words of the ancient prophets – typified by the grand proclamation of Isaiah we have just heard. What is needed is a recognition of the weakness and seeds of failure in all human plans. Divine grace is the only true and lasting counteraction; we are called to recognize God our Creator, teach ourselves his laws, repent of our mistakes and sins. Only our co-operation with divine grace will truly bring God's Kingdom on this earth of ours.

The Vision
Repentance brings forgiveness and mercy. Isaiah sees the day of the Coming of the Lord; God will usher in the perfect Kingdom. Often seen in the terms of freedom and redemption:

> *'Fear not, for I have redeemed you; I have*
> *called you by name, you are mine . . .' (43.1.)*

The Kingdom was often thought of in terms of a banquet, a feast, a time of unalterable joy: 'On this mountain the Lord of Hosts will prepare a banquet of rich fare for all the people' (25.6).

It is by faith that we believe this, and what we know of God in Christ gives us this confidence: 'On this day it will be said: See, this is our God, for whom we have waited that he might save us. This is the Lord; we have waited for him; let us be glad and rejoice in his salvation.' (25.9)

The Kingdom
The promise was fulfilled in Christ. He came preaching the Kingdom, and by his Advent the Kingdom came with power. By his death and resurrection we see evil decisively defeated. We see the fulfilment of the promise that 'death is swallowed up for ever'. And yet, the perfect Kingdom is yet to be. It waits the fulfilment of God's purpose, and will be brought into being by God himself. Meantime, our task is to make our lives more fitted for that perfect Kingdom, more just, more righteous, more compassionate, more loving. On differing political policies and parties we may be divided, but in doctrine and faith we are, as Christians, united. We work by divine grace, to permeate society with Christian ideals and standards, and so to hasten the coming of that perfect Day.

Fourth Sunday of Advent *Sunday next before Christmas*
24 December   Expectation
'Rejoice, daughter of Zion; I am coming and I will make my dwelling among you, says the Lord.' Zechariah 2.10 (ASB OT Reading)

Meeting
Advent is the Alpha and Omega, the Beginning and the End, of
our Christian foundation. In Advent our past and our future meet
and join with our present. Here we find the true meaning of
birth: for birth is the beginning of a present born out of the past,
which will change the future. Mary and Joseph knew and
accepted the realization of these facts in their lives. So it is that
we should be preparing in Advent to accept these realizations in
our own lives.

Advent is the time that we should look at and consider the
traditions that shape our Christian beliefs. Darkness and light;
hope and fulfilment; that First Advent – and the Second Advent;
the Promise, the End and the Beginning.

Waiting
Advent arrives after the leaves of autumn have fallen, when the
nights are growing longer; winter is here, yet thoughts of new
life stir vaguely, not clearly expressed, as yet.

Advent is our time of pregnancy, of expectation; our time of
waiting through the darkness, through the cold, through the
threat of the hazards of the approaching winter depths. And in
our waiting there is a strange silence. It is a silence of darkness
and light – the silence before the first cry of birth; the silence
before the cry of new hope and new life.

Listening
Advent is as though the world were listening; waiting with bated
breath, ears straining to catch the cry of a Child. The silence is the
silence of hope and of expectation; an attentive, urgent, anxious
listening and hushed waiting to hear the Word of God. It is as
when the Mother waits for the first stirrings of the birth of her
Child – she waits with anxious hope to be able to gaze on the
face of the One whom, for so long, so many months, she has
known without knowing, loved without seeing.

So we, during Advent, wait to see God's face in the Child,
hear in the silence the wonderful words of promise, of hope, and
of peace.

Peace
As in a favourite prayer – the second Collect at Evensong – 'Give
to your servants that peace which the world cannot give' – we pray
for the miracle of peace which only God can provide us with.

The cry of birth is the cry of a new promise; our world is hearing, one after another, new cries of promise. Cries that can be painful, as countries and peoples that have been at war and enmity, engaged in violence for years, yet struggle with the birth-pangs of letting go of the past, now looking to the future, while wrestling, agonizing, with the present.

The Way Through
God is the mother and the father holding us as we seek to find our way through the darkness into the light – as we wait in the strange silence for the new thing, the new-born miracle, the peace. The peace of God which the world cannot give; the peace that Mary found after the Annunciation, in the months of waiting, in the reconciliation with Joseph, in their journey to Bethlehem, with the growing Child who was to save his people from their sins, and in her fearful and awesome yet wonderful calling, to be the Mother of God.

The peace of Christ is not an easy peace; it is the touch of the Child whose hands will be pierced, whose feet will be nailed, whose side will be wounded. It is the peace of Mary doing what she knows to be God's will, bonded to her husband yet wounding him deeply, and her own soul pierced too. And she also deeply afraid, with a future of pain and love, of mystery and challenge; yet with the promise of joy and eventual triumph.

Not Easy . . .
No, it is not an easy peace; it is painful and demanding. Yet the peace of God can be found within all our own everyday struggles; when we seek for confidence in ourselves, for confidence and true self-love; when we struggle within our relationships to give of ourselves unselfishly; and within our world to strive to bring peace rooted in justice and love.

> *Lord, Child of Peace, give us peace.*
> *Lord, Child of Peace, make us instruments of your peace.*
> *Child of Peace, let me know that I will live in your peace,*
> *   a peace without doubt, difficulties and darkness.*
> *Child of Peace, welcome us to your peace.*
>
> S.W.

Advent 4 *Second Sermon* **Christmas Eve**

'In the morning you shall see the glory of the Lord.' Exodus 16.7, *or,*
'The glory of the Lord shall be revealed, and all humanity shall see it.'
Isaiah 40.5 *(ASB Sentences)*

What does Christmas mean to you?

Christmas means different things to us at different times of our
lives. In the beginning when we were little children, it meant the
presents we received. There was the Tree, decorated from top to
bottom, and around it were the presents, the most wonderful
presents in the world, in those days when just some nuts and
an orange in the toe of a Christmas Stocking seemed superb. As
we began to grow up, there was a change. Christmas began to
mean presents plus people. We began to think not just about the
presents that might come to us, but the presents that we could
get for other people. So, a new dimension was added, consideration for others.

   Then at school – Christmas meant chiefly a holiday, no classes
to attend, no homework; and there were parties and dances, all
the delights that fill the carefree period in a young person's life
– that period that comes, alas, only once. Presents were still
important, but it was people, friends, relatives, that were more
important.

People

As we grew older and one Christmas followed another, so people
began to mean more and more, and things – presents – less and
less. Our Christmas cards now mean more, much more, than our
presents for the simple reason that the cards come from relatives
and friends and people from all over, whose paths at one time
or another have crossed with ours. Sometimes there are messages
from those we have not seen for a long time, or from whom we
do not hear about at any other time. These are what make the
warmth of Christmas as we grow older, the warmth that lies in
the depth of the love or concern of those who care for us.

A Deeper Message

And as Christmas comes to mean that to us, so does the religious
message of the Festival grow more important, deeper and more
central. The Birthday has become the central thing about Christmas Day, and we come to church to kneel before the wonder of

the love of the God who could come into our world, with all its harshness, brutality and irresponsibility, and make himself known in the human shape, walk in our common way of life, carry our burdens, and enjoy the delights of our existence.

As that part of Christmas becomes more and more central, and as the years pass by, some of the people have gone, the presents fade and look shabby, and the parties are all over – but the figure of the Christ Child and the God whom he incarnates, grows in wonder and meaning for us. May that story become ever more fresh and alive and vital to all of us this coming Festival – then indeed we will have the 'Happy Christmas' which is the wish from your clergy and this church, to you all.

Christmas Day Monday 25 December
At Midnight or Early Day **A Cry for Peace**
'Glory to God in the highest and peace on earth, goodwill toward men.'
Luke 2.14 (Gospel, BCP & ASB)

Tonight
The message of the angels to the shepherds, and the words of the song of the Heavenly Host, 'Glory to God in the highest, and peace on earth, goodwill to all people' – these words, that message, is surely the pivot of this season of Christmas. Yet in the last months we seem to have so much evidence of the imperfections in human nature, while trying to achieve any sort of livable peace on earth, in so many places. Deaths, murders, war and cruelty, abroad and at home . . . Still so much violence and destruction . . . it seems almost impossible to find any kind of recipe for seasonal goodwill. Yet we must believe that underlying it all, and unreported in the news as it seems to be, there is a powerful feeling of urgency for the peace and goodwill the angels proclaim.

Conflict
It is true to say that it was not without cost that the Incarnation brought about a conflict of its own. Mary and Joseph and the baby in the humble – if not downright abominable – situation, like so many refugees today – an outdoor shed, draughty and cold, floored with rotten straw soaked in animal urine and drop-

pings, shut off from the overcrowded inn. They were not the first nor the last to encounter such aggressively brutal treatment in their time of need. Thousands of ordinary human beings, men, women and children, are still in need . . . are still being driven from homes or homeland by brutality and greed, by hatred and war.

Our Response
In part I am sure that perhaps largely unconsciously it is the thought of the suffering in our world, the memory of the TV pictures of children and adults at the end of their tether, the sick and the dying, the wounded and prisoners – that brings double and treble the attendance at our Christmas services in the Church – not only here but throughout the land. It is not just that we enjoy singing carols round the Crib for its own sake, or making the effort to come to the Midnight Mass, but because of a genuine and very human desire to know the message of the angels is to come true, in spite of the perilous mistrust of fellow human beings. Here is the challenge offered to the Church and to all of us by the angels – if we are to preach peace and goodwill, then we must so live. We must fight to be able to put down the weapons and mistrust that divide us, we must struggle to restore the common humanity between differing peoples and differing communities. There should be a great surge of pressure throughout the nations enjoying peace, for that peace to be extended to the present distress, hatred and cruelty that is rampant.

Meanwhile, may we all find much peace and goodwill during the Christmas Season; and may every blessing be upon you and those you love, as we kneel at the manger and implore the blessing of the Child.

FOR CHRISTMAS LIGHT

Blessed are you, Lord our God, Judge of all the earth:
your word endures for ever in heaven.
Yet in the stillness of midnight
the Almighty Word
leapt down from his royal throne
and was born in the likeness of man.

> In him, the Word made flesh, was life,
> a life that is the light of men:
> it brings to light what is hidden in dark
> and the darkness will never quench it.
> Rejoice in the light, you people of God.
> For by his light shall the nations walk
> till the whole earth is filled with his praise
> and every tongue confesses that Jesus Christ is Lord
> to the glory of God the Father. Amen.
>
> *(P.H.G., p. 14)*

Christmas Day Monday 25 December
Christmas Presents

'Mary gave birth to her first-born son and wrapped him in swaddling clothes, and laid him in a manger, because there was no room for them in the inn.' Luke 2.7. (A Gospel, ASB)

'The Season of Good Cheer'

The Christmas cards and Christmas calendars, in their jolly and enthusiastic way, call it 'The season of good cheer' – but let's face it, Christmas does tend to put a bit of a strain on pretty well everything, from family relationships right down to the bank overdraft. Whatever else it does, the season costs a lot – and especially when we reckon up the inevitable business of buying the presents. As Christians we are not immune to the problem, and I am sure that all of us here have had our share, one way or another, in the annual Yuletide stakes. Giving away and being given to, however, should make some kind of balance, and the pleasure we give needs to be totted up against the material view of expenses – and of course, what we ourselves received.

As Christians we are not immune from the problem but it is specially important that we, of all people, bear in mind the underlying significance of the annual ritual of giving and receiving of gifts.

God's Present to Us

First of all and most obviously, we give presents to others at Christmas, because it was at Christmas that God gave his present to us. That is just how St Paul describes Jesus Christ in 2 Corinthians (9.15) 'Thanks be to God for his inexpressible gift!' Even our Lord himself seemed to think of himself in such a way, to judge by his words to the Samaritan woman at the well: 'If you knew the gift of God, and who it is that says to you, "Give me a drink", you would have asked him and he would have given you living water.' (John 4.10) This idea of Jesus as the gift of God to humanity is the heart of the Gospel – 'God so loved the world,' as St John tells us (3.16) 'that he *gave* his only-begotten Son.' Only when we keep that fact in the front of our minds will our own Christmas giving make any real sense.

Our Budgets

We, of course, keep an eye on our budgets when we buy our presents. As often as not, we try to get something that looks expensive and good but is really rather cheap. And at the end of it all, we sit down with our receipts and cheque-book and cards, and try to count the cost of it. Not so with God! His was an act of complete self-giving, and one in which he refused to count the cost, as Calvary and the Cross so clearly show us. But, that gift also implies a demand.

An Obligation

Throughout the Old Testament we find the assumption that a gift lays the recipient under an obligation to the giver. Whether it is the Queen of Sheba's gifts to Solomon, or Jacob's gifts to Esau, there is the same underlying idea that it is necessary for the lesser to give to the greater, if he or she is to find favour. It may well, therefore, have been an unconscious 'insurance policy' that prompted the gifts of the Magi to the Christ-Child; but under the New Dispensation, both giver and receiver operate under new laws.

God's gift to us of his Son is a free gift, without any strings attached. There can be no question of buying the Christ-Child's favour with our gifts to the Crib. St Peter's retort to Simon the magician applies equally well to us: 'May your silver be lost for ever, and you with it, for thinking that money could buy what God has given for nothing!' (Acts 8.20)

Receiving Gifts

But Christmas, besides teaching us the right way to give presents, should also help us to learn the even more difficult lesson of receiving them. Most of us, I think, find it far easier to be the generous giver, than the grateful receiver. When it comes to Christmas presents, it may be comparatively easy to receive them in the right spirit. Even if we don't particularly like what we get, we can usually console ourselves with the reminder 'It's the thought that counts.' Where the lesson of the manger can help us, is in the hundreds of acts of receiving that have to be made in the course of a year. How often do we feel ourselves saying 'Oh, I hate feeling under an obligation.'

We resent feeling indebted, instead of seeing the whole exercise as an exchange of gifts, rather than of obligation. Mary did not *need* the gifts the Wise Men brought her Son, but she accepted them with courtesy, recognizing the greater need of the giver to give than of her to receive.

Those Presents!

Even when it comes to those presents which we can't stand – the hideous table mats from Dear Aunt Maud, or the useless cake knife that will join four others in the kitchen drawer – even then, perhaps, there is a lesson to be drawn from the Crib. I like to take Ronald Knox's advice at such times, and assume as a pious belief that it is quite likely that one of the Magi rode into Bethlehem on a white elephant!

The Gift of all Gifts

May God grant us all a happy and blessed Christmas, and the realization that he is, himself the gift to end all gifts as he comes to us in his Son. The true message of Christmas we can then see to be that what really matters is not the giving and receiving of things, but the giving of God himself to us, and of our acceptance of that gift, which we then celebrate in our self-giving to him, and to one another.

Sunday after Christmas
31 December   The Holy Family

'The parents brought in the child Jesus to do for him what the Law required.' Luke 2.27

Women in the Bible

Today we have something of a celebration of women in the Bible. In the first place, of course, we have Mary, the mother of Jesus, but also we hear about an Old Testament character, Hannah the mother of that great figure of Hebrew history, Samuel; and we hear, in the Gospel, something of Anna the prophetess who 'served God day and night' in the Temple, and joined with the devout old man Simeon – whose name we should bless every time we sing or recite the 'Nunc dimittis' – 'Lord, now lettest thou thy servant depart in peace . . .' – in praising God for the Child Jesus, the Saviour born for our deliverance.

Ancestors

If we look at the first chapter of St Matthew's Gospel, we find a genealogy of that Saviour, with a fascinating list of characters. The patriarch Abraham, Isaac and Jacob and Judah, then suddenly amidst the males, a woman – Tamar, mother of Perez and Zerah. A complicated story hers, which you can read about in chapter 38 of Genesis. Later we come to another woman, Ruth, surely one of our favourite Bible characters. She was an outsider, a non-Hebraic woman, a Moabitess, who yet clung to her Hebrew mother-in-law and insisted on returning to the land of Judah with her. Thus we see that Jesus had in his ancestry a mixed pattern, a mixture of races and a mixture of good and bad – like most of us, with the odd skeleton in the cupboard, we might say.

Race Problems

This surely gives to us all something to think about, in the world of today, where we see how over-emphasis on nationality or race, has caused and is causing problems, brutality and war in so many places. Do we look into our own hearts and find vestiges of prejudice against those of other races, other colours?

Here we should take to heart the words of Simeon, as he took the child Jesus into his arms; and praised God:

> *'My eyes have seen the salvation*
> *which you have prepared for all the nations;*
> *a light to enlighten the pagans*
> *and the glory of your people Israel.'*

Jesus for All
This is the praise of the Babe of Bethlehem, who came to be the
Light of the world – the whole world, all nations and all peoples,
'without any difference or inequality', as St Athanasius would
say; the truth of the message of Jesus is for all, as the fruits of
the Sacrifice upon the Cross were, and are, for all – as Anna, the
prophetess, spoke of the Child to all who looked forward to
deliverance. Indeed, that deliverance would come, and all
peoples, all races, would share in the benefits and the glory
of it.

Sunday after Christmas *Second Sermon*
The New Year – New Life

*'To all God's beloved . . . who are called to be saints: Grace to you
and peace from God our Father and the Lord Jesus Christ.' Romans 1.7
(ASB EP)*

The Good News
The New English Bible, and other modern versions, are nowhere
more helpful than in their translations of St Paul's epistles. Paul
is difficult to follow in many places, and yet – apart from being
the earliest of our New Testament documents – his letters are
extremely illuminating as to the faith of the earliest Christians,
and above all to what the Good News of Christ is all about.
Some of the difficulty comes from St Paul's own tendency to
compression, and some from the fact that his writings are all
letters, which by their nature emphasize one thing in one place
and another somewhere else. And, in addition, so much theological disputation has been based upon one-sided interpretations of
St Paul's rich and powerful mind, and his detailed descriptions
of genuine Christian experience.

St Paul wanted Christians to look forward – day by day and
year by year – to the glorious promise of eternal life. And in this
he is psychologically very strong, for it is now common knowledge that there is nothing more therapeutic than having something to look forward to – and this we have in God's marvellous
promise to us, of which our Lord's own resurrection is the pledge
and assurance. Without this wonderful hope to look forward to,

even the promise of forgiveness in this life would lose much of its importance.

The New Year

Here we are, at the beginning of this New Year, with a moment to look backward, for the lessons we can learn from the past twelve months; and more important, a moment to look forward, and with God's help make plans and take hope for the year ahead. What plans and resolutions can we sensibly think over at this turning-point? Outside observers have always been more impressed by Christian life and behaviour than by Christian faith and hope; but Christians must not live for observers. Our life is not a role that we are called to play; we are called to *be* something; we are called to be what God intends us to be, the new man or woman in Christ.

The New Person

It might well be said that the 'new' man or woman in Christ is the person who knows he or she is not good – but goes on trying. Not in sullen gloom, nor in arrogance or defiance, but out of our love of God. For if we have assurance that our best achievements in this world are not in vain, and if we have the promise of an eternal personal fulfilment, then surely we have a new hope, such as the world has never seen before.

Let us admit that this is a struggle; but even when the Christian wayfarer is most weary, we have the joyful assurance of what St Paul tells us – out of his own painful experience – when at the end of the eighth chapter of this letter, he writes: 'For I am sure that neither death, nor life, nor angels, nor principalities, nor things present, nor things to come, nor powers, nor height, nor depth, nor anything else in all creation, will be able to separate us from the love of God in Christ Jesus our Lord.'

Let us take this message and this promise and this hope, to go with us, and in the words of the old saying,

> *'I will go with thee,*
> *And be thy guide*
> *In thy most need*
> *To go by thy side.'*
> V.S.

24

The Wonderful Counsellor,
  boundless in might,
The Father's own image,
  the beam of his light;
Behold him now wearing
  the likeness of man,
Weak, helpless and speechless,
  in measure a span!
Then let us adore him,
  and praise his great love;
To save us poor sinners
  he came from above.

                                    (NEH 50)

1996
The Epiphany of Our Lord Saturday 6 January
A Child in the arms of his Mother

*'Where is he who has been born king of the Jews? For we have seen his
star in the east and are come to worship him.' Matthew 2.2 (ASB Gospel),
or, 'They saw the young child with Mary his mother, and fell down and
worshippèd him.' Matthew 2.11 (BCP Gospel)*

The Best-loved Story in the World

The story in our Gospel today is so well loved, and has captured
people's imaginations so remarkably, that it must be one of the
best-known in the world, certainly in the Christian world. Some
of us as children will have been Kings in the Sunday School
Nativity Play – oh, the enjoyment of dressing up and wearing
those gilt cardboard crowns, and if you were lucky, being the
King with the incense, and swinging the censer as you processed
across the stage. And everyone would be singing 'We three Kings
of orient are'. Whatever 'Epiphany' meant, it was all great fun.
So, what is 'Epiphany'?

The title comes from a Greek word meaning 'showing forth', or
'revealing', or as in the old Prayer Book, 'Manifestation'. (Incidentally you might notice another Greek word, the word 'Christ'
which we use so easily. It means 'Chosen', the One chosen by God,
anointed by God – since anointing was the mark of being chosen,
as it still is, in the anointing of a King or Queen at a Coronation.)

What was revealed?

St Paul tells us in his letter to the Ephesians – our New Testament reading – that God has revealed his secret plan. What is the plan? It is that God has sent his Son, Jesus the Christ, into the world to be our Saviour – not just a Saviour of the Jews, the Chosen People, but a Saviour of all peoples and a Light to all nations.

> *Guide them, Jew and Gentile,*
> *Homeward from afar,*
> *Young and old together,*
> *By thy guiding star.*
> *(NEH 50)*

It was to those Wise Men, Gentiles from the East, that the Star appeared and guided them to Christ. From their studies in the sciences of that time, they had understood that a great figure, a King, was to be born, in Israel, in or near Jerusalem. No doubt they expected to find this King surrounded by luxury in a palace, attended by servants and guards. Instead, they found him in a little town outside Jerusalem, and certainly in no palace. That was the first surprise. The second surprise was that, prince though he was, he lay in his mother's lap, a tiny, helpless infant. Whatever their surprise, they fell down and worshipped; then opened their treasures and offered gifts – mystical and symbolic. Gold for a king, incense for a God, myrrh as a sign of suffering to come.

Universal Light

The Church has always seen – following St Paul's exposition – in the visit of the Wise Men the beginning of that universalism, which the Old Testament clearly foreshadows, as the plan and purpose of God. The whole world was to be swept into God's redemptive purpose; all humanity would share in God's redemption through Jesus Christ his Son. All would be able to become members of the same body, the Church. So in the visits of the Bethlehem shepherds and the Magi to the crib of the Christ Child, the whole world is represented as worshipping the world's Redeemer. There is the vision that we have been given, there is the aim and object for which we are to work.

The Vision

Christ's vision was of people from all corners of the earth sitting down in the Kingdom of God, with the patriarchs and prophets of old, with Abraham, Isaac and Jacob. He talked of drawing all people to himself by the power of his Cross. As St Paul puts it, 'in union with Christ and through our faith in him we have the boldness to go on with all confidence'. We are the people to put into operation and bring to fulfilment that farsighted vision, and realize the foreshadowings, hopes and ideals of the Saviour of the world, making all peoples of all nations united in him.

First Sunday of Epiphany *or* The Baptism of Christ (PHG) 7 January   The Beloved Son

There came a voice from heaven: 'This is my Son, the Beloved, in whom I am well pleased.' Matthew 3.17 (ASB Introductory Sentence)

The Beginning
The public ministry of Jesus began with his baptism; the event is a major element in the Gospel records, and from the earliest days it has been a favourite theme of Christian pictorial art.

Yet, it was a puzzling event.

The obvious meaning of baptism – washing or dipping in water – is purification. Why should the Sinless One undergo a ceremony of purification? The embarrassment is reflected in the scripture texts. In Matthew, the Baptist seems apologetic: 'I should come to you, not you to me!' to which Jesus replies, 'We must do the right thing.' This gospel does not actually describe the baptism, although it is implicit in the narrative; and it is as Jesus comes up out of the water that the Voice from heaven is heard, declaring the Sonship of Jesus 'the Beloved', the one on whom the favour of God rests.

Acceptance
Jesus accepted baptism vicariously, we believe, associating himself with all sinful humankind, so that his baptism was prophetic of his whole sacrificial life and, above all, of his death. This is expressed in the solemn words that are echoed in our eucharist:

> 'Behold the Lamb of God,
> who takes away the sins of the world!'

In the old story of Abraham and Isaac, Abraham says, 'God will provide himself a lamb for the offering.' So, Jesus as a sacrifice is the gift of his Father to us.

> *'O Lamb of God,*
> *that takest away the sins of the world,*
> *have mercy upon us.'*

Behold! That is what we are to see and recognize in the Baptism and the Crucifixion.

All this is emphasized by John's saying, 'I saw the Holy Spirit descending upon him', and then plainly, 'This is the Son of God!'

Contrast

The Baptist makes a vivid contrast between *his* baptism – an outward act symbolic of purification, and the true purification – 'He will baptize you, not in water but in the Holy Spirit.'

So, we must recognise the inward meaning of our own baptism, as a sacramental sign and promise of our Christian life.

As we continuously use the words 'Behold the Lamb of God . . .' and look with faith and gratitude at Christ our Saviour and Redeemer, so we are re-created in our hearts by the Spirit. He in us offers faith to the Father; offers acceptance and forgiveness, healing and consolation to those who suffer and those who sin. And in all things and in all life, abandonment to the Will of God.

> *Almighty God,*
> *who at the baptism of Jesus in the river Jordan*
> *declared him to be your eternal and beloved Son,*
> *your chosen one, the Messiah:*
> *Let your Spirit rest upon us,*
> *that we may serve you with justice,*
> *and bring light and freedom*
> *   to those who dwell in darkness;*
> *through Jesus Christ our Lord.*
>
> (PHG 76, p. 357)

> *Almighty God,*
> *who anointed Jesus at his Baptism with the Holy Spirit*
> *and revealed him as your beloved Son:*
> *give to us who are born of water and Spirit,*
> *the will to surrender ourselves to your service,*
> *that we may rejoice to be called your children;*
> *through Jesus Christ our Lord. Amen.*
>
> (PHG Collect of the Day, p. 355)

First Sunday of Epiphany *Second Sermon*
'Repent!'

In those days came John the Baptist, preaching in the wilderness of Judea, 'Repent, for the kingdom of heaven is at hand.' Matthew 3,1 (ASB EP)

The Call

In the Old Testament we hear the prophetic call – 'Prepare the way of the Lord!' Right at the beginning of the New Testament we have John the Baptist crying out the same message, in the 'wilderness of Judea', the wild countryside round about the towns and villages. Yet the message was truly for the wilderness of human souls; and the metaphor 'The Way of the Lord' would be of vivid reality to all those who heard.

At that time, there would be no roads – in our modern sense – across the world's wilderness, upon which vehicles could be drawn easily and safely. Rough paths there were, often very rough, littered with boulders, sometimes steep, sometimes positively dangerous – in all probability made by and for, the passage of cattle. If some important personage was to pass that way, work would have to be done, a road made – even enough to take wheels, and clear enough to allow a vehicle – coach or chariot – to pass by, with its important human cargo.

Not Prepared

Applying this plain necessity to Messianic times, we can see that the world needed Christ, but was not prepared for him when he came. Is this still only too true of our human hearts? Preparation to receive Christ here and now is a vital necessity still.

At heart, the disease – if we may call it so – from which the world is suffering today, is spiritual in character. The peoples of the world have been so occupied with material things and physical things, the needs of life, the health and good condition of the body are unimportant. They are indeed very important, and especially important is the need for them to be fairly available and properly distributed.

Needs

Yet, the body and physical things should be seen as vehicles for the expression of the life of the Spirit. 'Soul culture' is of vital importance; conscious separation from God needs Christ the

Reconciler. Sin needs Christ the Saviour. Ignorance needs Christ the Teacher.

Yet, if we need Christ, Christ also wants us.

There is a hindrance which many experience, a hindrance of which our world does not seem aware. It is pride.

We want a Saviour from fear, from consequences, from punishment, from death, and from separation from God. But we want him on our own terms. We must go to Christ in humility, and from him receive the grace that he gives, for the life which is life indeed.

'I am come that they may have life, and have it more abundantly' – John 10.10.

Second Sunday of Epiphany 14 January
The Call of the Disciples
'Jesus said to the fishermen, "Follow me, and I will make you fishers of men."' Mark 1.17 (ASB Introductory Sentence)

The Call
Our theme this Sunday, is the call of the disciples; the call of God to those whom he wants to take on the particular and important task of leading his people in the ways that lead to salvation.

Our first reading is about the call of a very special person, one who became a strong leader, both in what we might call the ecclesiastical or church world, and also in the political world. The prophet Samuel; he was to have a powerful moral and spiritual influence over kings and priests and people. Yet our theme is 'The Call of the Disciples' – in other words, *our* call, God's call to you and to me.

Now consider the Gospel reading. This also seems to be about the calling of special people, very special people – the apostles Andrew and Peter, Philip and Nathaniel. Yet, none of these well-known figures – from both the Old and the New Testaments – started out as very special people.

Ordinary
It is true that Samuel had been dedicated to the Lord's service by his mother, even before he was born, and he was growing up in the sacred precincts of the Temple. Yet he seems a very normal, very human, little boy.

Andrew and Peter were unlettered fishermen, though certainly Andrew had been touched by John the Baptist's preaching and teaching, and was looking for something deeper than his ordinary life-style provided. Philip seems an ordinary enough fellow, and Nathaniel – although a member of the Sanhedrin – quite a timid young man. With all of them, it was God's call, God's grace, God's anointing with the Spirit, that changed them. By God's Spirit they were led to become in the end fearless, eloquent disciples; followers of Jesus, apostles, martyrs and missionaries.

And Us?
We are talking about disciples; isn't that exactly what we are? We claim to be followers of Christ; people who are trying more and more, day by day and week by week, in spite of hesitations and failures, doubts and fears, to come closer to God. From what we hear and read, it may seem that Samuel, Peter, Philip, Andrew had a head-start over us – but did they really? It may be an alarming thought for some of us, but haven't we been given the same potential as these early followers, the early Saints? Here is something to think about!

St Paul
Our second reading, from St Paul's letter to the Galatians, is a human story; not only was Paul well-educated, and brought up in a strict Jewish family, but he was a Roman citizen – a privilege and not bought, but by birth, as he himself made very clear when he wanted to (Acts 22, vv 27,28). Not only did he refuse to hear any spiritual voice, but as a 'boundlessly devoted' Jew he was a leader in savagely persecuting this new movement, which was seen as a heresy and a completely false and blasphemous new departure from the faith of the Hebrew nation.

But, then came the extraordinary event of his conversion. His blindness, a physical symptom of his spiritual state; his new view of the world and his own life – far from opposing Christ, Paul was realizing that he was to spend his talents, his education, his strength of character, his powerful mind – all in the cause of spreading the Good News throughout the Roman world.

Special
So, we are special, after all. Every one of us here has been called to serve and to glorify God, and to be temples of his Holy Spirit. If that seems rather frightening, we have to try and realize that

it is true; and remember, it is not something that we achieve on our own. God is the one who calls us, God is the one who enables us to do what he calls us to do. His grace and power enables us to become the very special people he designed us to be.

And what of the people whom he calls for particular tasks in his Church – or to some particular office or position? These people do not have a *higher* calling than anyone else; it is simply that their calling is different, their function is different. Not greater – nothing can be greater than to be God's disciples, called by him to do what he wants and directs.

Whatever the function, the state, the office the Christian is called to, never-the-less he or she is still a disciple, struggling perhaps, frail perhaps, very conscious of being unworthy.

There is an old hymn (by Mrs Alexander) which sums it up:

> *Jesus calls us, o'er the tumult*
> *Of our life's wild restless sea;*
> *Day by day his voice is sounding*
> *Saying, 'Christian, follow me.'*
> (NEH 200)

Second Sunday of Epiphany *Second Sermon*
God's Calling

The Lord said, 'Behold, I have put my words in your mouth.' Jeremiah 1.9 (ASB EP)

The Prophet
In the opening chapter of the book called by his name, Jeremiah tells how he was called by God to do special work for him. It was a tragic time in the history of Israel; Jerusalem had been captured by Nebuchadnezzar, the city destroyed, and most of the people taken off into captivity. Jeremiah came from a priestly family and God's call to prophesy was against all his thinking and hopes. To be frank, the priesthood was something of a higher caste than the prophets, who might indeed be almost anyone, and were often lacking in education and manners. Reluctantly, however, Jeremiah does accept his call, which turned out to be the preaching of repentance and the prophesying of destruction if that repentance was not forthcoming. Alas, his words fell on

deaf ears; those who bothered to listen resented his words and made him suffer for them.

He was of a sensitive nature, hence his unhappiness and lack of success told against him very forcefully. His words may not have had much effect during his lifetime, but after his death his influence was considerable. Not all his words were prophecies of doom; in fact he foretells the new covenant in words that might well have come from Isaiah:

'This is the covenant which I will make with the house of Israel, says the Lord: I will put my law within them, and I will write it upon their hearts; and I will be their God, and they shall be my people . . . For they shall all know me, from the least of them to the greatest, says the Lord; for I will forgive their iniquity, and I will remember their sin no more.' (Jeremiah 31.33–34)

The Apostle
Jeremiah, in the opening chapter of his book, says he was called by God to do special work for him from his earliest days. It would seem that he could hardly recall a time when he did not feel keenly that it was his duty to work for God. Peter, on the other hand, could have named the very day on which Jesus called him. Certainly, he had known Jesus for some time; they had practically grown up together (John 1.40–42). But there is no reason to suppose that this had changed him so far, for the better; he tells Jesus he is a sinner (Luke 5.9). His call was that of a man not hostile to religion, but certainly not specially pious.

In fact, Peter is more like the ordinary man-in-the-street; he does not show the piety of Jeremiah, and indeed we can picture him as a 'decent fellow' by ordinary standards, a hard worker at the fishing business and on his way up in the firm. But nothing more – until he came under the influence of Jesus, and the extra-ordinary moment of the incredible catch of fish.

When Jesus said to him, 'Fear not; henceforth you will be catching men,' that was the point when everything changed. 'When they had brought their boats to land, they left everything and followed him.' (Luke 5.11)

Peter, we may say with confidence, was a man of impulse and affection, rather than of calm, spiritual intuition, or careful, painstaking reflection. It was due to his forward and impulsive temperament that he generally spoke up for the others, and was so confident regarding himself and the future. Christianity owes much to St Peter and to those with similar characteristics, but they may well need keeping in check by more sober thinkers, and to become more disciplined by the lessons of experience.

It has been said, 'The world had many Peters, who wish to be wiser than Christ, and prescribe to him what it is needful to do.' But we must not be too hard on Peter; we rely also, perhaps too often, on human wisdom. The call is, first of all, to set our affection on the things above. If we can get our priorities right, then all will be well for us to engage in our work for the Lord.

The Confession of St Peter *('Promise of His Glory', p. 402)* 18 January

This festival begins the Week of Prayer for Christian Unity. It is observed in the Episcopal Church of the USA as a celebration parallel to that of the Conversion of St Paul. The two apostles thus begin and close the Week. Collect:

> *Almighty God,*
> *who inspired your apostle Saint Peter*
> *to confess Jesus as Christ and Son of the living God:*
> *build up your Church upon this rock,*
> *that in unity and peace*
> *it may proclaim one truth and follow one Lord,*
> *your Son our Saviour Jesus Christ,*
> *who is alive and reigns with you and the Holy Spirit,*
> *one God, now and for ever.*

Readings: Ezek. 3.4–11 or Acts 4.8–13
Ps 23
1 Peter 5.1–4
Matthew 16.13–19

Third Sunday of Epiphany 21 January
Christian Unity

'I appeal to you, brethren, by the name of our Lord Jesus Christ, that all of you agree and that there be no dissensions among you, but that you be united in the same mind and the same judgment.' 1 Corinthians 1.10 (Promise of His Glory, Unity Readings, p. 396)

Our Contrary Streak . . .

I suppose most of us have what might be called a 'contrary streak' – that is, when we are advised, or worse, told, to think or act in a particular way, we are immediately drawn to the opposite. Take those make-over features which we see in magazines about decoration and furnishings, when someone's kitchen or sitting-room is transformed – don't we often prefer the 'before' to the 'after'? And in films, why is the villain so often really much more attractive than the hero? In the Christmas Panto, I can't be the only viewer who preferred the Sheriff of Nottingham to Robin Hood. Would you say that this is an instance of evil being more attractive than good, at least on the surface – something Paul recognized, 'Be not overcome of evil, but overcome evil with good'? But I think it has more to do with the sheer contrariness of our human nature.

Unity . . .

Today we are in the midst of the Week of Prayer for Christian Unity, which began on Wednesday last and finishes on Thursday, the Feast of the Conversion of St Paul. Of course, we should be working and praying for unity, and rejoicing in the unity between Christians which has already been achieved. But I can't help rejoicing in our diversity as well. And I am in distinguished company; Dr Habgood, until recently Archbishop of York, and one of the presidents of the Council of Churches for Britain and Ireland, had this to say, 'Having witnessed the immense advances which have been made, my own belief is that a Church which is not concerned about Christian Unity is betraying the Gospel of Reconciliation. As I approach retirement, my prayer is that many more people will catch the vision of a Church in which difference can be celebrated without division.'

But Not Monochrome

I am glad he said that – 'Difference with Division' – because I, for one, would not be happy in a monochrome Church; and indeed I can't see how that could be achieved. There is plenty of diversity even within the Church of England – to say nothing of the worldwide Anglican Communion, and the whole Church of God. Yet we recognize members of other denominations as Christians like us, united in a common Baptism and our belief in the Gospel. How different from only a comparatively short time ago, when say in the 1950s, we did not mix much with Methodists, Baptists, Congregationalists, and Presbyterians – not 'Church' but 'Chapel'. As for the RCs, their Church was viewed with considerable fear and suspicion, and few Anglicans would dream of going into an RC Church – the culture was so alien.

Together
Not so long ago there was a picture on the front page of the 'Church Times', of two people being presented with the Freedom of the City of Liverpool. One was the Bishop, David Sheppard, the other the RC Archbishop, Derek Worlock. They are famous for their ecumenical partnership, by which they have literally overcome evil with good.

Liverpool had a long tradition of sectarian strife – consider its close links with Ireland – and it wasn't just that people from the different Churches avoided each other – they used to fight. For years David and Derek have worked and prayed together, bringing others together as they did so. A very true comment was made: 'Their work proves in action the Gospel insight that the way to joint mission is not to unite first and then serve our neighbour together but to go out together in love to further God's righteousness, and unity will be added.' (John Austin Baker)

Unity
True unity does not mean that we are identical in the way we go about our mission – we can be diverse, as long as we always keep in mind that we belong to one Church, as we work together to overcome evil with good.

We began with one greater worker for Christian Unity, St Paul; and we end with the prayer of another, Archbishop William Temple:

> *Lord Jesus Christ,*
> *you prayed for your disciples*
> *that they might be one,*
> *as you are One with the Father:*
> *Draw us to yourself,*
> *that in common love and obedience to you,*
> *we may be united to one another,*
> *in the fellowship of the one Spirit,*
> *that the world may believe*

that you are Lord,
to the glory of God the Father.
Amen.

Epiphany 3 *Second Sermon*
Conversion of St Paul

'Get up; go into the city, and you will be told what to do.' Acts 9.6
(ASB NT Reading)

Saints or –

To be 'religious' means that we wish to be approved of by our
God. Saul of Tarsus was extremely religious, that is, he cared
above all else to be perfect in the sight of God. Such people
may become saints, and be loved, or they may become extremely
unpleasant and be hated. Because they think 'It is in my power
to be perfect,' they are tempted to despise, dislike and even hate
all those who clearly are not perfect, are not even on the road to
perfection. Perhaps the trouble is, that however hard the perfec-
tionist tries, he has this inner fear that he is not quite making the
grade. This is the person who becomes a persecutor. The fear of
failing is taken out on others who are obviously not making the
grade, or worse, are opponents of all that the persecutor holds
sacred.

Saul

So Saul of Tarsus, highly educated, cosmopolitan, well-connected
from a wealthy background, trying with all his energies to be
perfect, observing his religious duties to the tiniest detail, scrupu-
lous in keeping every religious rule of the Jewish faith – is confronted by a rising tide of heretics. They were a pretty rough lot;
the leaders were Galilean fishermen, and their 'prophet' was a
carpenter who had been executed by the Occupying Power. He
had claimed to be the long-promised Messiah of the Hebrew
people, but his 'revolt' (if revolt it was) had come to nothing.
Now, his followers were leading ordinary pious Jews astray; they
must be liquidated. Saul was the man to organize the sup-
pression, and was making a good start.

Jesus

We all know what happened. Jesus appeared to Saul on the road to Damascus; the very same Jesus whose resurrection Saul believed was an ignorant and stupid lie. 'Who are you, Master?' – 'I am Jesus, and you are persecuting me . . .'

The important point to notice is that no word of reproach was added. No question of 'You have been cruelly opposing the true Messiah, the Son of God.' Christ says, 'Stand up! Go into the city and you will be told what to do.' Saul is commissioned as Christ's missionary; it is more than forgiveness, it is a great act of the Saviour's acceptance of Saul – as he is – and the giving to him of the trust of the Lord himself.

A Comparison

A comparison in something of our terms: the worst boy in the class, always interrupting, distracting, leading the others astray. The teacher, instead of nagging, shouting, punishing – gives the lad responsibility and a prefect's badge. It is a gamble; it may succeed in reforming the lad, or it may not. In Paul's case it was a triumphant success.

Conversion is a radical spiritual and moral change; it is a 'change of heart'. The person remains the same, but re-orientated as it were – what was once black is now white. All Paul's energy, enthusiasm, knowledge and gifts were now redirected. His conversion is one of the most striking examples of a 'work of grace in the heart'. He is always conscious of his conversion as an act of grace; it colours the whole of his outlook on the Christian faith. In his letter to the Colossians, for instance, he says, 'You have put off the old man with his practices, and you have put on the new man, which is being renewed in knowledge after the image of him who is his Creator.' (Col. 3.9,10).

The New Life

God does not say to even the worst sinner, 'You must be punished, and strain every nerve to reform yourself before I can accept you as my child,' but, 'My Son has borne the blame of your sin for you. I accept you – what you must do is to allow me to accept you like that, a new creature born from above' (John 3.5). It is not all at once complete, but is in a state of constant development by the indwelling power of the Holy Spirit. This process is growth into the image of Christ in the heart and in the life of every believer.

Lord Jesus Christ,
Son of the Living God,
teach us to walk in your way more trustfully,
to accept your truth more faithfully,
to share your life more lovingly;
so that we may come
by the power of the Holy Spirit
as one family
to the kingdom of the Father,
where you live for ever and ever. Amen.

(PHG p. 258)

Fourth Sunday of Epiphany 28 January
Barriers

Jesus said: 'God is spirit, and those who worship must worship in spirit and in truth.' John 4.24 (ASB Gospel)

At the Well

Jesus had walked into a hostile district; no sensible Jew would go through the Samaritan country any more than a Roman Catholic would take a trip through an Orange Protestant area. He would be afraid of running into trouble, for the two communities were bitter enemies.

Perhaps Jesus was hoping to make some kind of small breakthrough in the barrier between his own people and the Samaritans. In fact, he began to break down not one barrier, but two.

He had chosen to sit beside a well near a Samaritan village, one hot afternoon. 'Give me a drink,' he says to a woman who had come from the village to fetch water. She was startled; it was very unusual for a man to speak to a woman outside the home, and very definitely unusual for a Jew to ask a Samaritan for drinking water at a well, since the religious rules forbade a Jew from using a Samaritan drinking vessel.

Jesus was breaking both a social barrier and a religious one.

39

The Status of Women

We have to remember that the status of women was very low in most countries in ancient times. Certainly this was so among the Jews; one of the daily prayers a man would recite was 'O God, I thank thee that thou hast not made me a woman.' (Let it be pointed out that this has largely been dropped in our times!) It was the attitude of Christ to the women he met, that led the first Christians to give women more respect – though admittedly even among Christians their position was low by modern standards.

Slowly over the centuries the position of women in the world has improved, and in some countries there are few respects in which they are not equal with men. In the Church itself women have been holding all lay positions – from members of PCCs to Churchwardens, Readers, members of Synods, administrators of Communion, and now, of course, women Deacons and Priests, with no barriers to the Episcopate also.

Nationality and Race

Perhaps the most difficult barriers to overcome are those of nationality and race. What is unknown is often feared, and better communications and easier travel have greatly improved matters, but by no means set them right. The other great barrier is the one that exists between men and women of different colour in many parts of the world. Signs are that this also is becoming somewhat diminished, but it still brings great suffering and sorrow in many places. In our own country many immigrants feel very discriminated against, and in spite of what laws have been made, there is much bad feeling and resentment.

Here again the Church has not always followed the teaching of Christ in trying to break down national and racial barriers. This is something about which nearly all Christians have reason to feel ashamed, although many are coming to recognize more clearly what the Christian attitude should be, and to live up to that attitude.

Other Barriers

Jesus attacked the barrier between rich and poor, which in older days was very great, and today shows up in the sad sight of 'Cardboard Cities', of beggars on the streets, the homeless camping out night by night, and the squatters who have little else to hope for but taking over empty living space.

In healing the lepers and the insane, Jesus sought to break

down the barrier of neglect which fear had set up between these unhappy people, and those with sound minds and healthy bodies.

The Church has sometimes very nobly followed his lead, and sometimes failed lamentably.

Our own Barriers
We need to break down barriers like pride, and jealousy, and spite, that separate us from the people among whom we live. We need to break down the barriers of indifference and careless-ness about beliefs, that make us slow to help and serve the Church and good causes.

The greatest barrier Jesus tried to destroy was the barrier of sin. The sin which keeps us away from God and our neighbours, and can eventually shut us off from his love and his mercy and power. Let us unite with Christ our Lord and Leader, in fighting against barriers that separate us, and trying to destroy the sin in our own lives.

> Lord God, our Maker and Redeemer,
> this is your world and we are your people.
> We confess our sins and the sins of our society,
> in the misuse of your creation
> and in the abuse of your gifts and your people.
> We are full and satisfied,
> but ignore the cry of the hungry and the homeless.
> We live in peace and safety,
> but forget the refugees and the wounded,
> the sick and the desperate.
> Lord, forgive us and help us to do better.

Epiphany 4 *Second Sermon* **Anger**
'Take these things away; you shall not make my Father's house a place of trade.' His disciples remembered that it was written, 'Zeal for thy house will consume me.' John 2.16,17 (ASB EP)

The Coming of the Messiah
The Coming of the Messiah was a constant thought in the minds of the pious Jews; they were looking hopefully for the Day when the Saviour, the Old Testament declared God would send them,

would restore the Kingdom of Israel, would drive out the oppressors (the Romans) and set God's own people free. Many ideas were put forward, sometimes based on the Bible, sometimes strange ideas based on legends or simply invented. One of these ideas, for instance, was that the Saviour would suddenly descend from heaven by a miracle, and it was thought that he would probably make this descent into the very courtyard of the Temple, since this seemed a very appropriate place for the occurrence.

This popular superstition was the background to one of our Lord's temptations in the wilderness. If he had gone to one of the pinnacles of the Temple, thrown himself down, and miraculously been unhurt, the crowds of worshippers and visitors who were always to be found in the Temple precincts would then without doubt hail him as Messiah. What a wonderful short cut that would be towards winning attention and respect for himself, and interest in his message for his people!

Jesus did not follow the tempting voice which whispered to his inmost mind the help this short cut would be. But he certainly did visit the Temple several times, as recorded by John; and John places the drastic action of 'Cleansing the Temple' near the beginning of his gospel, rather than towards the end.

Sacrifices for Sale

The visitors who came to the Temple from far away and at rare intervals would naturally wish to offer a sacrifice there in this holy place; they would not be bringing animals for sacrifice with them, and even local people would find it troublesome, so they would all buy their sacrifices on the spot. Many visitors would come from outside Palestine, from Egypt, Greece or Rome. They would want to change their money into the Jewish currency, especially as all gifts for Temple funds had to be made in Jewish coinage. In no time then, a cattle market would be set up, and there would be tables with men ready to change money sitting ready at them. As time went on, these activities invaded the courtyards, and destroyed any pious calm with unseemly uproar – not to mention shady practices of various sorts.

Jesus, John tells us, made a whip of small cords; his action in the market was not a mere gesture but an effective driving-out of animals from the sacred precincts, a chaos among the money-changers, and finally an ordering out of the dealers in pigeons with their cages of birds. His reason for all this? 'You shall not turn my Father's house into a market-place!' Jesus' words are a quotation from Zechariah (14.21): 'There shall be no longer any trader in the house of the Lord of hosts on that day'; prophetically proclaiming that 'The Day' was imminent.

No Short Cuts
Perhaps the lesson for us is that we should be on our guard against what appear to be short cuts in life. Of course, they are not all wrong – let us save time and be economical when possible! – but some are to be avoided. Ways to make easy money, winning cheap popularity, may well be sinful or will lead us into sin. The popularity of gambling, especially the sheer chance of the Lottery, may not be absolutely condemned, but can bring problems and dangers.

If short cuts are wrong, so is inaction. Long before Jesus made his protest, the Temple authorities should have cut out the festering sores, right there on their own ground; and it was a sad lack of genuine devotion and care that allowed all that market to develop. We should learn from all this to be watchful and careful, not closing our eyes to what is wrong but showing clearly that we are on the side of what is right and good.

Ninth Sunday before Easter (Septuagesima)
4 February (Education Sunday)
Education or Indoctrination?
'Trust in the Lord with all thine heart; and lean not unto thine own understanding. In all thy ways acknowledge him, and he shall direct thy paths.' Proverbs 3,1–8 (ASB OT Reading)

Education or Indoctrination
Education or indoctrination? is an argument which has been simmering away for many years in relation to the teaching of religion, especially the Christian faith. Every so often the argument escalates from a slow simmer and begins to bubble furiously, and that is what has happened this year.

When I speak of religious education and teaching Christianity, I mean, in this context, statutory education – not the Christian nurture of children, young people and adults in a parish or church community. In the UK we have a long tradition of teaching RE in schools. This does not happen in many other countries, in fact.

RE in schools has been in the news, and the subject of much controversy; the guidelines – not a strictly defined regime for all schools to follow, but a set of guidelines on the teaching of each Faith, for local authority committees in the maintained system of Education (not the Church Schools) each with a working group representing that Faith – Christianity, Judaism, Buddhism, Islam, Hinduism, Sikhism.

A Storm!

A sensible arrangement you may think – but what a storm greeted the syllabus. There was too much Christianity, or not enough; primary school children would be muddled if they studied other faiths at all; some of the Christian protesters thought that other Faiths should have a *very* small slice of the timetable; they believe that religious education *is* indoctrination, and fear that whatever Faith is talked about, the children will be indoctrinated – so it had better be the one they support!

RE is not taught nowadays as 'Comparative Religion' – the old 'supermarket approach' to world faiths is out. People, including teachers, are more prepared to say what they believe. Church schools and colleges are more identifiable than they used to be, and the low-key stance once adopted has been replaced by a willingness to stand up and be counted. To quote a former General Secretary of my organization, the National Society for Promoting Religious Education, there is now 'No apology for theology'. Learning in all subjects, including RE, is now supposed to be exponential, not a distant view from the outside. It is no coincidence that the expression used in modern schemes of work is not 'Teaching about Christianity' or 'Teaching about Judaism' but 'Teaching Christianity,' 'Teaching Judaism', 'Teaching Islam' – there is an immediacy about this which is both attractive and alarming.

The Key

The key to right education, I believe, is motivation – what is the purpose of teaching Christianity, of RE and indeed of education in general? Why are we engaged in it, as teachers or learners, or both?

The answer for Christians comes from one sentence from St John's Gospel, the words of Christ: 'I have come that they may have life, and have it abundantly.' (John 10.10) *This* is the purpose of education – to enable people to have life abundantly, life in

44

all its fullness, both now and through eternity. Teachers who truly believe this will not quail at the trappings of modern education, where the language of scholarship has been replaced by 'charters', 'vocabularies', 'performance indicators', 'attainment targets' all open to a wider range of 'customers'. Please – human beings, people, engaged in a learning process which should equip all to live life more abundantly.

The Religious Dimension
RE as a classroom subject, and the religious dimension in education – including that other controversial topic, collective worship – if done in the right way, makes an enormous contribution to the development of the individual, and to the building up of community life. This kind of education is *not* indoctrination, but is helping people to develop. The philosopher R. M. Hare wrote that 'the educator seeks to turn children into adults; the indoctrinator tries to keep them as perpetual children.' Helping people to grow to maturity, to adulthood, in every way to continue developing, this is the aim of good education.

The Mystery
There is a mystery about the spiritual side of life – whether we mean religion or the arts or whatever else captures the imagination and speaks to the soul. We may perceive it only dimly, but we know it is worth pursuing.

> *'What no eye has seen, nor ear ever heard, nor the human heart conceived, what God has prepared for those who love him.'*
> (1 Cor. 2,8)

These things God has revealed to us through the Spirit; for the Spirit searches everything, even the depths of God.

J.M.Y.

(Shortened version of a sermon preached at Trinity College, Cambridge)

(Copies of the Education Sunday Leaflet 1996 can be had from the Promotions Secretary, National Society, Church House, Great Smith Street, London SW1P 3NZ)

9 before Easter *Second Sermon*
The Blessed Ones

'How blest are those who know their need of God; the kingdom of heaven is theirs.' St Matthew 5.3 (ASB EP)

The Saints

Most of the Christian Churches have an official, or at least semi-official, list of saints. The Book of Common Prayer gives an Anglican list in the Calendar, and in the 'Tables and Rules for the Moveable and Immoveable Feasts'; the ASB has a rather more easily set out arrangement, with 'Festivals and Greater Holy Days' and then 'Lesser Festivals and Commemorations'. Names come from the earliest days of Christianity and the latest, which for us means Josephine Butler, who died in 1907. Besides these names, other very good men and women, whose holy lives are well known, or who suffered for the Faith, may be commemorated; probably the list would include Andrew Kagura, martyr in Kenya 1953; Janani Luwum, Archbishop of Uganda, martyr in 1977; Simone Weil 1943; Pope John XXIII 1962 . . . to name only a few.

Jesus and Saints

Jesus did not speak of saints in the way we do. The Jewish Church in New Testament times had no list of official saints, nor have they one now. But in the course of his teaching and preaching, our Lord spoke of the great heroes of the Old Testament, and showed that he respected them, and valued the good deeds they did, and the wise teaching they gave.

The Beatitudes

In the Sermon on the Mount Jesus laid down very clearly a number of qualities, the possession of which entitles men and women to be called 'Blessed' in the sight of God. This helps us to form an idea of saintliness, and the list has been given the name 'The Beatitudes', because each item begins with the word 'blessed'.

The Blessed Virgin Mary

The Virgin Mary, the first Christian saint in respect of time, and most people would say in respect of eminence too, uses the word 'Blessed' of herself in the Magnificat – 'All generations shall call me blessed.'

46

Saintly Individuals
We would be mistaken to think of the Beatitudes as a formal list of qualifications, or to think that saints conform to them all – that would be too much to expect. But great Christians have been outstanding in two or three of them at least, working for the Kingdom, holy in spirit, merciful when others have been seeking revenge, or possessed in high degree one or more of the qualities which bring them into our Lord's list of 'the blessed'.

Ourselves
In the Beatitudes we have set before us a target of Christian living, set by Jesus himself; we should take time every so often to consider carefully how our lives and our conduct measures up against these standards.

Eighth Sunday before Easter *(Sexagesima)*
11 February   'A Thorn in the Flesh'
'My grace is enough for you; my power is at its best in weakness.'
2 Corinthians 12.9 *(ASB NT Reading)*

Action – and its Opposite
It's strange, isn't it, how often you may decide on a certain course of action – and then find yourself doing exactly the opposite.

Moral philosophers have a name for this – it's called 'Weakness of Will' – and when they are not pondering the true meaning of Goodness and Justice and Equality they might try to account for this all too human trait.

When I read some time ago that there was going to be a series of half-hour TV programmes from the RSPCA hospital in North London, I resolved firmly not to watch. Not because they were being presented by Rolf Harris – but I knew that I did not want to see animals suffering; especially as some of the cases would be bound to be the result of human cruelty – and anyway who can be keen on seeing into an operating theatre, animal or human, just about supper time?

All went well until Wednesday, when I switched on BBC1 by mistake; and there on screen was a tortoiseshell cat. I was hooked – I just had to find out whether she would be all right.

Towards the end of the programme an old Alsatian was

brought in on a stretcher. His owner had agreed that the kindest thing was simply to have the dog put down. He wept, Rolf Harris wept, and all over the country thousands of people were sniffing and gulping in front of their screens . . . Where animals are concerned, we are not afraid to show our emotions, are we?

There were other deaths – like the dog deliberately thrown over a balcony, who died in the operating theatre – but success stories also. A run-over cat had a leg amputated, but the nurse assured the owner cheerfully 'She'll manage very well with three!'

Parallels

There were so many parallels with human hospital dramas – the staff, professional and kind to patients and owners (but human enough to show their anger at cases of violence or neglect). The patients – bewildered, depressed or jolly and making the best of things according to temperament and the seriousness of their condition. And the owners – behaving exactly like family members when someone has to go into hospital.

And as with human illness and suffering, there are huge questions behind it all. Why are *these* animals ill or injured, while others are healthy and unharmed? All were being given the best treatment and care, so why do some recover and others not? There was the cat who had developed skin cancer on her ears, through being out in the sunshine so much – but plenty of cats sunbathe regularly and suffer no ill effects. Some people smoke all their lives but don't get cancer of the lungs; yet Roy Castle, who didn't touch cigarettes but was exposed to tobacco smoke when he played the trumpet in jazz clubs, died of lung cancer.

Sickness and Health

Questions about sickness and health are never far away when we read the Bible. Today's stories – about the healing of Naaman in the Old Testament days; about St Paul's 'thorn in the flesh' which he seems to take as a kind of retaliation for the 'visions and revelations' he has been granted, 'God's power is at its best in weakness' is something that we do see in hospital visiting, in our own time and place today. There are some very marvellous cases of ill people who are yet able with the power of God to display such courage, such faith and such hope, as to make the rest of us feel very poor examples of love and trust in God.

Our Gospel reading has two stories of the healing power of Jesus. The first certainly mentions animals, dogs rather than cats;

and it is interesting since Jesus seems to be displaying a certain petulance towards the Syrian mother. He had been having a difficult time from the Pharisees and scribes, and the people had been giving him no peace; probably, the scholars tell us, this was why Jesus went into Tyre, heathen territory, where the Hebrew folk would keep away. But even so, he was recognized as a Holy man and a healer, and this woman comes to him, begging his help. Jesus is tired, worn out, really exhausted; no wonder he just can't face any more demands – and here is this heathen woman going on and on. He takes a very Jewish attitude; but the girl melts the sharpness out of his response, and gains her point – the child is healed.

'Ephphatha'

The Lord is again in heathen territory – that of the 'Ten Towns' – and it seems most likely that the deaf and dumb man, and those who brought him, were not of the Jewish race. But Jesus is not to be restricted by conditions of race or religion: his gifts were – and still are – freely available for all. Today's story of the healing of the afflicted man, as did also the story of the mother and daughter, shows that healing does not depend upon the faith, or indeed even the hopes, of the suffering human being who is healed. The daughter of the persistent Syrian knew nothing of what was going on; the deaf and dumb was so cut off from ordinary human intercourse that he knew not who it was that his friends or relatives were leading him to. Remember the paralysed man who was carried by his friends and let down through the roof to the feet of Jesus? It was the faith of the friends that counted.

Praying for Healing

Praying for healing, in Jesus' name is what the Church does, and has done since the time of the Apostles. Peter heals a lame man 'In the Name of Jesus Christ of Nazareth' very early on (Acts 3). The Epistle of James recommends that 'the elders of the church (the presbyters, in the Greek, from which we get the word 'priests') should pray over the sick man 'anointing him with oil in the name of the Lord: and the prayer of faith shall save the sick, and the Lord shall raise him up.' What a key part is played by faith.

It is faith that brings about the transformation – it is not just the divine activity which counts, but the human acceptance of it.

The transformation may be a miracle cure; more often it is less dramatic, with the sufferer feeling a sense of peace and reconciliation, and coming to know and understand that God is with him or her in the suffering, as in any other part of human life.

Our Healing Services – Some Suggestions

Healing was a normal part of Christ's ministry, and it is a part of the Church's work too; we pray for the sick at every service and we also have a service of 'Laying-On of Hands'. This kind of service is more and more a usual part of the work of our churches, often combined with Anointing (James 5.14).

The service is very simple and straightforward, set in normal service of the Holy Communion. There will be special prayers for the sick, and there will be the opportunity for people to go forward again to the rail to receive, from the priest, the laying-on of hands. The priest lays his or her hands on the person's head, saying a brief prayer asking for healing in the name of God, and then moves on to the next. If there are those who cannot come to the rail, the priest will go to them. You can receive the laying-on of hands in this way either for yourself or for somebody else – it is quite usual to have the laying-on of hands by proxy; and it can be for any kind of illness or any aspect of a person which requires healing.

Of course, this is not an alternative to medical treatment, and you cannot count on feeling any different. But there are many people who, at some time in their lives, have received the laying-on of hands, and have realized – maybe later – that it has helped them in a profound way in their journey towards wholeness and closeness with God.

J.M.Y.

8 before Easter *Second Sermon* **Making Fools of Ourselves**

Isaiah the prophet asked, 'What did they see in your house?' Hezekiah the king replied, 'They saw everything; there was nothing among my treasures that I did not show them.' 2 Kings 20.15 (ASB EP)

The Wise and the Foolish

When we look back into past history, we find examples of wise politicians who had good ideas for the advancement of their country, but a foolish or evil-minded king, who held the real power, ruining their plans.

Just such a king was Hezekiah; he was far from evil and on the whole was a good man. The prophet Isaiah had some considerable influence on him, which may account for the religious reforms carried out in his reign – the destroying of the 'High Places' where pagan worship was carried on, and even the breaking up of the bronze serpent that Moses had made, because 'the people burned incense to it'. He held fast to the Lord, we are told (18.6) and kept the commandments which the Lord gave to Moses, 'and the Lord was with him'.

Disasters

Unfortunately the Assyrians advanced over Samaria and conquered it, taking the people off into exile. Then, some years later, the Assyrians 'came up against all the fortified cities of Judah and took them'. As a ransom, Hezekiah gave large quantities of gold and silver, much from the Temple and from the King's treasury, but the Assyrians were not satisfied and laid siege to Jerusalem itself. It seems that earlier, a conduit and a well had been made, thus the defenders of the city were able to have water; the Assyrians, for whatever reason, suffered from a sudden epidemic of violent illness which killed off very many of them. The king and the remnant of his forces retreated back to Nineveh, leaving the capital and the country half-ruined but at least with no more exhausting fighting to cope with.

A Blunder

On the whole Hezekiah was a good and God-fearing man, and he relied much on the advice of Isaiah. But kings who are good men personally may not be altogether wise rulers; and Hezekiah made a foolish blunder. Envoys came from the great Babylonian Empire to visit Hezekiah in Jerusalem, and the king was flattered and pleased. Anxious to make a good impression and to show that his country, however small, was not to be despised as poor, Hezekiah took trouble to have the envoys shown round the treasures of the city, and especially the beautiful Temple, now restored with costly ornaments.

Anger!

Isaiah was out of town, but when he came back he was furious when the king proudly described what had happened, and how he had impressed the men from the great city of Babylon. Isaiah gave him a savage dressing-down, telling him bluntly, 'All in your house, and all that your fathers have stored up, shall be carried off to Babylon; nothing shall be left, says the Lord! And your sons shall be taken away, and made eunuchs in the palace of the King of Babylon!'

The king, who had not been well, indeed almost at the point of death, at one time, murmured, 'Yes, yes, the word you have spoken is good . . .' and the chronicler adds, as an aside, 'He thought, Why not, if there will be peace and security for what is left of my days?' for the world and its concerns were slipping from him.

Pitfalls

A sad ending to the story of Hezekiah, but a lesson for us. For are there not times in *our* lives, when we are over-confident of our capabilities, or over-estimate what we have in the bank when some 'bargain' comes in view? Our anxiety to impress those about us, our conceit, can lead us into foolish behaviour, or even perhaps into sin.

There are shocking examples of money foolishly lost, and the behaviour of those responsible, even in Church organizations, as witness the folly of the Church Commissioners in our own Church of England, or the easy way in which the Salvation Army lost considerable funds quite recently.

On the other hand, what can one say about the scandal of Barings Merchant Bank, and Mr Leeson? Or the continuing battle at Lloyds between the unfortunate Names and the Management? Remember too the collapse of BCCI and the disastrous effects on so many Asiatic and African business ventures?

Humble Service

We are all trying to serve God to the best of our abilities, whether those abilities are great or small. Let us remember that we can make our acts of service more pleasing to God, more in accord with the teaching of Jesus, and more likely to be crowned with success, if we can do them with humbleness and not with pride, and with commonsense and not over-inflated visions of vast successes, so not ending up by making fools of ourselves and those who trusted us.

F.S.

Seventh Sunday before Easter *(Quinquagesima; Sunday next before Lent)*
18 February   'Be Merciful'

'Be merciful, even as your Father is merciful.' Luke 6,36

The Mercy of God
It would be untrue to say that the ancient Hebrews had no conception of the mercy of God, but there is something restrictive in their conception. It often appears that, in their view, God's mercy is restricted to the righteous. And the righteous are those who follow exactly and precisely the laws and prescriptions of behaviour, laid down in the Torah, the will of God revealed in the Pentateuch, the first five books of the Old Testament, written down – at least in theory – by Moses.

It would also be untrue to claim that mercy was an unknown virtue in the ancient world of Greece and Rome; but it was certainly not a major virtue, and many Classical moralists – and otherwise noble writers – are nothing short of contemptuous of mercy, as a sign of weakness and as a betrayal of the ideals of battle and war.

A powerful echo or reflection of this attitude hangs around in too many minds, making possible the slaughter of captured soldiers from the 'other side', the giving way to blood-lust in the treatment of 'enemy' wounded, the bestial behaviour to civilians – and especially women – which we hear and see so much of in our TV and newspaper reports coming from Bosnia and Croatia and other war-torn countries.

Death in the Desert
Our Old Testament reading today reflects not so much blood-lust, as a concept of God from early and highly primitive times. The individual was hardly recognized as such; he was a unit in a community, and it was this community which took the decisions, made the laws, enforced the customs. God's concern was taken to be with the people of Israel; his wrath fell upon the whole

tribe when some sin or crime was committed, hence the sinner or criminal must be rapidly exterminated. We think all this is crude and primitive – but we are still much motivated by ancient emotions, as appears all too often in the public reaction to cases of brutality or perversion today.

A Striking Story
Where the episode from the life of Jesus which forms our Gospel today, came from is not, the scholars tell us, at all clear. It is not included in some of the early copies of St John's Gospel, but is found in some old manuscripts of St Luke – and the style is certainly very like that of St Luke; and he is the evangelist who shows more concern for women, and relates more stories about the dealings of Jesus with women, than the others. But the point about the story is not so much that a chief character is a woman, but that Christ's opponents thought they could seize on a chance to embarrass him, to catch him out, similar to the attempt to involve him in the tax problem – if Jesus invoked the Mosaic law, he could be accused of over-riding the Roman law, for the Jews no longer had the right to impose the death penalty. If he did not stand up for the full penalty, he would be accused of not taking the Law of God seriously.

His Answer
We know his answer: he did not take lightly the power of the Law, but he invoked another principle of it which put things in a very different light. In a Jewish court, it was the character and trustworthiness of the witnesses which carried the main weight. The judges required not so much proof, as reason to believe the witnesses were trustworthy.

So, Jesus was challenging those who in this case claimed to be witnesses of the 'very act' of adultery. Had these zealous puritans thought that the court would expect the highest standards before allowing them to act as both witnesses and as judges? 'He who is faultless, let him throw the first stone.' Enough – one by one they crept away.

Sin no More
What of the hapless woman? Dragged out of her home, through the streets with jeering neighbours gloating over her half-naked condition, and hoping to enjoy the cruelty of stoning a 'soft target', she could hardly be aware of the subtleties of the argu-

ments going on above her head; but she knew that somehow the Teacher would save her.

'Where are they? Does no one condemn you?' 'No one, sir.' – 'Nor do I . . . Go, do not sin again.'

When we are tempted to 'take the law into our own hands', as we say – or to insist on 'our rights', or call for the utmost rigour of the Law in some matter, let us remember the words of the Saviour – he who would die upon the Cross for the redemption of that woman – and us.

> *Holy God,*
> *Holy and mighty,*
> *Holy and immortal,*
> *have mercy on us.*
> *Have mercy on your servants, Lord.*
> *Have mercy on us, Lord, in your kingdom*
> *and grant us your salvation,*
> *now and at the hour of our death. Amen.*
> *(PHG, p. 117)*

7 before Easter *Second Sermon*
A Beloved Brother

'No longer a slave but more, a beloved brother.' Philemon v.16 (ASB EP)

A Remarkable Letter

The letters of St Paul that we have in our Bibles are considerable compositions, dealing not only with local problems, but also with matters of doctrine and of prayer and teaching. Obviously these letters were not written on the spur of the moment, but are, rather, treatises intended for the instruction of the recipients, and probably are the results of several drafts in each case, until the final form was settled to the Apostle's satisfaction.

There must have been, if we consider for a moment how many churches Paul founded, in how many places, and how many and varied the problems must have been, a great many more letters, written by the Apostle than the eleven we have. What happened to the others, and how did we come to have the letters now part of our Bibles?

Part of the answer is possibly to be found in the shortest letter of them all, the letter of St Paul to Philemon, and in many ways the most remarkable.

The Runaway Slave

Philemon was, it appears, a Colossian citizen, of considerable wealth and influence, who supported the local church – he owed his conversion to Paul (v.19) and remained on good terms with the Apostle, who obviously had a high regard for him (v.7). One of Philemon's slaves had run away, perhaps with some stolen goods (v.18) and instead of hiding in the nearest big city – Ephesus – had made his way to distant Rome. Perhaps he had friends or relatives there, or perhaps he hoped to do what in fact occurred – meet his master's old friend and instructor. Did he know Paul already, and think he might find a sympathetic ear? We do not know, but we do know that Paul took Onesimus the slave under his care, taught him more about Christ, and baptized him (v.10 would seem to infer this). Paul makes a kind of pun over the slave's name 'Onesimus' – 'Useful' which was most likely tagged onto him by his master at the slave-market, when he was bought.

Useful

Now the interesting point here is, why did Paul find Onesimus really useful, and hint strongly that although he was sending him back to his owner, yet he (Paul) would 'be glad to keep him with him, in order that he might serve me' (v.13). There were slaves who had been educated, who could read and write, and even use the shorthand of the time to record their master's speeches, poetry or letters. Was Paul impressed with Onesimus's skill in this direction? and did he see – or indeed, was he needing a secretary and short-hand writer? What a help Onesimus would be with the constant flow of letters to be answered, questions resolved, and all the paperwork involved in 'the care of all the churches' (2 Cor. 11,28). Paul's hope in writing this letter to Philemon is delicately insinuated, but quite clear – please send Onesimus back to continue the useful and personal service Paul values so highly.

Later

Years later, a great figure of Early Christian history, St Ignatius, bishop of Antioch, having been arrested as a Christian, was being taken from his city to Rome, under sentence of death. On his progress, a progress that became a triumphal procession, he writes many letters to neighbouring Christian communities. To Ephesus he writes congratulating them on the good reports he has had of their bishop. His name? None other than Onesimus! We cannot be certain, of course, but if it is the same person, how richly fulfilled were the possibilities that Paul saw in that runaway slave.

For we may say with considerable probability that it was Onesimus who gathered together so many of Paul's letters, and responsible for the wonderful treasure contained in our Bibles today. Many scholars believe that it was the energy and devotion of Onesimus that gathered these precious writings together and then included, as a kind of personal guarantee, this short and touching letter about a man who ran away, but was saved by love and mercy.

F.S.

Ash Wednesday *The First Day of Lent*
21 February   'Return to Me with all your Heart'
'Return to the Lord your God, for he is gracious and merciful, slow to anger, and abounding in steadfast love.' Joel 2, 13 (ASB OT; BCP For the Epistle)

The Season of Lent
That great Anglo-American poet, T. S. Eliot, in his fine poem 'Ash Wednesday', wrote these lines:

> *Teach us to care and not to care,*
> *Teach us to sit still . . .*

Eliot's powerful questionings and haunting rhythms in his verse speak to us of time and place, and of rejoicing that things are as they are, of not hoping to return again, yet of praying not to be separated, and asking that our cry may indeed come unto the Lord.

Ash Wednesday is a special day. It introduces a season whose emphasis is on the great Christian truth that we are unique in our own time and in our own place. No one has ever existed before quite like us, and no one else ever will so exist; we are, each one of us, related directly to God – and that applies whether we lived in distant ages, or in mediaeval times, or today.

This season of Lent which begins today, is a time to sit still within ourselves; and it is a time to listen. Listen to the prophets and the apostles who are appointed to be read today. The prophet Joel tells us, 'Even now, says the Lord, return to me with all your heart.' The prophet Amos tells us, 'If you would live, resort to the Lord. Seek good and not evil.' The Apostle Paul tells us, 'Get into training!' and St James tells us, 'The nearer you go to God, the nearer he will come to you.'

Here are words we ought to recall and act upon; on Ash Wednesday we can sit still and listen to them, ponder upon them, take them into our hearts and minds.

Ash Wednesday
What is Ash Wednesday? What is today? It is for us, the beginning of Lent; it is the result of a kind of mathematical scruple on the part of early Christian minds. They started, away back in the fourth century after Christ, to count all Sundays as festivals, and so they excluded them from the forty-day fast observed in preparation before Easter, remembering Christ's time in the desert. To make up the ritual number, they added four extra days at the beginning of Lent; and so arrived at Ash Wednesday. So Lent begins today; and its name comes of course from the ashes placed upon the foreheads of the worshippers as they gather in church for the eucharist.

What of these ashes? They have a long history. We can read in the Old Testament of the turning of sinners to repentance, and how they repented in dust and ashes, in ashes and sackcloth. Rubbish, valueless, the lowest of the low. Job and his so-called comforters wept, rent their clothes, threw dust and ashes over their heads. When the prophet Jonah preached repentance to the people of the city of Nineveh, they put on sackcloth, high and low alike, and sat themselves in ashes. From the Bible stories, the custom grew whereby ashes were sprinkled on everyone as a sign of repentance. 'Turn away from sin and be faithful to Christ' or 'Remember that you are dust, and to dust you shall return' – recalling the Genesis account of Creation. A call to a new start and an abandonment of our old failings and mistakes.

Sit Still – and Hear

So on Ash Wednesday we begin to sit still for a time, to hear the ancient voices tell us what we know – that we can change, that we ought to be otherwise, that we can be better than we are, and that we can change – if only we want to do so.

If we pray, we can put aside our arrogance, our pride, our foolish anger, our mistakes and our failures: even in our fallen state we are what we are – that is, unique, and each one of us related to God directly, even at our worst, at our most foolish.

To quote Eliot again, from his 'Ash Wednesday' –

> *Suffer us not to mock ourselves with falsehood:*
> *Teach us to sit still,*
> *Even among these rocks,*
> *Our peace in his will . . .*
> *And let my cry come unto Thee.*

But, we do not need to read Eliot, nor even the ancient prophets – what we do need is to sit still, wherever we are, reflect on our arrogance, on our pride, on our self-centredness. And place ourselves before the Lord in humility and repentance; and remember that the Lord is *our* Lord, and to him our cries do indeed come.

ASH WEDNESDAY

> *Leafless trees in a scrub forest,*
> *daubed with paint for felling,*
> *we are scored for death*
> *by the priest's thumb*
> *that grinds soot into our foreheads.*
>
> *Ash underlines the wrinkles of the old,*
> *startles us by soiling*
> *lovely faces as well.*
> *Some crosses are off-centre,*
> *slightly clownish,*
> *like clumsy death-bed jokes.*
> *All are marked:*
> *black smudges, white albs.*

59

See us, Lord, like these candles we carry,
soot and spattering fat dripping away.
Help us to burn clearly before you.
                                        Roberta Berke

First Sunday in Lent 25 February
Sinful – yet Redeemed

'Through him you have given us the spirit of discipline, that we may triumph over evil and grow in grace.' (Preface for Lent, ASB Rite A)

Pessimism . . .

'Did you say the stars were worlds, Tess?' asks her little brother, star gazing as they drive to market in the early morning light. 'Yes,' she replies; 'they sometimes seem to be like the apples on our tree. Most of them are splendid and round – a few are blighted.'

'Which do we live on – a splendid or a blighted one?'

'A blighted one,' says Tessa.

We expect sentiments like that in Thomas Hardy's 'Tess of the D'Urbervilles.' His theme is splendidly pessimistic and thoroughly depressing, seeing in the chaos of life what he calls an 'everlasting nay', to faith in God and belief in a divine Providence. Much the same sense of pessimism and futility can be found in the minds of many other people of our century. In philosophy and in the arts there seem to be deep underlying currents of despair which suggest that humanity is indeed the creature of a blighted world, and that ultimately we are without hope.

Optimism

At first sight, the Church seems to be concurring in this diagnosis of the state of our world and of humanity in particular. One of the predominant themes of this season of Lent, upon which we are now entering, is the recognition that humanity is in a perilous state and that the world is dominated by the harsh and brutal realities of sin and death. But, unlike those who totally despair, the Church counterbalances the melancholy and pessimism with optimism and hope. As Pascal put it, 'Christianity is strange; because it bids man recognize that he is vile, and yet bid him to reach up to be like God.'

Lent

Lent is a time for wrestling with these twin truths for our human condition. Nothing should blind us to the fact that we are part of a fallen creation, deeply flawed by sin. Yet nothing should deprive us of the knowledge that God in Christ has reconciled this world to himself, and that we are redeemed. Our task is to unfold these two great truths, and apply them to our lives and circumstances in our approach to sin and redemption.

Austerity

From the top of the Mount of Temptation, the panorama is that of a glistening, cleansing desert, where nothing can be hidden and all is laid bare. It is not lifeless, nor is it harsh or unfriendly for those who are used to living in it. Like all deserts, it is teeming with life for those who have eyes to see and ears to hear. It is austere: yes, and that is its unique value. Everything is exposed, and light and shade come up in sharp relief. We may not have access to an actual desert this Lent, but we can simulate something close to it in our hearts and minds. It is in this manner of austerity that we will recognize the rights and wrongs in our lives with honest clarity. An austerity which does not repudiate life, but embraces that which – by its quality – enhances our own.

Opening Up

In an almost clinical way, we will need to lay open our lives to ourselves in the same decisive, caring way that a surgeon opens a body to reveal the diseased part. It will hurt, because it will reveal the nasty bits of ourselves that we would rather leave alone. But it must be done, because we cannot comprehend our need for redemption if we do not care to identify our sin. If we say that we have no sin – or sin that does not matter much – not only do we deceive ourselves, but we can have no gratitude – or very little gratitude for the Cross, because we will not see why we need it.

First then this Lent, let us reveal and acknowledge ourselves for what we are; personally and as a community. As a community, because together we help each other, pray with each other, and celebrate the Sacrament of Christ's love together; and the austerity of our repenters will be the antidote to self-indulgence.

'Man is bidden to recognize that he is vile', says Pascal; 'and yet also bidden to reach up to be like God.' And to that we can say an everlasting Yes; since during the Forty Days of our self-revealing and repentance, through it all, bubbling with an almost premature joyful hope, is the knowledge of the Easter certainty.

The Light
Like a steady guiding light shining in the distance, is the knowledge that life and the world is not a hopeless enterprise – because it is not our world, but God's world: and God's ways are higher than our ways. Where we have failed, he has succeeded; and he invests us with the glory of his achievement. This is the austerity and the hope, the pain and the healing, that God – in his grace and his wonder – offers us as the loving Father who sees his children in need.

Lent 1 *Second Sermon*   A Lent Course on Prayer (1)   Lord, teach us to pray – The Pattern

'Jesus was praying in a certain place, and when he ceased, one of his disciples said to him, 'Lord, teach us to pray . . .' And he said to them, 'When you pray, say: Father, hallowed be thy name. . .' Luke 11, 1,2

The Lord's Prayer
The question asked of Jesus is one that has been on the lips of his followers ever since. On these Sunday evenings in Lent, we shall be exploring different patterns of prayer that may be used by both the individual and the congregation. We begin by looking at the answer Jesus gave to his disciples, an answer that has become known as 'The Lord's Prayer'.

But, is it a prayer? Or have we been guilty of what Evelyn Underhill called 'incredible stupidity' in mistaking his *teaching* about prayer, for the words of a prayer itself. One thing is certain – we have made it into the best-known prayer in history. Let us look at three simple pictures:

First, peep into a child's bedroom in the evening: there is a little girl reciting the words of the Lord's Prayer like countless other small children, not exactly accurately at this stage, for she can understand hardly any of it. But nevertheless she is learning it as a prayer.

Now move to the other end of life, to the elderly in an Old People's Home. During the weekly morning service there, few are able to join in the words, as they cannot see to read; and many others look to be asleep. But halfway through the service, the celebrant begins 'Our Father . . .' and see what happens. A low murmuring begins; even those who seemed asleep begin to mouth the words of that prayer, which somehow remains in the memory, long after much else has disappeared. The third picture concerns a young woman who told the vicar that she hadn't been to church since schooldays – but always she found herself reciting the Lord's Prayer, again and again, whenever she felt frightened.

These illustrations could be repeated again and again, across the world and down the ages, and they show how we Christians have taken the words of Jesus, and made them into a formal prayer to recite.

But is that what Jesus intended?
Let us look at the two Gospel accounts where we find the Lord's Prayer. We began with the account in St Luke's Gospel, following on the question from one of the disciples: 'Lord, teach us to pray.' Notice that this came just after Jesus had finished one of his times of prayer – we read how he often went apart to pray. Now, his disciples want to share what he is doing.

They are asking a deeper question than what words should be used – they are asking about the whole approach to God, which is expressed in the manner in which we pray. Jesus' reply is not a 'mantra' – but a method.

This is endorsed if we look at the account in St Matthew's Gospel (6.7ff). Here, it comes in part of the 'Sermon on the Mount' where Jesus criticizes the hypocrisy of much contemporary religion; he attacks the 'vain repetitions' and 'empty phrases'. But are we not guilty of exactly the same thing in the way we so often use the Lord's Prayer, repeating it endlessly and often carelessly?

Perhaps so; yet, think of the girl who uses this prayer when she is frightened. You might say, she is using it almost as a magic spell; but it is more than that. It is a desperate cry to God from one who knows little of prayer (as she admits). Here the Lord's Prayer is the articulation of an inarticulate spirit. Just as flowers betoken the expression of love – for not all of us are great poets! – so the Lord's Prayer may be the token of a heart in need. And I believe that God is very ready to listen and respond to such a cry. But Jesus was trying to teach his disciples *how* to pray – so what he gave them was an *outline* of prayer, what we might call a template with which to work out our own meeting with God. It shapes up what is expected in that relationship of prayer.

Not a Prayer, but a Pattern
What Jesus gave his disciples was not so much a prayer as a pattern; a pattern with seven parts.

1. Our Father in heaven – From the start we realize with Whom we have to do – one remote and beyond, yet accessible as close as parental love. If we reflect on that idea of fatherhood we shall begin to appreciate the depth of love that holds us to God. Think also that we pray 'Our' father, and we open up the common humanity; our prayer begins to feel the pain of every human division, every oppression, every suffering.

2. Hallowed be thy Name – we begin to explore the whole place of adoration and awe as a ruling temper of our life.

3. Thy kingdom come – seeking to co-operate in God's creation and redemption, to enthrone him in our hearts and in our world.

4. Thy will be done – to give ourselves to his service, to seek his purpose; a part of prayer that is costly to reach; so often we say it glibly, without meaning or intention.

5. Give us our daily bread – we bring our every need to God, the ordinary and the extraordinary, spiritual and physical; our whole life is bound up with him.

6. Forgive us . . . as we forgive – the penitence we all need; the mutual sorrow and mutual recognition of our mistakes and shortcomings bound up in mutual love.

7. Lead us . . . deliver us – acknowledging our dependence on God; asking for his help and guidance and protection.

Here then is a pattern of prayer that should mould our every approach to God. We recite the prayer as a whole to remind us of this, but that is only the beginning; we then must pray the prayer in every detail. That is how we, like Jesus, may spend time apart, time in prayer with God.

But note just one thing from our look at this great prayer. Of the seven parts, the *first four* – in other words, the priority and main thrust of the prayer – are concerned with God; the last three concern us.

Do our prayers begin with God, or with ourselves?

Perhaps that is the best question to begin our reflections on Prayer, this Lent.

Second Sunday in Lent 3 March
God's Kingdom – here *NOT*

'No one who does not do right is God's child, nor anyone who does not love his brother.' 1 John 3.10

Saved!
Our first lesson seems to be about destruction over the whole earth, but we need to remember that the point of the story of the Flood is the command of God to Noah to *save*, to save his own family – thus saving the human race, and to rescue also male and female of every kind of creature, ensuring that none of them would become extinct. How very different from the present time, when so many species of animals are endangered, and indeed some have been wiped out already. The enemies of life are first, pollution – for instance the rivers of this country have lost, and are losing, their one-time magnificent fish populations due to industrial effluents, while the seas themselves are being emptied because of intense over-fishing by ourselves and other nations.

Every day we seem to be hearing about some beautiful animal in danger of being wiped out – dolphins, tigers, elephants catch the headlines, but how many others are there which do not get the publicity which may help to save them? What we need to guard against are the sins of greed and selfishness, and in particular the arrogant urge to snatch every opportunity to make money, regardless of the effects of our actions upon other human beings, upon the animal world, and upon the whole world of nature.

Such actions are sinful, and St John is telling us exactly how and why, in our second lesson. In particular, he points to the fact that we are called God's children, and as such we must abide by God's standards for us; sins are lawlessness, against God's will and intentions. If we take Christ as our standard, and take hope for the future, we will not be misled into arrogance and misuse of power and of God's marvellous gifts.

Strong Talk . . .
It was exactly these sins of arrogance and misuse of power that Jesus came up against, as related in our Gospel story.

Jesus, the compassionate and merciful, exercises his love and power to heal a deprived, handicapped man – both blind and dumb, we are told. How cut off this poor fellow must have been, how reliant on his fellow human beings for every need in a world that was confined, dark, stumbling.

Such a healing was, the scribes and theologians said, a sign that the long-promised 'Son of David', the Messiah who would restore the kingdom of Israel, had arrived. It was the prophet Isaiah who spoke of One who would be anointed by the Spirit of the Lord God, to bring healing, comfort and freedom to those who suffer, to the prisoners caged in the dark, to the sick and lame, and would restore the glory of Israel. Jesus himself, earlier, preaching in the synagogue at Nazareth, had quoted the prophet:

> *'The spirit of the Lord is upon me because he has anointed me;*
> *He has sent me to announce good news to the poor,*
> *to proclaim release for prisoners and recovery of sight for the*
> *blind . . .'*

Again, he had sent a message to John the Baptist in prison, saying to the followers of the Fore-runner,

> *'Go, tell John what you have seen and heard –*
> *the blind receive their sight, the deaf hear, lepers are healed . . .'*

These healings were unambiguous signs of the Kingdom. They were not performed by Jesus in order to witness to God's Reign primarily – they were done out of love and compassion, in the power of God, by One whose heart was touched by the sorrow and pain and distress he met.

Discord

These acts of mercy and love were well received by the ordinary people, the simple folk, the peasants and workers whose daily tasks mean that they are in contact with real life and real death, real pain and real pleasure. Not so the Pharisees, who attacked Jesus bitterly, accusing him of using the powers – not of God – but of the Devil, Beelzebub – or Satan, as we say.

Jesus is well able to show that such talk is nonsense; and interestingly he refers to followers of the Pharisees who themselves 'cast out devils', perform exorcisms, that is. Do they use the power of evil against itself? Of course not – be sure therefore that it is indeed the Spirit of God himself that is operative, and that truly this is a sign of the Kingdom here and now.

Other Sayings

Matthew has placed here some other sayings of Jesus, which appear in Mark (3.27 and 9.40), though this latter is given the other way round; and 3.28 to verse 30, a version of the saying about the slander of the Spirit, but Matthew, like Luke, has the additional words indicating forgiveness for anyone who speaks against the Son of Man. Those who turn something good, something of God, into something evil and bad, refusing to recognize the hand of God where it is plain to see, are indeed sinning against the Holy Spirit, and the Early Church could see no further hope for them 'either in this age or in the age to come'. A dreadful fate indeed, from which may the Lord in his mercy deliver us. 'Be not deceived, God is not mocked' (Gal. 6.7).

Lent 2 *Second Sermon*   A Lent Course on Prayer (2) 'Lord, teach us to pray' – Adoration

'Come close to God and he will draw close to you.' James 4.8

The Presence of God

God is everywhere and always with us. Whether we are in church or in a bus, whether we are making a cup of tea or saying our prayers, we are no less and no more in his presence. His fullness is always open to us. It is we who do not make ourselves available to him. 'Come close to God and he will draw close to you.'

So what do we mean by 'prayer'?

There are many definitions of prayer, but I prefer the most comprehensive. I think prayer is any human activity which attempts to make contact with God. It does not have to take the form of a solemn address to the Deity. A simple sign of the Cross is a form of prayer; reading the Bible or a book about God is a form of prayer; doing something special for Lent, or giving up something we like during Lent, is a form of prayer. Recognising God in his creation, whether in one's fellow human beings and their doings, or in the world of nature, is a form of prayer.

In all these things we are trying to break down the barriers which prevent us from seeing God's love shining down upon our lives.

Our Response

But when we do recognize that love, what is our response?

It seems to me impossible *not* to respond if we really see that God is there; and that response is what I mean by adoration. It is a simple movement of the heart towards God, a turning towards him which does not need elaborate words, perhaps does not even need words.

All that is involved is a greeting. Because it is God we are greeting, that must be an expression of gratitude. Sometimes we do not need to work out what it is we are grateful for; we do not need to spell it out. There is so much that can arouse our gratitude – the realization that whatever we are enjoying comes from God – whether it is our friends or our food or the sunshine or the music; the realization that it is he who has saved us from despair or evil; the realization that Jesus came to live our life, and die for us, and conquer death and wrong. All these things deserve our thanks, and all we need say is 'Thank You!' Sometimes we do not quite know why we are happy; sometimes we have to push ourselves to be grateful. But when we catch a glimpse of the Divine Love, we know we must give thanks; and when we see more than a glimpse it is not thanks that are in our minds so much, as simply wonder and praise.

At the Heart

This is what lies at the heart of the Church's prayer; it is not just asking for things. Since the Lord Jesus joined with the disciples at the Last Supper, we have had the pattern of actions he left us: to take bread and wine, to give thanks, to break the bread, to distribute it and the wine, and to consume them. Gradually we have developed sets of words to use, but the words are not as important as the actions. Jesus is there and we are there, making contact with one another in the bread and the wine. It does not really matter what words we use. This is the great Thanksgiving, the best way of thanking that we know, the Eucharist.

Although there is, of course, intercession in the Eucharist, that is not and should never be its principal purpose. The Eurcharist is there to bring the Lord to mind, to bring ourselves into his presence, and to receive what he gives. It is to be with God.

The same thing is true at home; we can kneel down and close our eyes and try to cut out everything which distracts us from God. Not everyone likes or is able to kneel; basically it is a question of finding a position which means, for us, turning to God, and which helps us concentrate on him. Other things can help us too – some people have a crucifix or a plain cross, to remind us of the Passion; the rosary reminds us of the life of Christ, his shared humanity. Some prefer to pray in church; we may perhaps just kneel or sit without saying anything, like the old French peasant who spent much time before the Blessed Sacrament. When asked what he did, he replied, 'I sit and looks at him, and he looks at me; and we are happy.'

Contemplation
That is contemplation or mental prayer – just knowing you are in God's presence and not needing to say anything. The worship of the Church does involve maybe too often, too many words; and all forms of prayer are betrayed by our inability to fix our minds on any one object for long, even God. St John of the Cross wrote about the 'dark night of the soul'; St Ignatius Loyola teaches us to bring quite elaborate pictures of Bible events into our minds; St Teresa of Avila wrote 'The Way of Perfection', 'Foundations', and 'The Interior Castle' classics of spiritual life.

We are too often inclined to set aside parts of the Christian tradition as beyond us. We suppose that adoration is best left to contemplative monks and nuns. We do not think of it as simply the natural response of any of us to God our Creator, our Saviour, our Sustainer, whenever we really manage to focus our minds on God. Too often, in our prayers, we are thinking much more of what we are praying for, than the God we are praying *to*. The practice of the prayer of adoration is designed to take our minds away from what *we* want and to put them at the disposal of God. All we have to do is, to be still. 'Come close to God, and he will draw near to you.'

Third Sunday in Lent 10 March
Decision
'From that time Jesus began to make it clear to his disciples that he was destined to go to Jerusalem and suffer grievously at the hands of the elders and chief priests and scribes, to be put to death.' Matthew 16.21 (ASB Gospel)

Steadfastness

The virtue of steadfastness is not a popular virtue of today. To be steadfast is too often castigated as stubbornness, mere bigotry. Toleration is praised in such a way as to present steadfastness as a grave blunder, if not a positive crime. In fact, one has a suspicion that tolerance is often used as a cloak for downright indifference.

Certainly, tolerance is a quality which is eminently desirable amongst us humans, especially in a democratic society. Yet, tolerance is a quality which is difficult both to acquire and to cultivate. It is a late development in the life of persons and in the life of societies. We can see many – far too many – nations today who have either never had real tolerance, or have lost it, or are in process of losing it. The growth of the call for reinstatement of the death penalty is an example; another is the increase of racial prejudice.

Indifference

Indifference is woefully easy. It flourishes when we 'cease from mental fight', and give up opinions of our own, simply to drift along with the opinions of the day. Headlessness of the distinctions between right and wrong fosters its growth. Those who give way to scepticism are prone to it when they ask, with Pilate: 'What is truth?'

Even neutrality can sometimes be indifference; yet there are spheres of life and action where there can be no neutrality. If we give way, we lose our integrity. Ernest Hemingway is reputed as a writer of tough, muscular, masculine themes; in story after story, his characters are confronted by what the bull-fighters call 'The Moment of Truth'.

Taking a Stand

A person of integrity is one who takes a stand, stands up to be counted, come what may, for his beliefs. Robert Jordan is the hero of Hemingway's book, *For Whom the Bell Tolls*. At the end of the book, set in the Spanish Civil War, Jordan – badly wounded – is left by his comrades to cover their retreat. As he looks along the road to where the enemy will appear, Hemingway gives us his thoughts. 'Now, finally and at last, there was no problem, however it had been . . . or would ever be. I have fought for what I believe in . . . a good cause, and worth the fighting . . .' His last task is to hold up, even for a short time, the enemy; even though he himself is inevitably to die. He has chosen to make his stand, whatever the consequences – and indeed seeing those consequences.

The Moment of Truth

Does it seem strange – or even blasphemous – to talk about a Hemingway hero and our Lord Jesus Christ in the same breath?

I hope not. Because, at this time in the middle of Lent, we have brought before us in the readings and teachings of the Church, the moment of decision for Jesus. His Moment of Truth.

That decision was, whether to continue on the road to Jerusalem, at the end of which he could clearly see death, or not. Jesus's answer is plain and definite.

'From that time, Jesus began to make it clear to his disciples that he was destined to go to Jerusalem and to suffer death . . .'

Every Decision is the Same Decision

It is true enough that, in a sense, every decision is the same decision. At every stage of the life of Jesus – and indeed in our small way also – there was the choice to obey the Father's will, or not. Jesus' loving obedience to the Father was the guiding principle of his life and conduct – yet it is clear that at this time, Jesus is particularly oppressed by the thoughts of the suffering that lay ahead, if he were to continue on his present course.

Not – let us be clear – that Jesus had a special ability to read the future, some psychic power as we might put it, but simply that he could see as any intelligent person could see – as Hemingway's hero could see – that in spite of the efforts, the heroism, the energy expended, the cause was doomed – humanly speaking.

The Tempter

Here again was the temptation with which he had been confronted at the very beginning of his career: to take the safe way out. Surely God does not expect one to go on to certain death, for failure, for nothing? Let's be sensible! 'Yet,' says our Lord, 'what will we gain if we win the whole world and lose our integrity?' – 'Get behind me, Satan! My path is God's path, not man's.' So what gives us integrity? Our standing by our beliefs, our faith, what we hold to, even if they lead us to apparent failure, even death.

So Jesus took his decision, and as St Luke puts it, 'set his face to go forward to Jerusalem' where he would meet his Passion and Cross; his Moment of Truth.

God help us to be 'truly human', to stand up and confront, to be counted, to keep our integrity and stand by what we believe, in the face of opposition, in the face of the 'soft option', in the face of betrayal, hatred, and even death itself.

Lent 3 *Second Sermon* A Lent Course on Prayer (3) 'Lord, teach us to pray' – The Litany of the People

'Let the priests, the ministers of the Lord, weep between the porch and the altar, and let them say, Spare thy people, O Lord.' Joel 2.17

The Litany

The purpose of our course on prayer this Lent is to explore some of the types and styles and forms we can use in our praying.

Today we are going to look at one particular form of prayer which goes back a long way in both Christian and Hebrew devotion – the Litany. You may not be familiar with it, or you may remember it from earlier days, when the Prayer Book form was used more often.

The title 'Litany' comes from the Greek and means 'supplication', a form of asking, devoutly and earnestly; so a litany is a series of requests made before God, led usually by a cleric or a cantor, and responded to in repeated forms by the people. Its great virtue is that it is a corporate prayer; it is a parish at prayer, or a group at prayer, or even just a few people gathered together at prayer. There is the sense of us *as* a group, *as* a body of God's people, standing or kneeling before God and seeking his help or giving him praise, united together in our aim.

Formal

At a time when much prayer is personal and private, or informal and 'off the cuff', and sometimes almost chatty, there is quite certainly a place for a more formal approach, a recognition of ourselves as creatures of God, coming before our Almighty Creator, in need of his care, consideration, forgiveness and grace. Hence our Litany is longer than the brief prayers we are perhaps more used to; and usually the words themselves can give us something to think about; we are trying to pray in depth as well as together.

Our Book of Common Prayer Litany is a superb piece of Tudor English, from that amazing time in our history when our language was at a special and particular peak – the Authorized Version of the Bible, the works of William Shakespeare, the Book of Common Prayer – these are masterpieces, representing a time when the newly-forged English language was in the hands of masters and our country was in a period of enormous power, wealth and activity. The Litany, which was put out in a separate book under Henry VIII, was the first instalment of the Book of Common Prayer of 1549, and was intended to be used before the Eucharist, Sunday by Sunday, in place of the old Procession. It was also appointed for the 'Perambulation of the circuits of Parishes' on the Rogation Days (Beatings of the Bounds – and sometimes beatings of the choir-boys!).

Together

As we join together in the Litany in a moment – for today this is not so much a sermon as a practical experience – let us use our imaginations and try and feel ourselves in the tradition of those worshippers long ago in the Temple at Jerusalem, those in the Early Church, often meeting under the threat of persecution, those bringing the Gospel to these islands – the early missionaries, those of the Middle Ages worshipping in our great Cathedrals, those of the Reformation times, those who held to the Church in the days of Cromwell, and indeed all who loved and followed the Church down the centuries.

Let us think of all those who have gathered together before God, seeking his care and his blessing; and let us feel ourselves to be a part of that great stream of worshippers. And let this event open our eyes and minds to another dimension of our meeting with God in prayer – the dimension of our corporate prayer, covering the whole range of our human living, our needs and our hopes, our care for others in trouble or despair, our concerns for the nation and the world. Together we present our intercessions before the Throne of Grace, with minds and hearts and voices united.

(See next page for Practical Details)

Careful planning is needed between Clergy, Organist, Choir and Servers. If the BCP is not available for the congregation, copies of the Litany need to be run off, with or without the music as may be decided.

A decision should be made as to whether the Litany will be sung or said; and whether it is to be in procession or not. If in procession, will this be for Clergy and Choir only or will the Congregation take part? Percy Dearmer (in *The Parson's Handbook*) wrote: 'No doubt the best way of singing the Litany is to do so in procession. This was the old custom, and there is nothing against it in the Prayer Book. It brings out the meaning of the Litany in a way that nothing else can do.' Cyril Pocknee in his revision of Dearmer, wrote: 'There are occasions when the whole congregation should be asked to take part. Anglican worship tends to be far too static, and anything that can bring ordered and purposeful movement is to be welcomed.'

Dearmer also notes: 'The omission of the *Amen* at the end of the Collect "O God, merciful Father" is a printer's error in 1662; corrected in 1928 and in the Shorter PB of 1948. The *Amen* should of course be sung or said at this point.'

Contemporary Versions

The ASB version of the Litany is on p. 99. It is interesting to see the revival of corporate prayer both in the ASB and in the other official service books: a short penitential Litany is given in *Lent, Holy Week and Easter* on p. 24, and an Intercession on p. 34. In *The Promise of his Glory* there is a Litany of All Saints on p. 59; Holy Dying on p. 108; Advent, p. 130; Christmas, p. 156; and Epiphany, p. 234. In *Patterns of Worship* there are excellent Litany forms for the Seasons in Section 51 (p. 138ff) and others can be found under Sections 63 and 65 (p. 179ff).

Fourth Sunday in Lent 17 March
Mothering Sunday

'Mary kept all these things in her heart.' Luke 2.19, or, 'Jerusalem, which is above, is free, which is the Mother of us all' Galatians 4.26 (For ASB see p. 170 – The Transfiguration)

The Family

We in the churches can be a little simple and sentimental about things; we tend to prefer second-hand answers, easy answers which do not take account of the actual climate; or giving answers to questions that people are not asking any more. And who listens then?

In thinking, then, about mothers and about families (as indeed we should, today of all days) we can run the danger of simplifying all too easily. Clerical meetings and groups do talk as if families are all like the one in some Ready-to-Eat food advert, a happy Mummy who stays at home and does just about everything; a happy Dad who goes to work in a nice car, a brother and sister to play together happily and do well at school, and a big happy dog which everyone pats on the street. The 'feel good' factor is here and of course God is easily found too. The ideal family strengthens the ideal world and leads us to the ideal God.

Problems

But, there is a problem. The ideal family is rarely met, except in the Bisto adverts, or when we follow their exciting lives in some soap opera. Real families are fragile things; they suffer setbacks, confusions, difficulties and hurts. In fact, some commentators say that this is why the TV soaps are so popular – so that we can join another family and feel part of it. We feel, by way of projection, that we do belong somewhere at least.

In reality, families are not often ideal.

The tensions can be hardly bearable; passions can die; love can grow cold; futures can look grim.

There are women who never see their husbands because they work all hours; there are elderly people who feel unwanted by the family, or forgotten by their own children. There are children in schools who cling to me because they don't have a strong figure at home since their parents separated early on. There are people who have never wanted to marry, who prefer solitude; and those who have never met a partner. There are gay partnerships; unmarried people who have often lived together for many years; there are the victims of nasty divorces and painful separations. Bruised people, wondering how to find self-respect again.

These are all people who don't get on the happy families adverts; and who all too readily become scapegoats for the ills of the world. If only they were ideal – we say – everything would be all right! We tend to think we can simplify the matter of the family just because we are Christian people.

Families are Vital
There is no doubt that families are vital to our physical and spiritual health. We are human beings, each of us with an enormous hunger to be spoken to, to be touched, to be judged and loved and forgiven. And most of us begin to learn these lessons of life within the warmth and space of our families. In the family we are talked to and touched into life, and into a sense of being valued and accepted, as we are, for what we are. And if these things don't happen at home, we have to learn them elsewhere at another time and in other places. If we never learn them, we are growing up as only partly human instead of fully human.

Yes, we clash with our parents, find it hard to remain friends, feel they are keeping us back. There is pain and frustration as well as joy and love. Our parents may feel equal frustration, or failure, or envy, or guilt. Our emotional lives are complex, and even more so within our family relationships. Don't let anyone kid you that family life is easy. It is not. Family life needs working at, it needs time, it needs patience – a lot of patience.

Discipleship
And this is why I claim that the learning within a family life is central to our spiritual growth. This is so because of the complex nature of Christian discipleship – the person who journeys with God often knows similar pains to the person who journeys within a family. Faith is not some sort of big spiritual grin we carry around – faith is a journey. And on a journey we move, we don't stand still. And because there is *movement* in faith, there is also growth and change; and growth and change can hurt, as families must know well. Yes, there are times when faith gives a joy in the heart, a joy we cannot find anywhere else, perhaps. But equally there are times when we can feel deserted, alone, frightened, angry with God, with our family and neighbours, and with ourselves. And there are days when God just doesn't seem to be there. We try and remain friends with God in darkness – what the spiritual writers call 'The dark night of the soul.' Yes, these are dry periods in our lives when we feel trapped, stale and cold.

Growth
When we look back we can often see what was going on. It may
be that we were being broken out of a mould we had grown too
closely into; perhaps we were being taught new truths about
ourselves, or about life, which we found difficult. Perhaps we
were getting too self-satisfied, too complacent or just plain selfish.
Or, maybe we were being taught that love proves itself in constant renewal, and renewal needs a bleak time to discover a new
energy.

For, as human beings, we live with knowing and not knowing,
with hints and guesses, with faith and fear; and we place these
together to make our 'collage' of faith.

The Cross
R. S. Thomas, a priest and a poet, describes such hard and dark
times of faith like this: (He is in church at night . . .)

> *There is no other sound*
> *In the darkness, but the sound of a man*
> *Breathing, testing his faith*
> *On emptiness; nailing his questions*
> *One by one to an untenanted Cross . . .*

Nailing our questions to the Cross!

Perhaps this is the way to see our Lent. For to us Christians
the Cross of suffering is at the very heart of the Divine Life we
believe we are called to share. It is there that we see Jesus alone,
touched and crying for God, with his Mother looking on. It is
there, in that damaged family scene, that we see the very, the
true 'body language' of God and his love. It is there that we see
the great contradiction, the paradox of Christian life, the paradox
that should make us suspicious of the ideal. And it is there that
we are shown that there are no easy answers – not to the real
questions of our existence.

Mothers
There is a Jewish proverb which says 'God couldn't be everywhere, so he invented mothers.'

Today should be a celebration of your life and all that it holds
– the memories of past joys and sorrows, of relations then and
now, the gift of a partner or of children, with whom you share

your love today. Hopes and faith for all that is yet to be accomplished by you and in you, and by them.

But it should also be a laying-down before God of the difficulties and pains that your life may also hold, not least the difficulties and pains in your parenthood, partnerships or solitude.

Our relationships are gifts from God. They bring us to life and love. They are celebrated by the God who became Incarnate, flesh of our flesh, life of our life, love of our love.

But because of their strength, their vulnerability is also to be acknowledged – and not only acknowledged but also owned, by those of us who journey with the God of Mystery and embracing Love, as it was owned by the Mother of the Lord, as she held the body of her Son at the foot of the Cross, on the bitter Mount of Calvary.

PIETA

They let me hold him in my arms; across my legs I felt the weight
Of my Son's bruised and bleeding form.
His pierced head with its matted hair I held close against my breast
Cradling it there.
Hungrily I held him to myself, and down within my soul
Deep groaning grew –
As once again my body knew the pain and wrench of labour.
But now it was not joy that came to birth
But sorrow wailing in the light torn from my leaden body –
Offspring of grief and fear.
'Eloi, eloi, lama sabachthani' – like him, I cried out in my pain.
Then I looked down, and saw that God was here –
Here, in all the blood and sweat, here in the midst of blasphemy and
*   sin –*
God was – And I could weep – and I shall sing!

Lyn Jennings

As Christian people, as parents and children, we are learning to sing with Mary.

M.O.

Lent 4 *Second Sermon A Lent Course on Prayer*
(4) 'Lord, teach us to pray' – The Prayer of Penitence

'I will arise and go to my father, and will say unto him, Father, I have sinned against heaven and before thee, and am no more worthy to be called thy son.' Luke 15.18,19

Early Days
In the early Church standards of belief and of conduct were rigorous. It took between two and three years to be prepared for Baptism, for instance, since in order to begin the new life in Christ you had to be totally rid and purged of the old sinful life. There would be the group known as 'penitents' who would be dismissed from the eucharist, along with those preparing for baptism, before the prayers and the communion. These 'penitents' were deemed to have committed sins serious enough to damage their part of the Body of Christ, the Church; and they were in effect excommunicated, albeit temporarily. They had to show publicly that they had a clear intention to renew and restore damaged relationships, and heal wounds, before they could again participate in the full common life of the Church. Depending upon the sin this could take from two to twenty years until they could be received back into the Church and be at peace with God.

In this early Church, you could not suddenly become once again, what you had failed to be; a period of thorough repentance and preparation was required before restoration.

The Middle Ages
By the Middle Ages penitence had moved into the realm of fear – the fear of dying with your soul in a state of sin. It was a time in which the 'Wrath of God' had been intensified by the images of Hell and Purgatory; this motivated people to assuage their anxiety by such means as pilgrimages, penance, devotion to 'holy' relics, ascetic exercises and the notorious 'indulgences' – by which the sinner could buy time out of Purgatory, and incidentally fund the Basilica of St Peter in Rome and pay the wages of the likes of Michelangelo. The Reformers rightly pointed to the abuses and superstitions that underpinned much of the penitential practice of the church at this time. Luther, amongst others, saw confession as neither necessary or possible (in the sense that

you cannot fully understand your sins); but the Reformers did not abandon confession, seeing that when made freely it could be an occasion of both consolation and counsel.

Thus General confessions and absolution became part of most Reformed orders of service; private confession was seen as a part of Christian ministry and pastoral care.

Today

Our contemporary views have moved far away from, on the one hand, excessively individualistic notions of sin and forgiveness, and also the connotations of judgement, punishment and retribution which seem to underly much mediaeval practice.

Does this mean that penitence is simply an antiquated device, which has never been properly thought out and decided how useful it is, or what to do with it? Certainly the queues once seen in major churches at festival times no longer appear; and in many places the tendency is to sit down together and discuss our problems face to face. And we cannot omit to notice the rise in counselling, therapy and analysis; then there are the opportunities today for making a retreat or going on a quiet day, when it is possible to talk with a priest should you so wish, on a more informal footing.

Encouragement and Comfort

Few of us would doubt the value of sharing problems and difficulties with friends or family; by doing so we not only share our fears and failures but receive hope, encouragement and comfort. Here is an important social interaction, which binds us in trust and love, and breaks the illusion of self-sufficiency.

But we may well need more than such encounters to know ourselves accepted, and something more fundamental than sharing our anxieties and guilt, to know ourselves forgiven. Where do we go with that sense of failure and weakness, that complicity in the injustice and darkness of this world, our broken relationships, our failure of choice and action, our inadequacy in response to God's love? Or our feeling of something that comes between us and God?

Recognition

What is needed is the recognition that no-one is free from failures and weaknesses, and that Christians are not called primarily to follow a law code, a system of rights and wrongs. We are called to respond to the God of love, to become fully human and fully alive in God, having faith in the Christ who told his disciples to forgive from the heart, and would not condemn the woman caught in adultery, but spoke of God as the father who welcomed with compassion and open arms the prodigal son. So where do we go and to what do we turn?

Many find our general corporate confession and absolution, within the Eucharist and the daily Offices enough; but some desire a more personal confession, expressing a personal repentance. So then, you can make your confession within a short service, in your own words, after which the priest may offer comment and advice, and suggest some prayer or action as a token of repentance and thanksgiving. This is not the place for discussions about morality, nor deep spiritual direction – that can be done at a more appropriate time and place. The priest is at your side encouraging you to open your heart to God in order that you can see yourself in all honesty. When the absolution is pronounced, it is less a blotting out of sin and more of a bringing of new life. Here is moment of grace in which we can know that God's love has found us, and that the unacceptable is accepted, absolved and redeemed.

Compassion and Mercy

The prayer of penitence has always had a place in the life of the Christian community. Sadly, there are wrong ideas and strange myths associated with confession and absolution, as well as abuses that have been made of it, but essentially the prayer of penitence is about believing in God's promise shown to us in the life, death and resurrection of Jesus Christ – a promise of God's love, compassion and mercy.

M.C.

'I tell you,' said Jesus, 'there is joy in the presence of the angels of God over one sinner who repents.' (Luke 15.10)

Lord our God,
grant us grace to desire you with our whole heart;
that so desiring, we may seek and find you;
and so finding, may love you;
and so loving, may hate those sins

from which you have delivered us;
through Jesus Christ our Lord.
                        (Lent, Holy Week & Easter, p. 46)

Fifth Sunday in Lent *Passion Sunday*
24 March   **Victory**

*'Grant that by faith in him who suffered on the cross, we may triumph
in the power of his victory.' (ASB Collect)*

Victory

That's a great word. All down the ages, when some sort of victory
has been won, people celebrate. We have been commemorating
the victories after World War II in Europe and in the Far East.
Parades and processions, fireworks and flags, balloons and
banners; throwing our hats in the air and lots of eating and drinking. Speeches and interviews, articles in the papers and programmes on TV. That's the public aspect, of course, but there is
also the private aspect. The sorrows and pains of those who
have lost loved ones; the sorrows and pains of the wounded, the
disfigured, the sufferers not only from shells and bombs and
bullets, but from fears and terror which can wound the mind and
the soul just as badly as guns wound the body. And we may
think especially of captives and prisoners of war, as well as the
civilian victims – all of whom may suffer as much if not more
than members of the armed forces.

Suffering

Haven't we all at some time been bewildered and affronted by
the fact of suffering? How can we square the suffering we see
around us, or experience ourselves, or view on TV or read about
– how can we square this with a faith in a loving God? Is there
an answer?

One answer is that there is no absolute answer to the questions
about God and suffering. We can flounder about with pious plati-
tudes or clichés, but for some or most we are left feeling angry
and disillusioned by it all.

What we *can* do – is to look at the Cross and see Christ dying
upon it, bruised, wounded, in agony, unable to do anything to

relieve the pain, and with the shadow of death closing down upon him; and to try and take in that. That was the greatest victory ever won; and the victory did not happen after his crucifixion, at Easter, on the third day, with the Resurrection. No, the victory was won at Calvary, through that death upon the cross, and all that led up to it.

Another Victory

Incredibly, with terrible ups and downs, passing through huge troughs of depression, through doubts and fears and unbelievable pain, Jesus won a victory; and those who share in whatever way in such pains and despair and terrors – they too with countless others, share in that victory. The human spirit can and will come through the depths, will survive, will not be broken for ever, and Jesus is the living proof of it, in his triumph in the midst of humiliation. It is a world-wide, humanity-wide, fulfilment of promises and prophecies.

Sadly, two of the disciples with Jesus – although he tells them all plainly what was going to happen, and although his whole demeanour as he led them along 'the road going up to Jerusalem' did indeed strike them with awe – seem to lose the sense of impending doom, and we see them pre-occupied with the foolish and inappropriate squabbling over who will be the best-off in the Kingdom. It was to take the disciples a long time to understand that the Kingdom of God was not like some earthly kingdom, with bickering for power and pushing for favours.

Jesus does not at once refuse their request, but asks a penetrating question: 'Can you drink my cup, can you be baptized with my baptism?'

The deeper meaning of these words does not come home to the questioners. Boldly they answer in the affirmative.

Jesus tells them that indeed they will share his cup and his baptism; but the seats of honour and power are not for him to grant.

Angry

The other disciples are angry with the two; not so much, it seems, for their lack of understanding of the nature of the Kingdom and the rewards to be hoped for, since all the disciples seem to think the same way, putting the kingdom of Christ on a level with earthly domains; but angry that these two are trying to stretch a march on the others.

Let us remember that we are part of the great problem and sin of the world as it is, problem and sin which continue to crucify God's purposes for this world and for ourselves. Come to him in penitence and receive his forgiveness, and then seriously follow the Lord's words: 'Whoever wants to be great must be your servant, and whoever wants to be first must be the willing slave of all. Our service is a measure of the extent and the reality of our acceptance of Christ's commission – to love and to serve, even if that may lead to the cross; and let us be clear, the cross is a sign and symbol of victory gained, a triumph won, and a sign and symbol that we can make our own.

> *Lord Jesus Christ*
> *who by your suffering and death*
> *upon the Cross*
> *delivered and saved the world,*
> *grant that by faith in you*
> *we may share in your victory*
> *and have a place in your kingdom.*
> *Amen.*

Lent 5 *Second Sermon* A Lent Course on Prayer (5) 'Lord, teach us to pray' – The Prayer of Intercession

'I am praying for them; I am not praying for the world but for those whom thou hast given me, for they are thine; all mine are thine, and thine are mine, and I am glorified in them.' John 17.9

Why did they ask?
Let us go back to the beginning; this series of sermons started from those words of the disciples to Jesus – 'Lord, teach us to pray, as John taught his disciples.' Why did they ask that question? Why did they ask for that teaching? Did they not – rather like us going to church – go regularly to their synagogues every Sabbath, and pray with the congregation? Didn't they – also like us – pray privately during the week, whether in a formal or informal way?

We may be sure they did – but, we are entitled to surmise that, again rather like us, their prayer often felt meaningless; it didn't seem to achieve anything. Their public and corporate prayer was, maybe, often wordy and repetitious, sometimes sufficiently so as to make them angry; while their private prayer lacked something, too.

To put it irreverently, for all their devotion they seemed to have no hotline to God; put more reverently their prayers seemed to fail to help them to get into tune with the Spirit.

Yet, as John's disciples must have thought about John, so even more so with Jesus – here were two men who really did seem to be in tune with the Spirit, really did seem to be able to talk with – and receive strength from – God, in a very real way. How was it done? 'Lord, teach us to pray.' What was Jesus' response? It was, as we all know, the Lord's Prayer.

Intercession

Now, we are to discuss intercession; but look at the Lord's Prayer. Nowhere in it do we find anything which is *directly* intercession, whether in the sense of interceding (or pleading, which is what the word means) for others – for the sick, the dying, the lonely, for peace in the world, and so on. Nor in the sense of asking anyone else – Jesus, Mary, the Saints or whoever – to intercede or plea for us. True, we ask for *our* daily bread and for forgiveness for *our* trespasses; and in so far as that 'our' includes everyone in the world, we might be said to be praying for others as well. But I believe that we are grouping ourselves with our fellow human beings when we use these words, and we pray them in a petitionary sense rather than acting as go-betweens, as intercessors.

Jesus himself did intercede, on two occasions in particular. First, according to St John in chapter 17 of his Gospel, Jesus said in prayer about his disciples:

'I am praying for them; I am not praying for the world but for those whom thou hast given me, for they are thine; all mine are thine and thine are mine and I am glorified in them.'

Here, Jesus interceded for his disciples because, surely, he knew the task that would be ahead of them after his death; he knew the strength they would need, and the temptations they would face as they were persecuted.

Is there not here, a pointer as to how deeply – and, I suggest, how much more deeply than we normally do – we need to pray for each other and for our fellow Christians, because if we and they are to live out the lives of followers of Christ we too shall face temptations, we too shall need strength.

The Greatest Word of Love

Now, the second of Jesus' particular intercessions is that sentence which is surely the greatest word of intercession, the greatest word of Love ever uttered, that sentence wrenched out of his agony upon the Cross, 'Father, forgive them, for they know not what they do.'

A prayer of intercession which went beyond his disciples to all the world – all those who through lethargy, or brutality, or foolhardiness, or negligence, or villainy – nail him to the Cross; as well as those of us, his disciples, who – if we are not already in one of those previous categories – help to place him there by our cowardice in all too easily running away.

Those two times of Jesus' intercession flowed from his union with God and from Love – Love for his disciples, Love for the world for which he was dying. And because those words of intercession flowed from Love, they were, we may have no doubt, effective.

So with intercession as with all our prayer.

It is our attitude, our intention, what is really going on in our hearts, which matters. And the Lord's Prayer, properly understood and properly prayed, will bring us into close communion with God, so that our prayers, too, will flow from Love.

True Value

None of us will ever become perfect in Love, but it is only as we pray from, and in, Love, that our prayers of intercession will be of true value; and to the extent that they are prayed from and in Love, they will have effect. That does not mean that they will be answered just as we have asked, for always they will be subject – as for Jesus in Gethsemane – to 'Thy will be done.'

And our intercession will be from and in Love if we truly pray in the Name of Jesus. Remember how he said 'If you ask anything in my name, I will give it you.'

Unfortunately, as it seems to me, not only do we rattle off prayers in church without truly *praying* them, but we add the words 'Through Jesus Christ our Lord' apparently believing that by the addition of those magic and pious words we have prayed in the name of Jesus. But have we?

Praying – and saying prayers

Two boys were involved in a bad accident; the parents heard of it in the middle of the night, and for more than an hour did not know whether the lads were alive or dead. Then the news came that they were alive but badly injured. The parents were reading the Bible and happened to turn to John 16, and read:

'Truly, truly, I say to you, if you ask anything of the Father, he will give it to you in my name. Hitherto you have asked nothing in my name; ask and you will receive that your joy may be full.' (v. 24)

For many years they had been going to church and saying many prayers – but when they read those words they said, 'Lord, you are absolutely right; hitherto we *have* asked nothing in your name. Now in your name, we *do* ask that these boys shall be well.' They did get well. But they would say that they can't say whether there was any connection, direct or otherwise, between the prayers and the recovery. Reason would tell us that there was no connection, for of course, many have prayed in His name that a loved one should recover, but in vain. But, at the very least, that heartfelt prayer in the name of Jesus had a deep effect on the parents, and as with so many things in prayer we come back to the words of Tennyson, 'More things are wrought by prayer than this world dreams of.'

But let us emphasize that the words are 'more things are wrought by prayer', and not 'more things are wrought by saying prayers'. Saying prayers only, whether of intercession or otherwise, will under God get us nowhere. Praying prayers will aid us, or others, somehow.

A PRAYER

Almighty and everlasting God,
the comfort of the sad, the strength of those who suffer,
hear the prayers of your people who cry out of any trouble:
and to every distressed soul grant mercy, relief and refreshment,
through Jesus Christ our Lord. Amen.
(Lent, Holy Week & Easter, p. 215)

Palm Sunday *(The Sunday next before Easter)*
31 March   'Hosanna to the Son of David!'

'He humbled himself, and in obedience accepted even death – death on a Cross' Philippians 2.8 (ASB NT Reading), or, 'He thought it not robbery to be equal with God, but made himself of no reputation, and took upon him the form of a servant.' Philippians 2.5 (BCP)

Robbery to be equal with God?

A strange expression – better perhaps in the NEB version, 'to snatch at equality with God'. St Paul is thinking back to the first book of the Bible, the Book Genesis. There he sees the 'primordial robbery' symbolized in the story of Adam and Eve. They reached up to pluck the forbidden fruit, the fruit that they had been told – by Satan – that would make them like gods. A story? A myth?

Yes indeed; yet a story with truth within it, a myth that has a lesson for us all, clever human beings that we are.

The great error of humankind is this – to suppose that by our own cleverness we can become Godlike, can control the natural world, can control our own destiny. All things are in our hands, and we can do anything – so we think, and so we go on.

Disaster

We fail, continually fail, in spite of the lessons we receive, the teaching we get, the warnings we are given – we fail to learn the lesson that this error of ours can only lead to disaster. Whether we think of the destruction of the rain forests; the expanding of the great gap in the upper atmosphere that is even now resulting in the melting of the polar ice, the heating of the seas; the destroying of so many species of animals and fish; the threat of atomic waste, and indeed of atomic energy itself; the constant threats of war and nuclear missiles – the world has suffered and is suffering from all this, the results of our human cleverness, human vanity, human attempts to be like God.

God's Creation

Yet, we were created that we should become Godlike, that we should follow his teaching, that we should be glorified, that is to say, precisely Godlike. Today's reading from St Paul's letter to the Philippians teaches us how this amazing purpose of God can be fulfilled. The divine Son of God descended from glory in order to reverse the false ways of humanity – the way of greed, the way of robbery, the way of destruction. Jesus came to teach and to show by his own example, the way of humility and obedience. A costly way, a costly obedience, leading to the eventual death of the Saviour, which we commemorate today at the promulgation of the Passion and Crucifixion.

Power

As St Paul puts it (1 Corinthians 1.18–25): 'Where is the wise man? Where is the scribe? Where is the debator of this age? Has not God made foolish the wisdom of the world?' How right these words sound today, do they not? Paul goes on,

'We preach Christ crucified, . . . to those who are called, Christ the power of God and the wisdom of God. For the foolishness of God is wiser than humanity, and the weakness of God is stronger than mankind.'

The way out of our problems and our troubles, our mistakes and our stupidities, is simply to put our trust in God and take his words seriously. By giving ourselves over to the Spirit of Christ; by letting his mind be in us, then we are certain of doing his will; we are carrying on the work that he began, and which he empowered his apostles to continue, in the Church of Christ.

The Church of Christ

Why do we trouble to maintain the Church of Christ, with all its imperfections, its troubles, its frequent foolishness, its incapacity to keep control even of its financial problems, let alone its spiritual ones? Why do we battle on against a sea of opposition and – worse than opposition – indifference? It is simply that we may continue to bear witness to the truth. In the first place to the truth that God is, and who God is, and what his plan for us all is; then, to bear witness to the truth of our real human vocation – that is, to conserve the world we are on and are part of; to make it and keep it in accordance with the will of its – and our – Creator. To save it, that is, to bring to it salvation. Salvation is a far different thing from a mere improved condition, whether for the human race or for the planet we live on. Salvation means a complete change, a complete acceptance of the saving grace of Christ, who came to save the world.

Here is our human calling and our human vocation. Sometimes that calling and vocation may seem almost too good to be true; yet truth is the basis of all that we do, or try to do. In the spirit of truth we are called to live and work to God's glory and the building of his Kingdom all our days.

Palm Sunday *Second Sermon* **Rejection**
'The very stone which the builders rejected has become the head of the corner.' Mark 12.10 (ASB EP)

Confrontation
Jesus has been confronted by the chief priests, the scribes, and the elders, as he was walking in the Temple. They want to question his authority for his preaching and teaching, and his attack on the traders in the Temple. 'By whose authority?' they ask. Jesus was teaching in the form of a new exposition of the Scriptures; such action was the prerogative of the qualified, professional lawyers. The question had a straightforward answer: Jesus had no official authority, and no doubt this was what they wanted to hear. But Jesus makes his answer a comparison with the preaching and teaching of John the Baptist; the people had taken John as a 'real' prophet, and his words were revered in popular opinion, more than the 'official' teaching and policies.

Put Down
Faced with the popular feeling, the authorities had no choice but to give way. Jesus follows this success with a sharply pointed parable, in which the owner of a carefully-prepared vineyard is disappointed of his natural and proper return from his tenants, who in the end brutally kill the servants he sends and – worst of all – the son and heir. The theme seems to be the vital necessity of recognizing the messengers of God, and with a change of heart repenting at once. The following text refers clearly to the rejection of Jesus, and then the restoration of the Lord as indeed the 'cornerstone' in the final version of triumph and victory, the Resurrection on the third day.

A Lesson
Here is a sad lesson and reminder to us, not only of the actual events which brought our Lord's ministry of love and healing, teaching and preaching, to a sudden, brutal and cruel end, but of the fact that we can all share in those events to a definite extent, by our rejecting or ignoring what Jesus teaches and stands

for. We would be very mistaken to see this parable only as a story allotting blame to those hard and deliberately one-sided priests and officials – concerned only for their own positions and power – who were immediately responsible for our Lord's death. The parable asks all of us the question which – in various ways and in various words – the Lord put to those who heard him during his earthly ministry. The question: 'What is your attitude to me? What do you think of Christ?'

Our Answer
How will we answer that question?

It is all too easy to turn away from Jesus, ignore what seems difficult or demanding, if not with violence like the men in the parable, nor like the Jews and Romans who brought the Lord to the dreadful Place of the Skull, but by our own indifference, our own love of self, or our own lack of the courage needed to follow Christ in the temptations of daily life.

PRAYER

Father, hear our prayer and forgive us.

Unstop our ears
   that we may receive the gospel of the cross.
Lighten our eyes
   that we may see your glory
   in the face of your Son.
Penetrate our minds
   that your truth may make us whole.
Irradiate our hearts with your love
   that we may love one another for Christ's sake.

Father, forgive us.
                    (Lent, Holy Week & Easter, p. 210)

Maundy Thursday 4 April
The Sacrament of Love
'A new commandment I give you, that you love one another, as I have loved you.' John 13.34

Sorrow and Joy

This evening is a strange evening. It's a time of mingled joy and sorrow. Like the disciples, we gather together to share in the Passover feast, the remembrance of the power of God displayed in the feeling of his people from the bonds of captivity in a strange land. It is an occasion of joy. But at the same time, we remember how the Lord Jesus and his disciples came together. There was a threat hanging over all their heads; they knew that the authorities – Hebrew and Roman – were preparing some action. What form it would take they did not know exactly – but arrest, imprisonment, torture, death, were all on the cards. It was an occasion of foreboding. Christ himself was in deep distress. He could see more clearly than the disciples the suffering that lay ahead; he must have been deeply saddened by the defection of Judas; and he must have been anxious lest he might be arrested before he had said and done all that he intended. No doubt they ate 'in urgent haste' (Exodus 12.11) after the manner of the first partakers of the Passover, expecting at any moment the hammering on the door and the shouts of the security forces sent to arrest them.

The Washing of Feet

First, however, the washing of feet; no servants here, but Christ himself signifying the love and care we are to have for one another. Our religion is one of service, let us never forget that. If our Lord and Master washed the feet of his followers, we also ought to do as he did – that is, be ready to serve wherever and whenever help is needed. This symbolic action done, they were ready to go on to the most important part of the evening's action.

'Do this as my Memorial'

'Do this as my memorial', said the Lord, over the broken bread and the poured-out wine. As we receive in our own time and place, the bread and the wine, the words of Jesus 'This is my Body' – 'This is my Blood' tell us that we are indeed partaking of the very power and strength of the Lord and Saviour, our Redeemer. Day by day, all over the world, in every kind of church or meeting-place, the followers of Jesus share the bread, share the cup. Here is the great act of fellowship, fellowship with Christ himself as also with our fellow worshippers and communicants. Down the ages the sharing of a common meal has always, in all places, been a sign of mutual trust, of goodwill, and of fellowship.

The Future

With the commemoration of the past goes also the looking to the future. 'We proclaim the Lord's death, until he comes in glory!' Yes, we look forward with fervent love and hope to the Day of the Lord. Maranatha! Even so, come, Lord Jesus. The Risen Lord is with us here as we give thanks for the Resurrection and look for the Coming of the Kingdom.

Anima Christi

Soul of Christ, sanctify me,
Body of Christ, save me.
Blood of Christ, refresh me.
Water from the side of Christ, wash me.
Passion of Christ, strengthen me.
O good Jesus, hear me.
Within your wounds, hide me.
Let me never be separated from you.
From the power of darkness defend me.
In the hour of my death, call me and bid me come to you,
that with your saints I may praise you for ever and ever.
(L.H.W.E.)

Good Friday
5 April   Life through Death

'Unless a grain of wheat falls into the earth and dies, it remains alone; but if it dies, it bears much fruit.' John 12.24

Death

In these words we have one of our Lord's own ways of describing his death, the death that we commemorate today. The occasion when he used these words was soon after his triumphant entry into Jerusalem, after Palm Sunday as we would say; some Greeks approach Philip, asking to see the Lord. The festival at Jerusalem not only drew a great crowd of Jewish pilgrims; people of other nationalities – whether they were full proselytes or merely sympathetically inclined to the Hebrew religion – also made the journey to the Holy City. To the Jews, it was convenient to refer to such people as Greeks, though they might come from almost anywhere in the eastern part of the Empire. The main thing was that these pilgrims were not Jewish by birth.

We do not know exactly what these men said to Jesus; but in all probability Christ expected that they would be likely to see him die. So he makes some very solemn and significant sayings, and is in fact explaining his approaching death, in the form of a parable of a tiny grain falling into the ground, and entering into the yearly cycle of nature, death and rebirth, as a new and rich harvest will follow.

The Necessity of that Death

It was not easy for Christ to show forth the necessity of his death, so soon to come, but it was even more difficult for his disciples to understand it. To them, death seemed to have marked upon it the stamp of weakness, failure, incapacity, and possibly even guilt. They had been so long with Jesus and they knew him so well – as they thought – that they must have been heart-struck to have to consider and accept that this one perfect human life, to which all the ages past had been pointing, could possibly end in death. All the people had been shouting, 'Hosanna! Hail to the King!' How could it come to this miserable, criminal's death, nailed to a cross . . . Laughed at, abused, jeered at, helpless . . . It was a terrible shock. When his enemies saw Jesus on the criminal's gibbet, they felt they had him in their power at last, here in the grip of death. This, they thought, settled all his claims. Here was stressed his impotence: 'He saved others, himself he cannot save!' The disciples seemed to have some kind of a trace of these thoughts in their minds. Peter had indignantly told the Master to put the thought of suffering from him – 'God forbid, Lord! This shall never happen to you!' (Matthew 16.22). Later, the disciples at Emmaus evidently expressed their disappointment in Jesus – 'We had hoped that he was the one to redeem Israel' (Luke 24.21). His death shattered their hopes. There is good reason, then, for St Paul's description of the Crucifixion as it made its impact on the two divisions of the ancient world – 'Christ crucified, a stumbling block to Jews, and folly to Gentiles' (1 Cor. 1.23) – the very negation of wisdom. It would also seem that those Hebrew Christians addressed in Hebrews had real difficulty in understanding Christ's death – 'Although he was a Son, he learned obedience through what he suffered, and being made perfect became the source of "dull of hearing" (v.11). Yet, to the

Lord himself, the 'seed' had to fall into the ground and die, before the New Life could come to be.

New Life through that Death

When Christ spoke the words of our text about the grain of wheat, he would no doubt have appealed to the witness of the prophets down the ages, if he had been speaking to those born as Jews. To instructed believers, like those addressed in Hebrews, he would no doubt have insisted that being made like unto his brethren, he must submit to the law of humanity for them, though with results which would far transcend our human deaths. But, as he was speaking to Greeks, who would not be familiar with prophesies, and who had no real understanding of his unique position, but were simply approaching what we might call 'a popular preacher' – he used an idiom and an explanation they could understand. He simply pointed to a fact of nature, which was enacted year by year in the harvest fields. 'He went on at once to lay down the law of life through death – the principle which lies at the very heart of the Gospel' (Temple). The caterpillar surrenders its form to become the butterfly in all its beauty; the seed decomposes, to rise again as a fresh and glorious plant. From death, there arises a new life.

Death as Fruitful

Jesus took on himself the form of a slave; he took on himself the human nature that is ours, the nature of the transient inhabitants of this tiny planet. By taking upon himself our nature, he stooped and laid aside all his power, all his liberty of action, and placed himself under the restraints and obligations of human life. The Master of all became the slave of all; and under that form he was willing to die. No one forced him to do this, but by his will to save the world, he was ready to do it for us. And the death he died was the cruel, brutal, callous death accorded to common criminals. Christ was willing to do all this, endure all pains, carry all blame, because he is God – and God is Love. If the Divine love offers so much, then indeed our human love ought to offer itself, in return, to God. Let us today, with the Cross so firmly in our minds and souls, place ourselves there, on the hill of Calvary, and with tears of penitence offer ourselves to the Suffering to the Suffering Saviour, our Redeemer, our Hope.

Easter Day
Sunday 7 April The Open Tomb

'The women saw that the stone had been rolled back already.' Mark 16.4 (ASB Gospel)

Our Festival of Openness

Easter for us should be the great Festival of Openness. The great stone which sealed the tomb has been rolled back – now the vault is open for all to enter and see! The crucified Christ, laid to rest in the tomb, is no longer there. The Cross of defeat has become the sign and the hope of victory. In the words of the poet Robert Herrick,

'We need fear the Cross no more!'

Suffering, defeat, and death itself are held fast in the open generosity of God's love. If you had come into church yesterday, about this time, the feeling was of dereliction, of nakedness, of everything shut and closed; but overnight – as it were – all has been transformed. The great high altar reredos – closed since the beginning of Lent – is now open for all to see its full glory; the Lenten veils hiding the pictures and statues, are taken away, as is the great hanging before the glorious Rood. Flowers decorate the building; the Choir is in full song; the banners are carried; the festal vestments are worn.

More, if we look outside at Nature and Creation, the glorious weather tells us its own Resurrection story; the sunshine has set off a Spring of immense power and love, whose glory sweeps away Winter. As Martin Luther wrote,

'God has written the Resurrection story not in books, but in every leaf of Springtime!'

Queen of Festivals

Easter, the Queen of Festivals, expresses eloquently the inexhaustible love, openness, and generosity of God; all leads us back to that central fact of God's grace and mercy. Easter is not about exclusiveness, but about openness. It demands of us our naked trust in that naked gift of God's love, expressed through the Cross. Sadly we brush aside the question of the Cross, and want to stay with the God we feel comfortable with, and who we can 'do business with'. But we cannot omit the symbol of the Cross, nor think only of a God who will be 'relevant', and whom we think will be pleased with our bustle of religious professionalism.

A Divine Beginning
The Easter event is a Divine Beginning; the Cross is redefined with Christ's arms outstretched openly in love for all Creation and all creatures. Let us take out the message in the words penned by John Donne:

'Blow the trumpets and arise from death!'

Easter calls for an honesty and an openness with God. Easter calls for an openness about our ministry as Christians; it calls for openness one to another, and a refusal to cover up. Rather, to abandon ourselves both to, and for, the other, so that all may have access and the opportunity of entering into the tomb, so that they too may see and believe.

Acceptance
There must be therefore, an acceptance, a sharing and a living, a time for laughter and for tears, but all under God. Let us gladly allow others to peer in and look; we must not monopolize God by false religiosity nor vague spiritualy – let us not block the entrance, but keep it open, for Easter is the Festival of Openness – and never Closing.

Then and then only will the Holy, the Divine, be set free from human boundaries and man-made conditions. Easter sets us free from our false picture of a manic and obsessive God, and a stuffy religion of the airless vault, where there is no light – and hence no growth. We must not cling to the old just for the sake of it, lest God is robbed of life and openness by our all-too-human web of management and administration. Let us not make our Faith a defended fortress of self-satisfied religion, but something of open imagination, where all is held in trust under God. Let us allow God room to move, to act, to overcome!

The Power of God
The Easter Story celebrates the power of God, the generosity of God, the love of God – and the openness of God. What we so often fear is our staleness, our incompetence, our vulnerability, our suffering and pain; but these inabilities are our strengths

when we learn to rely upon God. Nothing is more destructive and contrary to the Easter Story than the assurance, the arrogance, that we can cope on our own. Let us be open to God's Word and his Love, and be suffused by him. Above all, let us think of the 'Empty Tomb' as being the 'Open Tomb', for here is a positive title – the Tomb is open, it allows us to go in; let us clear the path for others, and clear our own inner vault to allow the power of God's love and light to shine in, to strengthen and to enable.

As that great preacher Leslie Weatherhead said,

'The supreme Message of Resurrection is not the event itself, but the power of God's openness and his love.'

Yes, Easter is the Festival of Openness. Let us roll back the stone of arrogance and proclaim 'Christ is Risen!' not in word only, but in example of life and living.

J.O.

Easter Day *Second Sermon* 'Unless . . .'

'Unless I see in his hands the print of the nails, and place my finger in the mark of the nails, and place my hand in his side, I will not believe'
John 21.25 (ASB EP Reading)

Faith

In his introduction to his book 'The Resurrection of Christ', Leslie Weatherhead writes, 'Part of the trouble in the Church today is, that young people who do come in are expected to believe a lot of difficult propositions without any evidence, by simply switching on to something miscalled 'Faith'. But Faith is not something to be turned on like the turning of a tap. We must point out that faith is utter loyalty to the trend of all the available evidence – and then a leap forward to the improbable, prompted by insight.'

During the period of Lent, many of us will have been journeying and questioning the teachings of Christ as recorded in the Gospels, and this journeying and questioning will have brought us to the fundamentals of our faith. What is it that is so distinctive about our Christian faith? Are answers to problems clear-cut and concise – or are they seen as varying, depending upon interpretations, upon traditions, upon answers given in other times and under other conditions, often very different from our own of today.

But our faith, we may be sure, has been strengthened by the insights we gain from one another, from discussion, from our reading and consideration; as the doubts of Thomas were dispelled by faith and experience.

Glory
One glorious Easter hymn starts,

> This joyful Eastertide,
>   Away with sin and sorrow.
> My Love, the Crucified,
>   Hath sprung to life this morrow.
>   (NEH 121)

The Resurrection which we celebrate at Eastertide is the very heart of the Christian message, and we joyfully leap forward to the improbable this day. The only proof of the Resurrection is, as Professor John Macquarrie puts it, 'is that in the living Christian community today, the person of Christ still lives, and the living God still acts through him to reconcile and make whole.' May this be a very blessed and happy Eastertide, and may we all be joyful proofs of the Resurrection, so that others may be led to faith through us.

J.O.

First Sunday after Easter *(Low Sunday)*
14 April   **'Bread of Life'**
'I am the bread of life. He who comes to me will never be hungry; he who believes in me will never thirst' John 6.35 (ASB Gospel)

The Eucharist
From the very earliest days of the Church, the believers in Christ have come together upon the Lord's Day for the Holy Communion. When we take part in the celebration of the Holy Sacrament, we are forging a new link in a long, long chain; a chain which goes away back to the Last Supper in the Upper Room, and our Lord's act of institution. That act is not explicitly mentioned in the Fourth Gospel, but the Christians for whom it was written

were already accustomed to holding a solemn supper at which the bread and wine were affirmed to be the body and blood of Christ; and they knew that the institution of this new and distinctive act of worship went back to the explicit teaching of Jesus himself. Earlier in the chapter there are hints towards such teaching ('Jesus took the loaves, gave thanks, and distributed' (v.11) and 'The bread over which the Lord gave thanks' (v.23) and then the words, so similar to those recorded as used by Jesus in the other gospels at the Last Supper, 'The bread which I will give is my own flesh; I give it for the life of the world' (v.51) Jesus is the bread of life, and we feed on him 'by faith with thanksgiving'.

He who came down from Heaven
Jesus declares that what God requires is faith in his Son: 'This is the work that God requires: that you believe in him whom he has sent' (v.29). In answer to this claim the people ask for a sign. Moses had given the children of Israel, as they journeyed through the wilderness, food from heaven, 'Manna'. No doubt they believed that when the Messiah came, he would do the same. Jesus replies that it was not Moses who gave them the bread from heaven, but 'my Father who gives you the real bread from heaven' (v. 32).

It is Jesus who is the bread from heaven, the bread of life: 'Whoever comes to me shall never be hungry, and whoever believes in me shall never thirst.' (v.35) The reference is to Moses, striking the rock and the water gushing out. But now there stands in their midst a greater One than Moses. Man is a spiritual being, with spiritual needs; and Jesus satisfied all those needs; in him we find fulfilment. The life that comes from him is eternal life, beginning here and now, but finding its fulfilment in the life to come.

The Will of the Father
Jesus comes to do the Father's will: 'All that the Father gives me will come to me; and he who comes to me I will never turn away.' God's will is that all shall come to him: 'It is his will that I should not lose even one of all that he has given me, but I will raise them all up on the last day' (v.39).

Yet, God respects the freedom he has given. So, Christ's coming brings always mercy and forgiveness; but it also brings judgement, the judgement that must come when we reject the light, and turn to darkness.

How hard it is to understand why so many find it difficult to believe, and reject God's love in Christ. But this has always been so; it is a part of the mystery of our human freedom to choose.

There is a divine pressure in one sense, on us to accept our calling in Christ: 'For it is my Father's will that everyone who looks upon the Son and puts his faith in him, shall possess eternal life . . .' (v.40) God's love is such that he seeks to draw us into fellowship with himself – but, we remain free to choose, and – the power of evil being such in the world – to reject his love. What we need to remember is that God's calling to us all, is to salvation, to that fulfilment which he makes possible for us in Christ.

> For Unity in the Church
> Lord God,
> the source of truth and love,
> keep us faithful
> to the apostles' teaching and fellowship,
> united in prayer
> and the breaking of bread,
> and one in joy and simplicity of heart,
> in Jesus Christ our Lord.
> (Patterns for Worship, p. 162)

Easter 1 *Second Sermon* **Doubt and Belief**

Jesus said: 'Because you have seen me you have found faith: happy are those who never saw me and yet have found faith' John 20.29 (ASB EP)

Religion and Modern Thinking

Many people today feel that science has made it impossible for an intelligent human being to accept the great doctrines of the Christian faith. The climate of today's thought is unfavourable to belief in any religion. On the other hand, scientists have dropped, generally speaking, the old-fashioned attitude of a harsh kind of dogmatic anti-religion. Instead there is a sort of vagueness, a kind of fogginess that prefers not to deny but will not assert – either a religious view or a non-religious view, of life.

Perhaps the most striking example is the famous Dr Stephen Hawking, author of *A Brief History of Time* – a best-seller to beat almost any best-seller. Yet it deals with the abstruse questions of time and space, creation and the end of all things. Widely regarded as the most brilliant theoretical physicist and cosmologist since Einstein, yet with a crumpled and almost useless body, speaking by means of a mechanical voice-reproducer; yet Dr Hawking will not, and refuses to give, any kind of definite judgement as to whether he believes in God or not. The 'Space-Race' and the wonderful lift this has given to astronomy, in particular the Hubbard telescope with its enormous range, still has not even begun to unlock the enormous mysteries of the universe.

The Vastness of Space

The more we learn about the universe, the more vast and astonishing becomes this strange entity, space itself. We think of the size and apparent emptiness of the universe, and we cannot escape feeling that humanity is insignificant and puny. We come – we know not where from; we go – we know not where to. Do we really exist? Is there another life, perhaps somewhere in this vast universe? How can we believe that God knows or cares anything about us? How can we matter to him? Yet, if we think a little more, we are reminded that it is not just size that matters.

A Point of Light

Although we are encompassed in mystery, we know that there is a point of light in the surrounding darkness. Christ came to tell us, once and for all, that we are not orphans and castaways, driven about blindly on the boundless sea of the universe. He came to tell us of our Father, who is in heaven, even God. We know, unless all human knowledge of the past is merely a vain and useless dream, that Christ did indeed rise from the dead; and we also know that this great and almost unimaginable event has changed not only the course but the whole aspects of the world and of human life in general. Christ is our Elder Brother, and his life is the pattern of what God wills our lives to be. As he rose, so we also will rise if we are joined to him in true faith. He is our refuge, then, our only refuge, from the agonizing mysteries of the world. He is the one certainty, and he reaches out to us, while we reach out to him. Christ is not only the Resurrection and the Life, he is also the Light of the world. Let us be true and real about the call to go to him who is the world's Light. Without him, life has no point, no object, and all our efforts and hopes are fruitless. But with him, we have confidence, we have

certainty; he is with us as our spiritual power in our course
through the storms, the perplexities, and the pains of life.

Father of Lights,
from you come every good and perfect gift:
keep us in the light of Christ,
to shine in your world,
that all may believe in you
through Jesus Christ our Lord.
              (Patterns for Worship, p. 164)

Second Sunday after Easter 21 April
The Good Shepherd

'I am the good shepherd; I know my own sheep and my sheep know me'
John 10, 14 (ASB Gospel)

The Shepherd

A favourite picture, is it not? The shepherd following along
behind his flock perhaps on the Yorkshire moors or the Sussex
Downs, with his dog running out on one side, then the other,
to keep the woolly creatures on the straight and narrow. What a
dream of England as it was, but not perhaps quite so definitely
so, today; probably the shepherd is on a mountain bike, and he
possibly will be talking into his portable phone and keeping in
touch with the farm.

But the skills and the knowledge the shepherd needs still
remain much as ever; the most important will be that he knows
his sheep. Each one of them is an individual with their own
funny ways, habits – bad and good, shape and structure easily
recognized by his experienced eye.

If a shepherd can know every one of his sheep, how much
more can God know every one of us?

God

Can God know every one of us? Can he? But that is what we mean
by God; there is no limit to his vision, his power to see into the least
little details of his Creation. Even into our own souls . . .

We belong to him. We are his property. The contrast of Christ's parable is between the shepherd-owner, and the hired hand. Unlike the hired hand, the owner notices and seeks out the lame, the sick, the damaged – the sheep whose woolly coat has been torn by thorns or barbed wire, the sheep with a bruised leg or a split hoof, the sheep who is sickening for some stomach upset. He is prepared to face the thief, or the destructive killer dog gone wild, and takes the risk to himself of limb or even life.

Knowing the Shepherd

The sheep know their shepherd. In the East, the shepherd goes first along the track, looking for good grass or for water, and leading the flock so as to avoid difficulties – rough raw rock perhaps, slimy dangerous pools, steep slopes which could easily let the sheep lose its footing. The sheep know their shepherd and trust him day by day to do what is best.

What do we know about God? Can we say 'Jesus is our friend'? Do we know him and trust him, day by day, week by week?

Do we allow him to guide our footsteps? Do we ask him to show us the path we should take? Is he a friend who is taken into our confidence?

The Same –and not the Same

Jesus is the same and not the same – as, for instance, the man who walked and talked with his friends in Galilee. That man was cruelly treated, that man carried his cross, that man was nailed to the cross and died, there in the heat and the sunshine, with the enemies cat-calling round about, in the Place of the Skull, Golgotha.

Now he is risen, now he is glorified. He has returned to his friends to greet them, to assure them he is still with them, to encourage them to take up his task on earth, the guidance and care of his flock. That flock for which he laid down his life – the good shepherd making the final and greatest sacrifice – that is the most precious legacy he leaves to his friends, in trust and in hope.

Other Sheep

Notice too the reference to 'the other sheep'. Many commentators take this to be either a reference to the Gentiles – as 'other sheep, not belonging to this fold', i.e. the Hebrew nation – or to other religions, meaning those who by following the tenets and instructions of their leaders and their own holy books or scriptures, with good intentions and high aims, will find themselves indeed 'sheep belonging to the One Good Shepherd' all the time.

In our age of space travel, another possibility seems feasible. Could it be that in years to come, if advances continue to be made in methods of space exploration and increases in the speed and range of space vehicles, we will reach other inhabited planets and discover other races of non-human creatures yet still intelligent and – for want of a better word – spiritual? And was this other race, or races, redeemed? Was there another Fall in another world? As a poet has put it,

> 'Nor, in our little day,
> May his devices with the heavens be guessed,
> His pilgrimage to thread the Milky Way,
> Or his bestowals there be manifest.
>
> But, in the eternities,
> Doubtless we shall compare together, hear
> A million alien Gospels; in what guise
> Hetrod the Pleiades, the Lyre, the Bear.
>
> O be prepared, my soul!
> To read the inconceivable, to scan
> The million forms of God those stars unroll
> When, in our turn, we show to them a Man.'
> – Alice Meynell

Easter 2 *Second Sermon*   The Writer – St Mark
'The pen of a ready writer' Ps 45.2.

Dedication
In the total of parish churches in our Church of England, we are told by expert church-haunters and church-tasters, who John Betjeman-like traverse the country and whose eyes miss little, that the number of churches dedicated to St Mark is between 100 and 200; certainly far less than St Mary the Blessed Virgin (2,000), All Saints (1,200) but more than Holy Cross, St Catherine, and St Cuthbert (100 each), St Augustine, St Barnabus, St Anne (50 to 80) or St Bride, St Hilda, St Alban, and St Jude (20 to 40).

In one of the churches dedicated to St Mark, a fine building near the London Zoo, we can see when we visit it, an interesting stained-glass window. The evangelist is shown in the act of writing down what he hears from the other figure in the design, St Peter. And to be sure, St Peter's reminiscences are at the core and heart of St Mark's Gospel story. By tradition Mark – whose festival we observe on Thursday next, April 25th – drew his information from the remembrance and teaching of St Peter, probably in Rome. In his First Letter, Peter refers to 'my son Mark', which shows the close relationship between the two.

World-wide

But Mark does not merely hear the story and write it down - he begins its transmission throughout the world and down the centuries. He acted in a way that was within his grasp. He was not a literary genius, but he was a writer, a compiler like the editor of this book. Mark was not called upon to do something impossible for him – he was not the non-swimmer called in to rescue the drowning man. A genius is quite different from an apostle; the genius cannot do other than practise his art – the apostle often complains at being chosen for apostolic work, but knows quite simply that it has been laid upon him to do it.

A Pattern for Us

And this pattern of hearing and doing is a pattern for each one of us Christian people, young or old. We are not required to be geniuses; we are called instead to respond with whatever God has given us, individually, in the way of heart and mind and soul and strength. And this individual response, made in the way that only each one of us can make it, must never be 'collectivized' as though there were only a few acceptable ways of the hearers doing or responding.

On the other hand, there are categories of response which it can be useful occasionally to list: First, our response is to try and follow the example of Christ in daily life, and to try and bear witness to him. (There are more ways of bearing witness to Christ than we generally think of; they become apparent often more in conversation than in summoning them up ourselves.)

Prayer, Worship, Service

Then we respond in prayer, opening our hearts to God; next we have to read the Bible, using such helps as we find good for us in explanatory books and in the BRF notes or other such commentaries. Then there is worship, Sunday by Sunday, joining in prayer and praise; and most important – receiving the Holy Sacrament with regularity and devotion. We are told to give personal service to Church and to neighbours and to the community; and we are to give money to the needs and work of the Church both at home and overseas. And, my friends, the time will come when we will no longer be able to make these responses and contributions; therefore notice this – The time for making our responses is now 'while we have time'. A last thought: in our stained-glass window, the two figures are linked in the relationship of speaker and hearer. Each of us has heard the gospel; we are each linked to one another and to the first apostles by the chain of hearing and doing.

Third Sunday after Easter 28 April
New Life in Christ

'Jesus said, "I am the resurrection and I am life!"' John 11.25 (ASB Gospel)

Lazarus

The story of Lazarus, the friend of Jesus, is a particularly vivid and powerful one. Jesus tells his disciples (v.11) 'Our friend Lazarus has fallen asleep, but I shall go to awake him out of sleep.' It is a dangerous trip, into 'enemy country' we might well say, and the disciples are, very reasonably, afraid. They may all be arrested, they may be stoned, they may be killed – it is not a prospect to look forward to. And if Lazarus is dead, what can they – or the Lord – do about that? It seems a foolish venture.

Surprisingly, perhaps, it is Thomas – he who was to be known, rather unfairly, as 'Doubting Thomas' when he could not accept the account of the appearance of the Risen Lord – 'I must see the marks of the nails, and place my finger in them, and my hand in his side, before I will believe' – He it is who boldly challenges the indecision and fear of the others, calling out, 'Let us also go, that we may die with him!' (v.16) Effective, because this roused the others from their fears and they all set off, ready to face death if needed.

At Bethany
Arrived at Bethany, Martha gives the assurance 'Your brother will rise again.' She thinks he is referring to the Last Day; Jesus reminds her – 'If a man has faith in me, even though he die, he shall come to life, and no-one who is alive and has faith will never die.' Striking words indeed, and does she believe this? 'Lord I do; I now believe that you are the Messiah . . .'

Jesus shows tender sympathy with the sisters; he sighs heavily and is deeply moved. Then comes the astonishing miracle, with the great cry, 'Lazarus, come forth!' and the command, 'Loose him, let him go.'

Lazarus hears the voice of Christ – and lives. This is what Jesus promised should happen: it is the time 'when the dead shall hear the voice of the Son of God, and all who hear shall come to life.' (John 5.25)

Resurrection and Life
Our service of Christian burial begins with a thunderous note of assurance: 'I am the Resurrection and I am the life; he who believes in me, though he die, yet shall he live, and whoever lives and believes in me shall never die.' (John 11.25, 26; ASB) Here is a trumpet call to faith – this is not just an aspiration, a mere pious hope. Jesus *is* the resurrection and the life, because he died and God raised him from the dead. It is a partial truth to say that Jesus was the kind of person who couldn't die: we believe that the Resurrection is something that actually happened, and our faith is based on complete confidence in this. Because he lives, we live too.

Easter 3 *Second Sermon* **Uncertain**
'Simon Peter said to the disciples, "I am going fishing"' John 21.3 (ASB EP)

Baffled and Uncertain
The disciples had by no means taken in as yet, the nature of their future. Yes, they had seen the Lord – or most of them – but the great work that lay ahead, the spreading of the news of the Resurrection, the making clear of its meaning, the sheer size of the task – all this took time and thought to understand. Were they under the impression that they were to make the great news

known only in the familiar surroundings, and among the familiar faces, in the villages and towns of Galilee?

Another possibility may be considered. In spite of the joy which our Lord's resurrection brought them, were they afraid of its consequences for themselves? Jesus was back – wonderful! – but what fresh demands was he making upon them? Did they feel that he expected far too much from simple fishermen than they were able to perform? And how were they to support themselves? They were not rich, and they could not trespass too long upon the hospitality of Mary, the mother of John Mark, in Jerusalem, nor of Martha and Mary in Bethany. So it seemed best to go home, pick up the threads – or rather, the nets – of their old life.

Again, was an element of timidity, and of lack of enthusiasm for a task that seemed too hard and too vast for them, one of the motives that moved Peter to go back to the well-known routine of fishing, and the rest to agree to go with him.

Christ's Appearance

If they were mistaken in whole or in part about the Lord's plans for them, or if they lacked the courage or the drive to put those plans into action, there was only one thing which could put matters right: another visit from Jesus.

This was precisely what took place.

St John's Gospel describes how Jesus was waiting for them on the lake shore – but they did not recognize him. Instead, he acted as any local bystander would, if the fishermen were having no luck. It is a fact, still reported by visitors to the Holy Land in our day, that from the beach it is possible to see a school of fish, which those out on the water cannot spot, owing to a trick of the light; so the man on the beach shouts directions and enables the fishermen to make their catch.

'It is the Lord!'

Following the instructions of the stranger, the disciples make a huge and unexpected haul. John recognizes who it is that has directed them, but it is Peter who takes action, throws on his tunic, and splashes into the water. Thoughtfully, Jesus has prepared a meal for them; and no doubt they listened and questioned while eating that open-air breakfast, and found reward courage and strength of will in his presence. It may well have been the case that when Jesus left them, all seven knew that their days and nights of fishing in the lake were over for good, and that their future milieu of work was wider, and their task far greater than they had thought ever possible.

Turning to Jesus
There are times in our own lives when we mistake what we should be doing, or we are too timid to go forward boldly, or too slack to bother, or too selfish and filled with our own ideas, to sit down and think out what is the Lord's will for us.

With us, as with those apostles in the early days, the remedy is the same – to go to Jesus; let his gentle but firm voice speak to us as we turn our thoughts to him, seek him in prayer and meditation, and take strength from the holy Food he supplies in the Eucharist to try harder to carry out, not our own limited plans, but his far better and greater purposes.

> For the Work of the Church
>
> We pray for the coming of God's kingdom, saying,
> Father, by your Spirit
> *bring in your kingdom.*
>
> You came in Jesus to bring good news to the poor
> and salvation to your people.
> Father, by your Spirit
> *bring in your kingdom.*
>
> Send us to tell the world
> the good news of your healing love.
> Father, by your Spirit
> *bring in your kingdom.*
>
> Send us to proclaim that the time is here
> for you to save your people.
> Father, by your spirit
> *Bring in your kingdom.*
>
> *(PHG, p. 236)*

Fourth Sunday after Easter 5 May
Many Dwelling-places

'There are many dwelling-places in my Father's house' John 14.2 (ASB Gospel)

Stately Homes

All over the country there are – or were – many large country houses. Some were built in Victorian times, most were built in earlier days and reflect the styles and the conditions of periods when transport was on foot or by horse or in a coach, depending on your place in the social scale. Such houses reflect the society of the time, and the tastes as well as the wealth of the owner or the family who lived in them. But many of these great houses have gone now, some pulled down and some turned into flats or institutions, while many survive through the National Trust as 'stately homes' open to the public for viewing at a fee. The Authorized or King James Version of the Bible translates our text today as 'In my Father's house are many mansions,' but this does give something of a false impression, suggesting that Jesus was talking about 'stately homes'; and modern Bibles use the more modest word 'dwelling-places', as being more in line with what Jesus must have meant. Our version today comes from the New English Bible.

What did Jesus mean?

A great many Christians have taken these words to be a promise concerning life after death; Jesus is saying that there is a place of happiness and rest prepared for us in the life to come. The Lord said earlier in the same talk to his disciples 'Where I am going you cannot follow me now; but one day you will.' (13.36) The word 'mansion', if not a very accurate translation, does suggest something important about the future life. For although the large country houses are all too often almost empty today, in the great times for which they were built, they were full of people and busy with all kinds of activities. There was the owner's family, there was a large staff of servants and craftsmen, gardeners and carpenters and plumbers, painters and plasterers and artists, as well of course as workers in the farms, shepherds and ploughmen and dairymen. So our Lord was telling his apostles of a future state into which all can enter, and where all who do enter will be in fellowship with one another and with God, and will be working busily in God's service. May it not be that those who were prevented – for whatever cause – from taking up a desired career or particular employment on earth, will find a new chance given to them, and a new opportunity to make use of gifts and talents left unused on earth.

The Journey through Life – and Beyond

Archbishop Temple preferred to translate 'mansion' or 'dwelling-place' by the word 'resting-place'. Travelling along the roads of Palestine and the East in the time of Jesus, travellers could find rest overnight on their long journeys in 'Rest-houses' or 'Resting-places'. Prosperous travellers would send forward an agent or servant each day, whose job it would be to make preparations at the next of these stopping-places, so as to ensure as much comfort as might be possible.

Our life then is a journey, as so often so described in the Bible and elsewhere. We are not travelling alone nor unprovided for, since Jesus himself describes himself as the servant who goes before – 'I am going to prepare a place for you' (14.2). 'I will come again and take you to myself, that where I am you may be also.' (14.3)

If, on the journey of life, we set ourselves in the right direction, and take our travelling seriously, we will have God's support and the fellowship of the Lord Jesus as we go through the world. And that support and fellowship will not cease when we enter the new and astonishing world on the other side of the boundary of death.

PRAYER

God and Father of our Lord Jesus Christ,
bring us to the dwelling which your Son
is preparing for all who love you.
Give us the will each day
to live in life eternal.
Let our citizenship be in heaven
with your blessed and beloved,
the whole company of the redeemed,
and with countless angels
praising, worshipping and adoring him
who sits upon the throne for ever and ever. Amen.
(PHG 10, p. 107)

Easter 4 *Second Sermon* **The Future**

'Peter asked, "Lord, what will happen to him?"' John 21.21 (ASB EP)

Discussions

As we heard last week, after Jesus had risen from the dead, Peter and some other disciples found themselves in a kind of No Man's Land; unable to know exactly what to do, they returned to their old trade of fishing. Jesus appeared to them in the early light of the morning, on the shore, and guided them to make a good catch; then called them to breakfast which he had prepared. He would have had much to say to them, much to encourage them, many questions to answer, and he must have transformed their attitude from discouragement to hope and strength. In particular, Jesus had a special talk with Peter when breakfast was over. John was within hearing range, but seems to have said nothing. What Jesus said to Peter may be summed up by saying that it was firstly, about the past, then secondly, about the future.

Threefold

Peter had made a threefold disowning of Jesus during the trial, as all four gospels faithfully record. It seems the intention for that sad disowning to be wiped out by the threefold profession of love of Jesus; and certainly Jesus' final command 'Follow me' would seem to refer back to his saying 'You cannot follow me now, but one day you will.' (John 13.36)

Peter is given a great task for the future; Jesus entrusts to him the care and the leadership of the Christian Church. Up to now, Jesus has been the only shepherd; the Lord's words 'Feed my lambs' and 'Feed my sheep' are taken to mean authority and leadership, though the precise extent which they imply is not agreed by all parts of the Church.

The Future

Jesus also speaks of Peter's personal future. The saints' martyr-dom is clearly pointed to; he would find himself as helpless as an old man, in the face of those who would put him to death, a martyr to his faith. Recent excavations under St Peter's in Rome seem to confirm the tradition that Peter was executed, and that his body was buried below what is now the place of the high altar of that great church.

It seems that Peter wondered if John, the 'beloved disciple' whom 'Jesus loved', who was close at hand and was able to hear the conversation, would also become a martyr. Christ gives the mysterious answer, 'If I will that he remains until I come, what is that to you? Follow me!'

This would seem to be a rebuke; Jesus cuts Peter short. We are not to be too inquisitive about our neighbours, their past, their present, and their future. We can also be too curious about what lies ahead, not only for others, but for ourselves. Jesus gives us good practical advice when he told us not to worry too much about possible troubles in the future, and said, 'Do not be anxious about tomorrow; tomorrow will look after itself. Each day has troubles enough of its own.' (Matt. 6.34)

The Catch
'Simon Peter went aboard and hauled the net ashore, full of large fish, one hundred and fifty-three of them . . .' (John 21,11).

The scholars tell us that we have here a rich piece of symbolism. The evangelist can hardly intend us to think that someone present counted and remembered the exact number of the fish. A round number would have been just as impressive. What is the meaning therefore of the number given? It happens that the sum of the numbers $1 + 2 + 3 +$ and up to 17 is 153; $17 = 10 + 7$, and ten and seven were each numbers signifying (in the symbolism of numbers of the ancients) a perfect whole. By such reasoning, 153 could be understood as standing for a symbol of the whole of something (perhaps the whole of mankind, or the whole of the church). Alternately, the explanation may be that some natural-ists (perhaps influenced by the arithmetic rather than actual observation) allowed for exactly 153 different species of fish in the seas of the world. In this case the number would again be a symbol of totality.

And we can hardly be wrong when we see in another quite unimportant detail – 'the net was not torn' – another symbolical statement. Perhaps, if the fish in the net represented the totality of people to be brought into the Church, then the fact that the net was not torn would stand for the unity of the church – no division, no schism.

All this may seem rather recondite; but it was Jesus himself who started the metaphor: 'I will make you fishers of men' (Mark 1.17). All the rest is an elaboration of this promise.

Fifth Sunday after Easter *(Rogation Sunday)*
12 May   Understanding the Future

'Who shall separate us from the love of Christ? Shall tribulation, or distress, or persecution, or famine, or nakedness, or peril, or sword? . . . No, in all these things we are more than conquerors, through him who loved us' Romans 8.35,37 *(ASB NT Reading)*

At Supper . . .
Our gospel is part of Jesus' final speech to his friends at the Last Supper. The subject: The Future. Jesus with his grasp on reality, his understanding of God's will, is helping his friends to understand the future. The future will be different from the past; but some of the features of the past will continue still, but in a changed mode.

Nothing fishy about this change – it isn't something done with mirrors, but something definite happening upon the stage of human life. 'The same but different' sums it up – and if we cast around for something with which to liken it, on the small stage of our personal lives, we could say: It is life before and after a hospital operation, or a change of occupation, or a bereavement, or the birth of one's child, or the first falling in love, or our marriage; perhaps the first day when burdened with satchel and sandwiches and sharp pencils, we went to school for the first time.

The Same but Different
Each of these events can be reduced to their barest or basic details – the date, the time, the place. Some details concern Jesus – his death, his resurrection and his parting from his friends. But, St John is concerned with helping us to understand what these things mean. So, he has us overhearing the supper talk. He has the perfect ear for the thought processing questions of people who are depressed and who are out of their depth; they need clarity of the either/or sort. 'Let it be the same' – their future, or not the same; but not 'the same but different'. And so they keep batting back and forth their questions about 'A little while, and you will not see me; again a little while and you will see me.'

Coming Clean . . .
Now in today's reading, they may feel that Jesus is, so to speak, 'coming clean'; momentarily they grasp at least that his departure from them is linked with a return to the Father. And this return

to the Father will be a prelude to the release of a new kind of 'Jesus factor' in their lives. And this cloud of uncertainty that was over them from Good Friday until his Parting from them, was to be dispersed only by the gale force winds of Pentecost.

Preparation
Jesus is therefore overheard in the last paragraph of today's gospel, as preparing them for this change; the old ways of seeing, hearing, touching, were to be exchanged for new. And this was part of God's plan for his world – nothing less. Of course, he had yet many things to say to them; of course they could not bear them then. But instead of fobbing them off with mere dates, mere times, mere place names, he draws them into his own understanding of the New Era we call the Christian centuries. (In the Old Testament the writer of Job attempts a similar exercise, when Blake-like he imagines himself into God's thinking at the first creation of the world – ch. 38 & 39.)

Understanding
You and I read and hear today's Gospel.

For us, for each of us, there lies ahead deeper understandings of God's purposes, opportunities for humble obedience, forgiveness such as to purify us in order to see him more clearly.

And all this is not for our individual improvement, but in order that his will for his world may use us for its outworking. And all this he will do by the power of his Holy Spirit.

'It is not so much the word of Jesus knocking at the mind's door, that secures his admittance; it is the God within, drawing the bolts with invisible fingers. When your pride, he says, when your self-sufficiency has been shattered by the experience of my death, the Spirit will secure the admittance of all the truth you need to know.'

Second Sermon *'St Matthias'* p. 253

Ascension Day 16 May   Holy Thursday

'He who descended is no other than he who ascended far above all the heavens, so that he might fill the universe' Ephesians 4.10 (ASB NT Reading)

The Last Great Prayer

In the first lines of the 17th chapter of St John's Gospel, we have what is the most profound and yet the most simple exposition of the life of Jesus Christ. We are told that Jesus came from God, and returned to God, to the glory that he had before he entered our world. Eternal life is to know the true God and Jesus whom he sent (John 17.1–5).

The fact is, that everything we say about God must be in parables. Our deepest intuitions, those moments when we are aware of an infinite love, of our need to be forgiven, and of the assurance that we can be, and are, forgiven, and can be united with God; when our prayer and worship is most real, we are simply *with God*, God who is so unlike us, who is infinitely good and infinitely great. These moments can only be spoken about in parables: they can only be pictured, only expressed in intuitive language, given in hints and suggestions.

'God Up There'

Ascensiontide concerns us with questions – How far can we use the great parable that God 'lives up there'? In using the word 'heaven' – which originally meant the sky quite simply – we are using language which was once taken literally; blessed by its use by Jesus himself – above all in the great universal prayer 'Our Father in heaven'. Can we still repeat such phrases? And what then do we mean? In our age, in our time of space exploration, with the knowledge that we have of the vast mysteries of millions of light-years and of the structure of the universe, we are forced to see these expressions in symbolic terms. 'Up there' means a sphere that cannot be contaminated with evil, with misery and sin, as contrasted with 'down here' – only too heavily contaminated.

Christ brought heaven in that sense down with him – he genuinely suffered all that evil could do to him, yet remained heavenly.

Mystery and Worship

If we are to understand at all the mystery of God, and are to worship him, we need to see that Christ reveals God as the One who cannot be contaminated by evil, and yet really endures and suffers from evil.

The other side of all this, and the great practical point, is that we can already *be* heavenly people, since Christ has won for us the gift of the Holy Spirit. We, living in this world of ours, tempted, fearful, agonized, afraid – yet if we trust sincerely and deeply in Jesus Christ, we can be free from the contamination of sin. Yes – that, and 'heaven too' when we are completely liberated from all that makes it hard to see and love God our Father.

The Sunday after Ascension Day 19 May
Exalted

'We have a great high priest who has passed through the heavens, Jesus the Son of God. Alleluya!' Hebrews 4.14 (ASB Introductory Sentence)

The Resurrection and the Ascension

St Paul rightly sees the Resurrection of Jesus Christ as the peg, the essential point, upon which the whole of the Christian Faith hangs. It is in the light of the Resurrection that we look back and ask questions about the significance of Jesus' earthly life; but, we also look forward because the Resurrection has opened up the possibility of new life for all of us. Without the Resurrection, surely, any mission of Jesus must be reckoned a failure?

As an *event*, the Resurrection faces us with some historical problems. It is no good saying that this doesn't matter, or that nothing may be proved one way or another. The Resurrection may not be *proved*, but it must be open to historical investigation, because Christianity is not a myth, but a religion in which God reveals himself in and through historical events. The Crucifixion was a public event; it took place – historically speaking – 'under Pontius Pilate'. But the Resurrection is, in the last resort, a matter of faith.

However, the New Testament evidence concerning the empty tomb, the early tradition of the 'Third Day', as well as the Resurrection appearances and the growth of the Early Church, makes the Resurrection the most plausible explanation of the facts.

The view that the appearances were hallucinations, or that the

Church grew out of the disciples' wishful thinking goes against the evidence we have – and I think is more difficult to believe.

Raised by God
In all this, we have to remember that the Resurrection is not a possibility simply within the world of human experience. We are born and at the end of our lives, we die; but the Resurrection is part of the freely-willed activity of God. Jesus did not raise himself, he *was* raised by God. In the same way that the Creation did not just happen but was brought about by God, so the Resurrection is not a consequence of history – but is God acting, as God, in and through it. The statement 'Jesus is risen!' is, then, historically justified, because it can withstand historical investigation – though that is not to say, that any 'final' proof about the facts can be attained.

If the Resurrection is talking about the 'final' activity of God (that is, about what for us is still 'future' life) then it is not surprising that it remains controversial and difficult to explain and interpret solely within the terms of our limited human experience.

Not the Revival of a Corpse . . .
The Ascension develops the idea of the Risen Jesus further. Christianity does not assert the revival of a corpse – Jesus does not rise from the dead in order to die again. He is, in the language of theology, 'exalted' – 'enthroned with God'. The Ascension points the Resurrection in a Godward direction. Humanity is now taken into the life of God himself. As a result of the Incarnation, the Resurrection and the Ascension, life within the Godhead is different. Through these events, the possibility of our sharing in God's life is opened up to us.

Completion
The Ascension seen as the completion of the whole Incarnational process, also helps us to achieve a more balanced doctrine of the Person of Christ. It isn't that God 'becomes flesh' and that is then that – for if we overemphasize the Birth of Christ, that is just what we end up with; whereas seeing the Incarnation as completed in the Ascension reminds us that Christ's own nature is One 'not by the conversion of the Godhead into flesh, but by the taking of humanity into God' (Athanasian Creed).

All this has consequences for the Christian life. Christians do not believe in the Greek doctrine of the immortal soul which survives death, but in a God-given, qualitatively difference life which transcends (but not avoids) death. We believe in a God who brings life from death ('Resurrection') and takes that life and makes it part of his own life (Ascension). Both of these become possibilities for us, when we are incorporated into the dying, risen, ascended Lord through our baptism, and then sustained in him by our life in the Church.

At the Ascension

Thanks and praise be to you, Lord of heaven,
for Jesus Christ your Son our Lord.
You gave him the name above every name,
so that we say,
Jesus Lord of all
We worship and adore you.

King of righteousness, King of peace,
enthroned at the right hand of Majesty on high:
Jesus, Lord of all
We worship and adore you.

Great high priest, living for ever to intercede for us:
Jesus, Lord of all
We worship and adore you.

Pioneer of our salvation, you bring us to glory
through your death and resurrection:
Jesus, Lord of all
We worship and adore you.
                              (Patterns for Worship, p. 202)

Sunday after Ascension *Second Sermon* Saintly Brothers

'That the God of our Lord Jesus Christ, the Father of glory, may give you a spirit of wisdom and of revelation in the knowledge of him, having the eyes of your hearts enlightened, that you may know what is the hope to which he has called you' Ephesians 1.17,18 (ASB EP Reading)

John and Charles Wesley

On Friday we remember with praise and thanks, two remarkable brothers, John and Charles Wesley. The one – John – famous as a preacher and for his founding of the Methodist Church; the other – Charles – famous for his wonderful hymns. They were sons of an eccentric and impecunious clergyman, Rector of Epworth in Lincolnshire, Samuel Wesley, and his wife Susannah. They were the fifteenth and eighteenth children of the couple! (There were no ideas of family planning, it seems, in those days; and what a loss there would have been if there had!) What inspired these brothers?

John gave his answer in his old age: 'Surely never in any age or nation since the Apostles, have these words been so eminently fulfilled: "The poor have the gospel preached unto them!" Sinners have been converted to God, changed both in heart and in life, not by tens nor by hundreds, but by thousands. God is arising to maintain his own cause, and to set up his Kingdom . . .'

How did it all begin?

John developed early; his father admitted him to Communion at the age of eight. At Oxford, he was ordained deacon in 1725; and with his brother Charles formed a group who attended the Eucharist each week, studied the Bible together, visited the sick and prisoners, prayed together systematically, kept the Church's feasts and fasts; some laid stress on private confession. All was done 'methodically' – hence the name 'Methodists' soon became attached to them.

There then appeared the retired General James Oglethorpe, whose special work was with debtors, badly treated under the existing English laws, and for whom he was founding a colony in Georgia where a new life could be started. He invited the brothers to go out there to help; difficulties, mistakes and frustrations produced a lack of success. John wrote in later days: 'I who went to America to convert others, was never myself converted to God.'

Conversion

That conversion took place in London on May 24th 1738 – 'I felt my heart strangely warmed; I felt that I trusted in Christ, Christ alone, for salvation' and he had the assurance of sins forgiven. About the same time, a similar conversion took place in the life of his brother Charles.

John now joined the remarkable George Whitfield, greatly impressed by his open-air preaching at Bristol. 'The devil does not love field-preaching. Neither do I; I love a commodious room, a soft cushion, and a handsome pulpit!' wrote John; but soon 'submitted, and preached in the highways to about 3,000 people'. From this developed his tireless journeyings, over roads deep in mud, strewn with boulders, full of ruts. He averaged 5,000 miles a year on horseback, preaching fifteen times a week, for fifty years. A quarter of a million miles and 40,000 sermons!

Sometimes in Danger

Cornwall, among the tin-miners: 'The mob burst into the room, roaring and striking . . . I went into the midst, and brought the head of the mob with me to the desk. I received but one blow on the side of the head; after this we reasoned till he grew mild and milder, and at length undertook to quiet his companions.'

He was not welcomed by the Established Church, so gradually preaching houses were built around the country, though both John and Charles maintained their High Church views, and made it clear they intended a Church revival, not a separation, even though John declared: 'I look upon the whole world as my parish.' Charles continued to preach, but his fame rests chiefly upon his glorious hymns; he is said to have written over six thousand. The English Hymnal contains twenty, including 'Hark! the herald Angels sing', 'Love's redeeming work is done', 'Author of life divine', 'O thou who camest from above', 'Jesu, Lover of my soul' to mention only a few.

Separation

Still protesting his dislike of separation, John took the decisive step of 'ordaining presbyters' and 'setting apart' Thomas Coke as 'superintendent' for the Methodists in America. The organization of the Methodist Church was John's principal concern for his later years, though in 1789 he declared his determination to 'live and die a member of the Church of England'. He died in 1791. Sadly, although much goodwill and hard work has been devoted to bringing the two bodies together, formal unity seems still some way off. Let us pray that it will not be long before that unity is achieved.

Author of life divine,
  Who hast a table spread,

Furnished with mystic wine
   And everlasting bread,
Preserve the life thyself hast given,
And feed and train us up for heaven.
   Our needy souls sustain,
      With fresh supplies of love,
   Till all thy life we gain,
      And all thy fullness prove,
And, strengthened by thy perfect grace,
Behold without a veil thy face.
Charles Wesley (NEH 274)

Pentecost *(Whit Sunday)* 26 May
The Holy Spirit

'I will pour out my Spirit upon all flesh; yes, and on my menservants and my maidservants in those days, I will pour out my Spirit; and they shall prophesy' Acts 2. 17, 18 (An ASB NT Reading), or, 'Jesus said unto his disciples, If ye love me, keep my commandments. And I will pray the Father, and he shall give you another Comforter, that he may abide with you for ever; even the Spirit of truth' John 14, 15 (BCP Gospel), or, 'They were all filled with the Holy Spirit' Acts 2, 4 (BCP and ASB)

Importance

Pentecost or Whit Sunday, can truly be called, in some ways, the most important of all the Church Festivals throughout the whole year. It is certainly just as important as Christmas and Easter from the point of view of the Church; since this is the Festival and Commemoration of the descent of the Holy Spirit upon the Church – the coming of the Spirit of God upon the apostles, and upon the whole Christian people.

The Son of God came down, the Son of God was made man in the womb of the Blessed Virgin Mary. The Holy Spirit came down, the Holy Spirit was made human in the souls of Christians. When Jesus was born, he was to grow up and be himself; he left his mother behind. He outgrew her protection, he outgrew in time her person, and he outgrew in time her mind. Every mother has to see, and should encourage, her child to outgrow her care, sad though the process may sometimes be.

123

But as the Holy Spirit grows in us, it is not He but we who grow. He does not grow up and leave us behind, we grow up into Him. He, in the intention of God the Father, becomes the spring and the substance of our minds and hearts. He is the Spirit of Truth, the Counsellor, who will be with us for ever. And it is the Spirit who will lead us deeper into the love of God, and this love it is which will unite us to each other. And, not only to each other but to Jesus and the Father. This is the work of the Spirit.

Less Emphasis . . .
Perhaps the lessening of emphasis on Pentecost as a great Feast of the Church, is partly because the festival comes so soon after Easter, and then is followed very rapidly by Trinity. If we were to revive and take on once again the custom of the earlier Church, and continue with red for hangings and vestments, this might remind us visibly Sunday by Sunday that we are in the realm of the Holy Spirit. Indeed the ASB makes this clear, in the way that all the following Sundays (after Trinity) are now named as 'After Pentecost'.

(The name 'Pentecost', incidentally, simply means 'Fiftieth Day', and was the Greek name for the Hebrew harvest festival which took place seven weeks after Passover. Jesus' crucifixion was at Passover; the Church's mission began at the next festival, seven weeks later.)

Symbolism
The symbols for Christmas are the new-born Babe and the Star, easily understood as birth and hope; the symbols for Good Friday and Easter, for death and resurrection, the Cross and the Risen Person of Christ are very clear. By comparison the symbols for Pentecost seem less solid – though powerful indeed: Wind and Fire. Two powerful forces which cannot be fully controlled – indeed sometimes not at all controlled – by human effort. Good symbols for the Living God – disturbing, challenging, sometimes destroying, yet also purifying and healing, refreshing and warming, sometimes life-saving. These, with the gentle image of the Dove, show something of the vitality and the power of the Spirit.

Birthday of the Church
Pentecost is also called 'The Birthday of the Church', since it was at Pentecost that the followers of Christ were given new light, new understanding, new power, with confirmation and affirmation of all that had happened in the mission of Jesus – in his life,

death, resurrection and ascension. Pentecost is the event which brought a fresh inspiration, empowering and enthusiasm to those first Christians. To that tiny band of very ordinary, very frail, often fearful, men and women, which was transformed overnight, as it were, into the Body of Christ. The individual members of that Body were imbued with enormous courage, with power and strength in preaching and spreading the Gospel, the Good News of the Kingdom of God.

Was it really – for instance – the same man, Peter, who on the night preceding Good Friday, had vehemently declared, even sworn, that he 'didn't know this Jesus' – was it really him who now, at Pentecost, was able to stand up and without a sign of fear, address in the strongest terms the great crowd of assembled Jews and others from 'every nation under heaven'? And more astonishing, they all – so we are told – understood him; the curse of Babel was removed, and the new message seemed to be already clothing itself in the languages spoken in every part of the world, and therefore destined for world-wide proclamation.

The Power of the Spirit
As we commemorate the coming of the Holy Spirit to the apostles, we are reminded that not only did the Holy Spirit come to them on that special day, but he comes to us as well; a source of power in our lives, unique and different from the other sources of power we know, and remaining with us as long as we are willing to receive him, and guide us as long as we are willing to listen to him.

> You came to the disciples in the upper room,
>   and turned their fear into courage.
> For your love and mercy we give you thanks,
> *We praise your holy name.*
>
> You came to the disciples by the lakeside,
>   and turned their failure into faith.
> For your love and mercy we give you thanks.
> *We praise your holy name.*
>
> You came to your disciples on the Emmaus road,
>   and turned their despair into hope.
> For your love and mercy we give you thanks.
> *We praise your holy name.*

You come to your people now,
 and turn our weakness into triumph.
For your love and mercy we give you thanks.
We praise your holy name.
                                    (Patterns for Worship, p. 182)

Pentecost *(Second Sermon)*
The Help of the Spirit

'The Spirit comes to the aid of our weakness' Romans 8,26 (ASB EP).

The Promise

It is plain that when our Lord made some of his promises, the
disciples did not – at that time – fully understand. He clearly
wished his followers to know that his final withdrawal from the
world, the end of his days in human form on earth, was not
a withdrawal of his presence. A spiritual presence in 'another
Comforter' is promised – 'I will not leave you bereft; I am coming
back to you' (John 14.18). It was to be that in this way he would
fulfil his final promise to be with them to the end of the age. His
words had been: 'I will ask the Father, and he will give you
another Advocate, to be with you for ever, the Spirit of truth'
(John 14.16). He had just spoken of himself as in the future acting
as a helper or advocate at the heavenly throne, 'Whatever you
ask in my name, I will do it, that the Father may be glorified in
the Son; if you ask anything in my name, I will do it' (John
14.13,14). This other Paraclete would be with them for ever. It is
very clear that St Paul is speaking out of his own vivid experience
of the Holy Spirit's help when he wrote: 'The Spirit comes to the
aid of our weakness.'

The Experience

In the Holy Spirit's mission, we experience the fulfilment of the
promise of the Lord – 'He dwells with you, he will be in you'
(John 14.17). His is a present and a permanent indwelling; he is
to be with us as an ever-present Light, Help and Comforter. In
this way the coming of the Spirit was also to be a coming of the
Lord himself; though not in visible form, such as the disciples
had experienced in their earthly companionship, along the dusty
roads of Palestine. Mary Magdalen had been greatly reminded

of the changed state of the Lord's presence, on that Resurrection morning. 'Touch me not,' he said, 'for I am not yet ascended to the Father' (John 20.17) All were to be made aware of that change, but the abiding Presence was a spiritual reality.

It is in fact in this abiding presence of the Holy Spirit, that we experience the reality of the Three Persons of the Trinity. The Spirit's presence is thus the presence of the Father and the Son. The Son requests the Father, the Father gives the gift, and the gift is the Spirit. Christ had said: 'Anyone who loves me will heed what I say; then my Father will love him, and we will come to him and make our dwelling with him.' (John 14.23) Here is an understanding for us, of the Christian life. The prophets of the Old Testament had a hope of God being immanent in his world; this is a present reality for the believer in the Spirit's work and mission. Here and now, the Divine comes into our hearts, and in that gift we can truly live and truly rejoice.

Trinity Sunday *(First after Pentecost)* 2 June
Revelation
'Holy, holy, holy is the Lord God almighty; who was, and is, and is to come.' Revelation 4.8 (ASB Introductory Sentence)

The Trinity
The Father, the Son, and the Holy Spirit – these three Persons in a wonderful Unity represents to us the Triune God. Yes, it is a great mystery, but then mystery attaches to all life. 'The wind blows where it wills, and you hear the sound of it, but you do not know whence it comes or whither it goes; so it is with (not 'The Spirit,' but) everyone who is born of the Spirit.' (John 3.8) There will always be something surprising in such a one, to those who are merely born of the flesh. Now, if this is true of human beings, how much more must it be of God?

If we really could explain and know all about God, then for sure it could be said that God was merely the creation of the human mind. But so far from discouraging the search after the knowledge of God, this element of mystery is a stimulus. It is easier to believe in God as a Trinity than as a Unity. This may sound a paradox, but it becomes clear if we remember the way in which the human mind first came to believe in a Trinity within the Godhead.

Revelation from the Human Life of Jesus Christ
Those who walked the dusty roads of Palestine with Jesus were sure that they were in the presence of more than man. 'I indeed have baptized you with water,' said the Baptist, 'but he shall baptize you with the Holy Spirit.' 'He spoke with authority' not as their own best teachers, the Scribes: 'never man spoke like this Man'; 'You have the words of eternal life'; 'My Lord and my God'.

Who could this be? No mere man, certainly; equally to Jews it could not be anyone who contradicted their central doctrine: 'The Lord thy God is One God.' So, they turned to himself; and he answered that he and the Father were at one; his work was the Father's work. So, now they knew much more about God; all that they had seen in the human life of Jesus was a revelation of the Father.

Revelation from Reality
But we have not yet reached the concept of a Trinity. For that, a new historic fact became the starting-point. The time came when the followers of the Risen Christ became conscious of a new influence upon them, a new power. They felt knitted together in a common purpose; they found themselves of one heart and mind; they were filled with boldness and zeal. The new power transformed their lives; they were made like to the image of Christ; they had a new message; they had the power of utterance; and it was a message that they found went home at once to people of every nation.

Surely this too, they felt, is God's own action; this Spirit is the Lord; it is teaching us the very teaching of the Lord Jesus, which he said was a revelation of the Father. It is knitting us together as he knit us together; it is giving us the power to do God's work; this must be God's power, and 'the grace of the Lord Jesus Christ, and the love of God, and the fellowship of the Holy Spirit' became the common form of their blessing.

So the doctrine of the Trinity sprang out of historic facts; and when theology attempted to define it, it was felt that it was not sufficient to say that it is the work of one God acting in different ways at different times; it is something deeper than that; it had its origin in the eternal life of God. At that point it passes into mystery.

The Best Analogy that has been suggested is the analogy with our own nature. In that we are conscious of our inmost self, with its thoughts and wishes known only to itself; then there is the desire to express ourselves, to put out by word or gesture that which we are willing that others should know – the revealing self; and there is also the effect produced upon others by our revelation of ourself – the self reproduced. So we get some faint analogy to Father, Son and Holy Spirit; Life, Love and Power, these are consciously working together in the Divine Nature. No doubt but the analogy fails in exactness; yet if we try to picture to ourselves the best man or woman that we know – pure in thought, happy in giving out life, then we have something upon which we can build our conception of a Divine Person, the perfect embodiment of life, ever in love giving out its life, ever receiving back again. Human life, human love, human power to draw out life in others – these are not merely analogies; they are the steps up which we climb to the comprehending of a Divine life, a Divine love, a Divine power.

Trinity Sunday *Second Sermon*
Waiting upon God

'They who wait upon the Lord shall renew their strength' Isaiah 40.31 *(ASB EP)*

The Bounty of God

On the Thursday after Trinity Sunday, we keep the Feast of Corpus Christi. When this festival was established in the Middle Ages, its chief focus was the sacramental presence of our Lord in the Eucharist. However, in the present century, the Church has come to focus, ever increasingly, upon the mystical nature of the Christian community as the Body of Christ.

So the Feast of Corpus Christi (which means simply 'Body of Christ') now speaks to us in three different ways.

First, it teaches us that in Jesus Christ, God took our human nature to himself, and experienced to the full what it means to live in this world, where the material and the spiritual things co-exist together. Secondly, it teaches us that God so consecrates the material world by his incarnation, that he makes bread and wine the vehicles of his communion with us. Thirdly, still drawing upon the language of St John (ch. 6) it teaches us that God will dwell within us through the Holy Spirit, making us his mystical Body.

There is a development here which reflects the thought of St John in our gospel. Chapter 6 begins with the physical feeding of the five thousand; then, Jesus speaks of his sacramental presence as the 'Living Bread', and finally he uses the language of mystical indwelling.

Our Model
Here is a model for all Christian life.

We must all begin by getting things right at the material level – a proper ordering of our daily lives and work, our pattern of human relationships, and the right use of time, of money, and of what gifts God has given to us.

Upon this moral foundation we can begin to make progress in the sacramental life – seeing that material things are always the outward and visible signs of the spiritual dimension.

Through the Eucharist we learn that God uses material things to make himself present to us, thus hallowing the whole material universe. And finally we must all strive for the mystical experience of immediate union with God, through the Holy Spirit.

Increase – Decrease
There is a saying of John the Baptist which is exactly right at this point. As the Forerunner of the Messiah, he said of Jesus,

'He must increase, I must decrease.'

And this is precisely the mysterious process which takes place in each one of us, as we increasingly surrender ourselves to the indwelling of God. In no way do we cease to be ourselves, but rather we become more and more truly, the person that God intended us to become, and still calls us to be – men and women made in his image, made to be the carriers of his presence in the world, made to live to his praise and glory.

Corpus Christi *(Thanksgiving for the Holy Communion)* Thursday 6 June
Sacred Mysteries
'I will receive the cup of salvation: and call upon the Name of the Lord'
Ps 116

The Assembly

How very difficult it must have been for our ancestors in the Faith, in times of persecution, to come together for their Sunday service. There would be the fear of arrest, the accusation of assembling illegally for a conspiracy, for a plot, for some subversive plannings together against the government, against the State. At the best of times, their small body of believers would be allowed to meet, with the officials giving a cynical half-laugh, half threat – 'We know what goes on; don't forget you are being watched. Any trouble and you will be for it!' Depending on the attitude of the Emperor, or even the local ruler or Roman prefect – and depending very much on whether there was a need for some distraction of the people from increased taxes, or from lack of food supplies, or from a rise in prices – the small Christian community could find itself the scapegoat. Brutal arrests, beatings-up, destruction of goods and clothes, evictions – and in the worst times, tortures and cruel deaths. And the old heathen religions were still active, or gave the excuse for persecution – if any excuse were needed.

Times Past – Times Present

Those times are past; yet there are today persecutions of Christians in many places, as exemplified by Pakistan and the Sudan and other countries where the Christian faith is despised and Christian teaching is forbidden, and carries extreme penalties if discovered. In Iran and Iraq and other countries where extremism is the established rule, Christians have many problems and difficulties. Let us remember them in our prayers tonight and every night, and exert our influence as and when we can, by letters and protests to those in authority in this free and unsectarian country of ours, and by supporting those organisations who help and succour the victims of imprisonment, torture and distress.

Here and Now

Tonight, here and now our assembly has gathered together not with fear of arrest, not with a crowd outside shouting bitter and brutal slogans, nor with armed police openly jeering at us.

We have come together to thank God for all that he is, and for all that has been for us in Christ and by Christ. The crown of all that we do here tonight is in our act of Holy Communion, our Eucharist, our Thanksgiving; for we are a royal priesthood, God's own people, called out of darkness into his marvellous light

(1 Peter 2.9) and we share that as well as our offering made together. We claim it, since it was given to us by our Lord, and by it we assert our one-ness with him in this Body of his, the Church.

We also demonstrate our utter dependence on him, our Head, and we announce, to all, our unity in him and with one another.

Forgiveness
We do not come to Holy Communion as to the means of forgiveness of sins. That came to us originally at our Baptism; and it is given to us again by our repentance, our confession of sin, and our absolution. Like athletic players in a Saturday afternoon game, we go as it were to the sidelines, to have our wounds, our cuts and bruises attended to; not to the centre of the game, the altar. That is the place of the thanksgiving, that is the stage for our celebrating; there is the presence of our Host, the Lord Jesus. A wedding breakfast is no occasion for going over past failures; it looks instead with hope and confidence to the future as it celebrates the joy of the present day.

Doing what Jesus wants us to do
We come here tonight to thank God for sending his Son Jesus Christ; for his life on earth, his teaching and healing, his love and his offering of himself for us upon the Cross. And especially tonight we remember that last night before his arrest; how in noble and wonderful words and actions, he showed his love – first, in the amazing humbleness of the washing of feet, an acted parable of how we too should behave, loving one another and serving one another. Then secondly, taking the bread and the wine, breaking and pouring out, he declared that here was his Body and his Blood, broken and shed for this world, to be shared by us – all unworthy as we are – whenever we come together in his Name and for his purposes.

A PRAYER

God our Father,
you have invited us to share in the supper
which your Son gave to his Church
to proclaim his death until he comes.
May he nourish us by his presence,
and unite us in his love,

who is alive and reigns with you and the Holy Spirit,
one God now and forever. Amen
(Lent, Holy Week & Easter, p. 183)

Second Sunday after Pentecost *(Trinity 1)*
9 June   **A Full House**

'Happy the man who shall sit at the feast in the kingdom of God!' Luke 14.15 (ASB Gospel)

Interruptions

Some years ago, a mother brought her daughter to church. (Not this church, let us be quite clear.) Now the daughter, alas, was not only physically handicapped but not too good mentally. Mother thought it would be a good idea to take the girl – in her wheelchair – to church; a local church had the reputation of being friendly. So off they went; Iris (the daughter) beaming at everyone they passed, and gurgling if anyone said 'Hullo!' or 'Goodmorning!' In the church, as was her wont, Iris not only gurgled but did a bit of shouting now and then. No one appeared to mind very much; and certainly, after service, people were welcoming and friendly. Iris certainly enjoyed herself.

Alas, the next Sunday, the churchwarden (on instructions, it was learnt) met our friend at the door and, explaining it was too distracting for the congregation, turned mother and daughter away.

Of course, many people do lead stressful lives, and come to church for a bit of peace and comfort and quiet. One can see the problem with Iris. And the folk at the Sabbath dinner we hear about in our Gospel for today, may have felt a bit embarrassed by the noisy chap who shouted 'Happy the man who shall sit at the feast in the kingdom of God!' But they do not seem to have wanted to throw him out; quite the contrary, Jesus took up his contribution and made a parable of it.

Inclusiveness

The story of Iris and today's Gospel do have one important thing in common. They both speak to us of inclusiveness, and exclusivenenss. Jesus' story is not just about church-going; it is about God's invitation to enter his kingdom. Our theme this Sunday is 'The Church's Unity and Fellowship' and we heard in the reading

133

from Acts, how the very first Christians changed their lives. After accepting the Word preached to them, they were baptized, and soon formed a real community. Their fellowship was shown in several ways – they met frequently to hear the Apostles teach, they shared a common life, they met to break bread and to pray.

Now we are told that there were some three thousand of them; it is difficult to believe that amongst that number there were none with mental disturbances or physical handicap like Iris. We might remember St Lawrence, the Archdeacon of Rome and therefore the keeper of the Church's treasures. He was ordered by the heathen magistrate to produce them. The next day he appeared at the tribunal attended by a large crowd of beggars, the mentally disturbed and cripples. 'These', he explained, 'are the treasures of the Church.' Alas, he was burnt to death on a gridiron. But certainly the early Church, with Jesus' words of invitation to everyone – 'The poor, the crippled, the blind, and the lame' from the 'streets and alleys' and from 'the highways and hedgerows' – ringing in their ears, were not exclusive. 'Come to me all you who are heavy laden' and 'Let the children come to me, forbid them not!' These words of Christ ring in our ears, as in the ears of our forefathers.

The Parable
Let us look at the parable of the banquet again.

It is about people getting – or not getting – their priorities right. The feast in the story represents the heavenly banquet, that is, the Kingdom of God. The host in the story had sent out plenty of invitations; each invitation would, in the custom of the times, be followed up by a call from a servant to tell the guest that the meal is ready, and would they please come now. Unhappily, all the guests produce their excuses, some feeble, some reasonable. The host is furious and sends out his servants to bring in cripples, blind and lame – some no doubt just like poor Iris. Still room? The servant is sent to bring in those poor creatures outside the walls, living in hedges and ditches. (The Early Church took this part to mean Gentiles and other despised non-Jews who really were 'outsiders', when the pious and respectable people of Israel found it hard to respond to the call to 'enter the Kingdom'.)

Our Response
No-one here would want, knowingly, to turn away poor Iris; we may be sure some arrangement would be come to, so that she

could be happy and yet the congregation could be able to concentrate at their important moments. Let us ask for help in reaching out, and in accepting, so that many may come to Christ's table and taste of the Lord's Supper.

> Lord Jesus Christ,
> in the days of your flesh
> the sick were brought to you for healing:
> hear us as we bring to you in our prayers
> the ill in body or mind;
> may your Presence be with them
> relieve their suffering
> comfort their distress
> restore them to fulness of life
> for your love's sake.
>
> Frank Colquhoun

Pentecost 2 *Second Sermon*   **A Good Man**

'He was a good man, full of the Holy Spirit and of faith' Acts 11.24 (ASB Introductory Sentence)

St Barnabas the Apostle

We commemorate on Tuesday a remarkable man, St Barnabas, who did very remarkable work – 'he brought Paul to Antioch, and for a whole year they met with the church, and taught a large company of people; and in Antioch the disciples were for the first time called Christians' (Acts 11.26). And 'much people was added to the Lord' (v.24). Yet, he was a very humble-minded man, who was content to be over-shadowed by his friend and companion – the greatest of all Apostles – St Paul. Barnabas was in fact responsible for Paul being accepted by the disciples and the Jerusalem church – 'they were all afraid of him, for they did not believe that he was a disciple'. No wonder, when one thinks of the persecution he brought and 'the havoc he made in Jerusalem of those who called on the name of Christ'. It was Barnabas who persuaded the infant Church to receive the man who would be the greatest force in spreading the Gospel.

What was the message of St Barnabas to the new converts at Antioch?

Be Steadfast of Purpose

These new converts had just come under the influence of the grace of God, and they so manifested it in their lives, that they certainly gladdened the heart of St Barnabas. But to their new-found faith, they needed guidance and direction; and so the Apostle urges them to have real purpose in their lives, 'to remain faithful to the Lord with steadfast purpose'.

Faithful to the Lord

The 'steadfast purpose' was to show itself in 'remaining faithful to the Lord'; and none of us today in our time, can afford to neglect that exhortation. 'Faithful to the Lord' let us be; then, whatever the temptation, the trial or the difficulty by which we are assailed, we shall be safe. 'No one is able to snatch them out of my hand' (John 10.28) is our Lord's own description of the safety of those who follow him.

Christians in Name and in Service

The life and service of the new converts must have been quite marked, since we are told how 'in Antioch the disciples were first called Christians'. (v.26). They became a separate body of people; and from that time onward the followers of Jesus Christ have been known by that name.

It was for them a distinguishing adjective: is it ours? Well, of course we are 'Christians', and we would be indignant if anyone said we were not – but 'Christian' does mean 'a follower of Christ'. Do we answer the test as well as those early converts at Antioch?

If we are to prove worthy of the name of Christian, then we must 'with steadfast purpose' remain faithful to the Lord.

Third Sunday after Pentecost *(Trinity 2)*
16 June   The Lord our Helper

'God has said, "I will never fail you nor forsake you." Hence we can confidently say, "The Lord is my helper, I will not be afraid"' Hebrews 13.5,6 (ASB Postcommunion Sentence)

A Strange Question

Jesus asked, 'Who touched me?' He was in the midst of a crowd; on every side people were pushing or were pushed close up against him. It was like a TV picture of some famous figure in the middle of a crowd of fans, all pushing and shoving, so anxious to be near, if possible to touch. But Christ was asking about one particular touch – the touch of faith. For a moment, the Lord was somehow drained of energy and power. We can get a glimpse of the kind of strain that his daily life entailed – the constant queries to be answered, the attacks to be turned aside, the calls for help and healing, the demands on points of faith . . . The need to re-charge, to have a moment's rest and quiet, a space to pray, to meet his Father. We can follow the example of the Lord, if we will – take time to make a 'quiet day', go away 'on retreat' – or just drop into a church we know, in the middle of the day's problems and demands, to join in a brief service, or for just a few moments of recollection and peace and quiet.

Faith
The healing power of Christ was released by faith. The power that was strong enough to cure a long-standing illness; strong enough to drive out some evil spirit; strong enough to raise a little girl from her deathbed.

On one occasion we are told that the Lord could work no miracle because of the lack of faith of the people of the district. Today, the child was raised because of the *father's* faith. The truth seems to be, that faith creates an opening for the power of God to enter. It opens the door that seemed to have shut fast; it may be another who opens *our* door, we may open another's.

Refusal
There are those, who like the mourners in the room with the dead child, refuse to believe Christ's words, and laugh at them. These are those who refuse to accept that our life here, compared with the future that is promised, is only like a sleep, a dream, from which we will be awakened by the touch of Christ. Death, they think, is a dead end; but we are to be like Peter, and John, and James. They stayed to witness the power of Christ, and rejoiced to see it. Even William Blake could say,

> *'Do what you will,*
> *This life's a fiction,*
> *And is made up of contradiction.'*

But life is not all darkness; it has its crimson dawns and its golden sunsets. It is not all clouds, and after all, some of the clouds have silver linings! The Christian is sure that life has purpose, that faith contains the power of resurrection. It raised to new life the daughter of Jairus; here is a sign that faith can raise all who believe in Christ, from death to life eternal. Faith transforms what was ugly and corrupting, into a beauty and a glory beyond our human imagination or understanding.

PRAYER

Lord Jesus Christ,
Son of the living God,
teach us to walk in your way more trustfully,
to accept your truth more faithfully,
to share your life more lovingly;
so that we may come
by the power of the Holy Spirit
as one family to the kingdom of the Father,
where you live for ever and ever. Amen.
(PHG, p. 258)

Pentecost 3 *Second Sermon* Summer Course of Sermons on 'Belief'
(1) 'I Believe in Jesus Christ'
'We walk by faith and not by sight' 1 Corinthians 5.7.

Belief
We can, of course, say that we believe things, meaning no more than that we see no particular reason to question them. Religious belief is usually rather different. In this series we are not merely seeking your assent; we are seeking your allegiance. Or, more often, we seek a renewal of a commitment made in the past.

Belief in Jesus Christ, if it means anything serious, should affect your life, both your attitudes and your behaviour. Because Christianity is not primarily just a series of propositions, to which we might say 'Yes' to some and 'No' to others. Christianity, the Christian Faith, is rather a way of approaching our experience in life, with all its problems, whether expressed in terms of ideas and concepts, or of our relationships.

The significance of Christian belief is found in the way in which the Christian believer reacts to life and its problems. The Christian takes account of the love of God as expressed in Jesus in his life and teaching; that is to say, the love of God for each one of us. Belief in Jesus involves various statements *about* Jesus, made in various contexts; but, far more, it involves belief and trust in a Person, a whole person like a close and dear friend, or a loving and ever-helpful and hopeful spouse. But statements *about* Jesus will be useless to you or indeed to anyone, unless you bring yourself to recognize – or God brings you to recognize – that far from being statements from history books, they are true and real for you, and that you have made them part of your own way of tackling life and its problems, its riches and its difficulties, its joys and its sorrows. At this point, belief becomes what we call Faith, another word for Trust and Love and Hope.

Creeds

The Creeds are established formulations of Church teaching. The Book of Common Prayer contains three Creeds (so called from the Latin word *Credo* – 'I believe'). They all have misleading names. The 'Apostles' Creed', which is said at Matins and Evensong, was not compiled by the Apostles; it can be traced back to the end of the second century, in primitive form, when it was composed in Rome for use at Baptisms. It was developed over the years in Gaul, and was eventually adopted as a basic common form in the Western Church at the beginning of the 9th century, probably under the powerful influence of the emperor Charlemagne. The Athanasian Creed, also known by its first words *Quicunque vult*, 'Whosoever will be saved', was not in fact composed by Athanasius, a violent bishop of Alexandria; it was written about the year 500, probably by Caesarius of Arles. It firmly promises hell-fire for anyone disagreeing with it, and was removed from Roman Catholic service-books by the Second Vatican Council, amongst many other sensible and long-over-due reforms in 1900; our own 'Shorter Prayer-Book' of 1948 omitted it as does the Alternative Service Book of 1980. It is generally ignored by Christians these days. The third Creed is the one we say in the Eucharist, and is called the Nicene Creed, referring to the Council of Nicaea in 325 AD. However, the text which that Council produced was amended and finalized at the Council of Chalcedon in 451. (Chalcedon was a suburb of Constantinople.)

(The Nicene Creed is discussed next Sunday evening (Pentecost 4). A modern version of the Apostles' Creed is given here)

Do you believe and trust in God the Father,
who made all things?
We believe and trust in him.

Do you believe and trust in his Son Jesus Christ,
who redeemed the world?
We believe and trust in him.

Do you believe and trust in his Holy Spirit,
who gives life to the people of God?
We believe and trust in him.

This is the faith of the Church
This is our faith.
We believe and trust in one God,
Father, Son and Holy Spirit. Amen.
                              (Patterns for Worship 4.2)

Fourth Sunday after Pentecost *(Trinity 3)*
23 June   Lost – and Found
'Rejoice with me, for I have found my sheep which was lost.' 'Rejoice with me, for I have found the coin which I had lost' Luke 15.6,9 (ASB Gospel)

Lost!
In the gospel today we hear of two things being lost, and being anxiously searched for by their owners; the first a missing sheep, the second a missing coin. But as we listen to the two little stories, however, we may not realise how great in fact was the loss of the sheep and the coin to their owners.

The Lost Sheep
Farming today is mainly conducted on a large scale. A farmer with sheep will have a large number, and the loss of just one out of the flock is not really very significant. The Palestinian shepherd in Jesus' time was in a very different position. His flock often amounted to only a few animals, thus the loss of one of them would be quite a serious matter, for he was a poor man. In

140

addition it was a disgrace amongst shepherds to neglect or lose even one of the flock; thus he was prepared to go to a great deal of trouble to find the missing animal.

The Lost Coin
In the villages in the Holy Land in New Testament times, a married woman wore on her head-dress a circle of coins. It was worn we may be sure by the women in Nazareth, and so would have been a familiar sight to Jesus; he would see the coins on Mary's head every day.

The coins were given to a girl by her parents on her marriage, and would be big or small, gold or silver, as the wealth of the family permitted. The head-dress of the favourite daughter of a rich father would be valuable indeed. Apart from any value in money, the coins were of special value to the wearer for they marked her as a married woman, and it was counted a great disgrace to lose the head-dress or even one of the coins. The wearer would value it as much, and guard it as carefully, as any woman today would guard her wedding ring.

The Great Search
Both stories describe the great searches for what had been lost. At some danger to himself, the shepherd tramps over the hills, expecting to find only the mangled remains left by a wolf, or a lifeless body at the foot of the cliff – but at last! the relief! – he finds the sheep, not dead but alive. Almost as dramatic, though less dangerous, is the search for the coin, with the woman bustling about, sweeping here, there, and everywhere; even lighting a lamp at mid-day to enable her to see into dark corners more thoroughly, and then – at last! she glimpses the coin, shining where it lies. We all know that those searches teach us, that far as the shepherd walked among the hills, and long as the woman peered and swept, the earnestness of their searches is far surpassed by God's desire to win back a lost soul, and to return even a single sinner to the way of righteousness.

The Third Story
There is a third story in the same chapter of St Luke, which contains the stories of the Lost Sheep and the Lost Coin. This story is usually called the Parable of the Prodigal Son, though maybe better, the Story of the Lost Boy. It teaches us the same

lesson of God's love for the sinner, and his hope and his efforts for his repentance.

The Fourth Story
Well-known as these three stories are, and effectively as they teach their lesson of God's love and forgiveness, there is yet another story in the Gospels which teaches even more forcefully and more vividly, and contains even more power and tension than they do. Moreover, the three stories are not records of fact, but only parables that Jesus used as illustrations of his teaching. The fourth story tells us of events that really happened and people who really lived.

This great story is, of course, the story of Christ himself, of his life on earth and above all, of his death on the Cross. This true story proves far more strongly than any parable can, that God loves us and wants us to be with him for ever. 'There is no greater love than this, that a man should lay down his life for his friends,' said Jesus himself; and by his death he showed us this great love.

Pentecost 4 *Second Sermon* **A Summer Course of Sermons on Belief**
(2) Our Creeds
'God has sent his only-begotten Son into the world, that we might live through him' 1 John 4.9

The Nicene Creed
This Creed was formulated under all kinds of political and personal pressures, with shameful struggles for power between the leaders of the Churches in Alexandria and Antioch and Rome. Echoes and relics of these struggles have led to promoting the divisions of Christianity ever since. It is a sad and painful time to look back to, and a mournful reminder of how the unhappy rivalries and enmities of our all-too-human leaders – then and now – have resulted in strife and bitterness. What can we learn from all this today?

At the Council of Nicaea the doctrinal problem at issue was the central intellectual puzzle of the Christian Gospel: How could Jesus be, at one and the same time, God and Man? The answer given was that he had two natures in the same person.

Today

Now, we don't at all want to downgrade what was decided at Chalcedon. The Nicene Creed has lasted over one thousand five hundred years, and worn well; it is still affirmed regularly at the Eucharist by millions of Christians. (Though here in the Western part of the Church, we have an unfortunate interpolation about the Holy Spirit 'proceeding from the Father and the Son' not accepted by the East, away back in 589; which, however, is becoming less and less regarded as essential and therefore from time to time quietly dropped.) Frankly, however, does this Creed really have much appeal for people today? The trouble is that it deals in categories like 'being' and 'substance', which for most of us are just gobbledygook – and even for the theologians, are only comprehensible in fifth-century Greek. And what is the distinction in meaning between 'God from God' and 'true God from true God'? I can't tell you!

Conviction

I do not want you to think that belief in Jesus Christ involves necessarily believing in the exact text of the Creeds. But of course, what they are about is still important. The Fathers of the Early Church wanted to express their conviction that Jesus Christ was both God and human, and so do I. But, some of them put their belief in terms which suggested that Christ was not quite of the same essence as the Father, and that there was a time when God was there, but the Word was not. This makes something of a nonsense of the wonderful beginning of St John's Gospel, about the pre-existent God. Others believed that Jesus was – we might say – something like a god in a space-suit, contrived to *look* like a human being, but underneath, knowing everything and feeling nothing. In fact, it seems to me that the Fathers of Chalcedon, being so anxious to be respectful to the Divinity, overdid it and erred in this direction. They insisted that the Blessed Virgin Mary was the 'Theotokos', the Mother of God, a title which seems to leave very little room for the manhood of Jesus in all these definitions.

Different Points of View

One of the reasons why the Early Fathers had such difficulty in defining their belief in Jesus, was that they attached equal weight to every word in the Bible, as divinely inspired and infallible – and failed therefore to see that the different writers had differing points of view. The outcome was bound, therefore, to be confused and contradictory.

I don't think that we shall understand anything about Jesus unless we begin with the fact that the New Testament is about a human being, a human being who let God shine through him, who acted on behalf of God, and who spoke for Him – but all the same, a human being.

I do not think we can believe in an impassive God in a space-suit, because that – certainly for me – would undermine the whole significance of the Crucifixion; and I don't think we can believe that Jesus was some kind of subordinate being, which would take away his Godhead.

Belief in God
We are to believe in the Eternal Intelligence of God, the Word, as having set aside those things which made him separate from human beings, and as having been born to share our human condition – to share the weakness of infancy, the limitations imposed by a particular culture and a particular time and place – poverty and the status of an inferior native in an Imperial Empire ruled by foreigners. On top of all this, he bore prejudice, torture, repudiation and finally a cruel execution – but many of those who met him found him to be a clear glass window, as it were, showing to them the glory of his Father and his love – love which issued in healing, in truth, and in forgiveness. Love which in the end convinced them that eternal life was to be found in Jesus, and in Jesus alone.

God with us
We may suppose that the Word, outside our universe, is, and always has been, a person; and a person with the characteristics of a human being, just as we believe we are 'in the image of God'. I do not doubt that this Word was human in Jesus. The point where I differ most strongly from the Early Fathers is that I believe that, in Jesus Christ, God suffered. They stated at Chalcedon that this was not true.

The most important point I want to stress is that – as Paul said – 'God was in Christ, reconciling the world to himself.' We should not think it needful or wise to try to fathom God's methods further. Christ came as a man to demonstrate that God is love, and that God loves every person whom he creates. I am sure about this because he accepted death on the Cross, and rose again

– and because of the impact on humanity which the story of Christ has had ever since. He was truly human and truly divine, and he was all love.

Consider . . .
In order to be a Christian you don't have to accept my statement of belief in Jesus Christ our Lord, any more than you have to accept that of the Nicene Creed. All I urge is that you should consider carefully the message of Jesus, and ask yourself whether you have responded sufficiently to it. If Jesus Christ is indeed the Eternal Word, as St John said, is He speaking to you?

> We believe in God the Father,
> who created all things:
> *for by his will they were created*
> *and have their being.*
>
> We believe in God the Son,
> who was slain:
> *for with his blood,*
> *he purchased us for God,*
> *from every people and nation.*
>
> We believe in God the Holy Spirit –
> the Spirit and the Bride say, 'Come!'
> Even so, come Lord Jesus! Amen.
> *Rev. 4.5,9; 22.17. (Patterns for Worship, 4.5)*

Fifth Sunday after Pentecost *(Trinity 4)*
30 June   Unity in Christ
'Your people shall be my people, and your God my God' Ruth 1.16 (ASB OT Reading)

In Christ
The Christian life is a life in Christ. St Paul, the great example of a convert, someone who saw that Christ encompassed all that had been taught as religion, and yet had more, spoke of the Christian life as 'walking in the Spirit'. The Christian belongs to Christ, and the Holy Spirit builds up the life of Christ in us.

The Christian life is a response to the divine love. It is the opening of the heart to the love of God. It is the realization that God accepts us as we are, and by our response to his love, the work of transformation can begin. The greatest of all gifts is love, the divine love in us, which leads to a loving concern for all human beings, of whatever race or country or indeed religion. We see in the extract from the Book of Ruth, how the love of Naomi worked upon Ruth, and Ruth of her own free will, accepted the change to a foreign country, and the change to a foreign religion. The interesting point for us, is that Ruth is noted as an ancestor of David, and therefore an ancestor of Jesus. St Matthew makes this quite clear in the first few lines of his gospel (Matthew 1.5). Jesus therefore shared a common inheritance with a foreigner, a Gentile; and our second reading shows St Peter making it quite clear to the members of the Jerusalem Church that the call of Jesus is made to the Gentiles as well as to the Jews.

A Further Seventy-two

The gospel reading, from St Luke, makes all this even more clear. In the previous chapter Jesus gives the Twelve 'power and authority' and sends them out 'to preach the kingdom of God and to heal'. But in our reading from chapter 10, the Lord is recorded as appointing – not another twelve, but Seventy, no less, to preach the Gospel 'in all the towns and villages', specifically naming Gentile places. This seems particularly important to Luke, the historian and bringer of the Gospel to the non-Jewish world. The gospel reading is, as it were, a back-up to the story of Peter and his vision, which makes it very clear that the Gospel message is for all peoples and all nations.

The Christian and the World

We Christians are in the world and we must live our lives in it. We are not to be conformed to the world, but rather, we are to transform it. Our life is to be a response to the Divine love; it is the opening of the heart to the love of God in Christ. It is the realization that God accepts us as we are, and by our response to his love, the work of transformation can begin. The greatest of all gifts is love, the divine love which leads to a loving concern for all people and for all this world in which we are placed – every aspect of life, animal, vegetable and human must concern us.

Fellowship

The Christian life, above all, is not an isolated, solitary one. It is – or should be – a life lived in true fellowship. We are not to be conformed to the world, certainly; we are in the world but yet not of it. The Church is 'the Body of Christ' and we are called to be active members of it. We are responsible for one another – the law of Christ is fulfilled by 'bearing one another's burdens'. We live by the higher law of Christ, the law of love.

As St Paul puts it, 'As God's dear children, try to be like Christ, and live in love as he loved you, and gave himself up for you, as an offering and sacrifice.' We need always to remember that God has given us so much, for he has given us Christ; and that means that much must be asked of us. Yet, as we turn to God, we shall find the inner resources, which will carry us through all temptations and dangers, will give us the strength to do the will of God; and in confidence that God will vindicate the right.

Pentecost 5 *Second Sermon* A Summer Course of Sermons on Belief (3) 'I Believe in the Resurrection'

'The truth is, Christ was raised to life – the firstfruits of the harvest of the dead' 1 Corinthians 15,20.

The Heart of our Faith

Here we are not only at the heart of our faith, but also at the very beginning of our faith; for, while from the viewpoint of his Resurrection we may look back to the birth, life and death of Jesus Christ, it is only at his resurrection that our faith begins. It does not begin at his birth. Had there been no resurrection, the birth of Jesus might possibly have been of interest to some of us – historians for instance – if indeed (which is highly improbable) we had ever heard of such birth at all.

Had there been no Resurrection of Jesus Christ, his life – again if we had heard of it – might be quite interesting to us, if at least some of his teaching had been handed down.

But without the Resurrection, his birth, life and death – if known to us at all – would have been then of limited significance, and would remain so today. 'We preach Christ crucified, said

St Paul – and rightly so – but he could preach that only because of the Resurrection in which he firmly and truly believed.

What Happened?
Now, as we read and ponder the New Testament, we may differ on what actually happened at the Resurrection. In what shape or form Jesus appeared to his disciples, or what actually happened thereafter to his physical body, and so on; that's OK and we should not be shy of considering such questions. But if we are only saying 'Perhaps there was a Resurrection of some sort, but it really does not matter much, and I can believe in the man Jesus anyway' then we are missing the point. I am very aware that too often we may encourage people to see things in black and white, without being willing to permit them to accept the existence of grey, or indeed more colourful areas.

There are, I believe, grey areas in relation to the Resurrection of the sort I have mentioned – Why, for instance, did Mary Magdalene not recognize Jesus near the tomb but think he was the gardener; why did Cleopas and his friend not recognize the stranger as he walked along with them; what happened to him, when he vanished out of their sight at the supper-table; and how did he just 'appear' in the Upper Room when the doors had been locked?

Yes, these are grey areas – at least to myself – which we can speculate upon; but whether or not the Resurrection happened (however it did) is not grey; it is pure black and white.

The Central Fact
If there was the Resurrection of Jesus, we truly have the basis for faith in him. If on the other hand there was no Resurrection, then – let us make no mistake – as St Paul said, 'Our preaching is vain, worthless; and furthermore if our hope is for this life only, we are the most miserable of creatures.'

The centrality of the Resurrection to our faith we cannot avoid; we cannot get around it and still talk of the importance of Jesus Christ. This is the central fact of our belief, our faith, our religion.

The Gospels
The four gospels are all implicitly written – and in the case of St John's work, explicitly written – 'that you may believe that Jesus is the Christ, the Son of God; and that by believing you may have life in his Name' (John 20,31). When John says this,

he is not referring to belief in a man, Jesus, who died – finis! – but to belief in, trust in, the resurrected Jesus, for these words of his follow immediately the passage in which the Risen Lord appeared to the disciples, and after Thomas had gasped out those break-through words – 'My Lord and my God!' If you have moments of doubt – if you feel, like Thomas, that you need proof, that you would want to see the prints of the nails in the hands and the feet – remember not only what the Gospel writers tell us about the Risen Christ or about Thomas's reactions, but remember also the words of St Paul, written many years *before* the Gospels, and indicating the experience of the Church in the *earliest* days.

'I handed on to you of first importance what I had in turn received; that Christ died for our sins, in accordance with the Scriptures; and that he was buried; and that he was raised on the third day, in accordance with the Scriptures; and that he appeared to Cephas, then to the Twelve, then to more than five hundred brothers at one time, most of whom are still alive, though some have died. Then he appeared to James, then to all the apostles. Last of all, as to one untimely born, he appeared also to me.' (1 Cor. 15.3–8)

Paul's Faith
Paul bases his faith partly on the experience of others, partly on his own – and it is faith in Christ who has risen from the dead. He knew some at least of the appearances to other disciples; he itemizes them in the verses I have read, and it seems inconceivable that he has not talked about them with some of the disciples to whom the Risen Lord had appeared. Most were, he says, still alive at the time he wrote.

Paul had heard Stephen's dying speech (Acts 7.58) in which he speaks to Jesus as alive and powerful – 'Lord Jesus, receive my spirit' and 'Do not hold this sin against them.' This must certainly have stuck in Paul's memory and formed part of the growing pressure that eventually brought about his conversion. Next Sunday we will look at the Gospel writers, and see what they have to say about the Resurrection.

Sixth Sunday after Pentecost *(Trinity 5)* July 7
Truth in Jesus

'You did not so learn Christ! – assuming that you have heard about him, and were taught in him, as the truth is in Jesus' Ephesians 4.20 (ASB NT Reading)

Put off your old nature

The letter we hear a part of today, is clearly written to Gentile members of the Church by a Jewish Christian writer; for he shares the assumption that Gentiles were only too ready to fall into the vices of paganism. They did not, after all, have any strict moral code of their own to start with, and did not respect the Hebrew Law. 'But this is not how you learnt Christ!' says Paul, meaning in this case the instruction before Baptism; the Sacrament is in itself not only teaching the truth as it is in Jesus, but putting off the 'old nature' and putting on the 'new nature' so that the whole pattern of life is changed.

Believing in God

It is not easy, is it, to believe in God in face of the suffering and pain and evil in the world. A young boy whose mother was sadly killed in an accident on the roads, said: 'I can't believe in God, if he allowed this to happen to my Ma.' We can easily understand how he felt. What makes the difference is that we see God's love in Jesus. In his life was suffering indeed, but in the end it was triumphant suffering. We know, because he tells us so, that in the end it is goodness and love and God's purpose which will prevail.

Jesus tells us . . .

The true way of life is what has been shown us in Jesus. It is the way of love: 'leaving your former way of life, and putting aside the old human nature, which, led astray by its lusts and desires, is sinking towards death. You must be made new in mind and spirit, and put on the new nature of God's creating, which shows itself in the devout and loving life called for by the truth. To know this is to commit oneself to it. To learn, we must follow the way of Christ. Only once we are actually in that life, can we begin to understand it.

The Will of God

What matters in the end is God, and the doing of his will. And it is this will which must prevail – as we see in Jesus. What mattered for him was the Will of the Father. This brought him to the death on the Cross – but God raised him from the dead. The last word is with God. St Paul speaks of the mighty power which raised Jesus from the dead.

We think of the power of the Holy Spirit at work in this world, bringing life to what seems dead. In history the Church itself has seemed lifeless and dead, yet always the mighty power of the Holy Spirit has been at work to revive and renew. Think of the time in the sixteenth century, when the Church seemed hopelessly degenerate and corrupt; but great reformers protested against the abuses, putting their trust in God and standing firm because they were sure of the truth of God, as they saw it in Jesus. Or the time in the eighteenth century, when the Church seemed lifeless and dead, a mere appendage of the political placemen of the ruling party. Then came the great stirring under the reviewing breath of the Spirit, in the evangelical revival under John Wesley. 'The Church as it now is, no power on earth can save' was said in the late 1700s – but Bishop Blomfield was appointed in 1828 as Bishop of London, and life returned. How often have we heard the Church written off, and always there has come renewal and life from the dead!

Trusting God

To despair is to leave out God and his Holy Spirit. So often we fret and despair and worry. We have to learn when we have done our utmost, to leave the final issue to God. We must be content to leave the future to him in calm and confidence. So the prayer expresses it:

> God grant us the serenity
> to accept the things we cannot change,
> The courage to change
> the things we can,
> And the wisdom
> to know the difference. Amen.

Pentecost 6 *Second Sermon* A Summer Course of Sermons on Belief' (4) Everlasting Life

'These things are written, that you may believe that Jesus is the Christ, the Son of God' John 20.31.

The Empty Tomb

With all their differences on many matters, each of the Gospel writers lays emphasis on the Empty Tomb; each one considers this of great significance. Let us look briefly at what they say.

Matthew records that the Chief Priests and Pharisees, remembering that Jesus had said that after three days he would rise again, ask Pilate (28.62–66), 'Command that the sepulchre be made sure until the third day, lest his disciples come by night and steal him away, and say unto the people, "He is risen from the dead:" so the last error shall be worse than the first.'

To this Pilate responds 'Go and make the tomb as secure as you know how'; and they went and made the tomb secure by putting a seal on the stone and posting a guard.

Then, according to Matthew, when the women ('Mary Magdalene and the other Mary') came to the tomb, they found the stone rolled away, and an angel told them that Jesus was going ahead of them to Galilee. When the empty tomb was reported to the Chief Priests, the guards were bribed to tell people that the disciples came during the night, and stole the body away while the guards slept.

Mark tells us that the women found the tomb empty, with the stone rolled away; and a young man in white told them 'He is risen; he is not here – See the place where they laid him. He is going ahead of you to Galilee.'

Luke also tells of the empty tomb and of similar words being spoken; but he gives us also the story of the two disciples on the road to Emmaus, in which Cleopas tells the stranger who had joined him and his companion, about what had happened in Jerusalem, saying, 'In addition, some of our women amazed us. They went to the tomb early but found no body; then they came and told us they had seen a vision of angels who said he was alive.'

John tells us the beautiful and moving story of Mary Magdalen's visit, when finding the tomb empty, she runs to Peter and 'the other disciples' – taken as meaning John 'whom Jesus loved' – and they run and find the tomb indeed empty, with the added evidence of the folded or wrapped together linen cloths.

No Significance?
There are those Christians today, even some in high positions, who appear to attach no significance to the empty tomb, or who appear to doubt it. Now, as I have said, there are 'grey areas' about the Resurrection – what actually happened to the physical body, and so on, and indeed why – even allowing for the different ways in which witnesses see things – the stories should be told rather differently but there is no 'grey area' I believe, in the fact that the tomb was empty and that this was for the Early Church very significant. If it had no significance it is inconceivable, to my mind, that all four Gospel writers should mention it.

For Today
It is true that for you and I today, the empty tomb is not significant because of our own experience – we did not actually see the empty tomb three days after Jesus' burial – but it is significant as a strand of history handed down to us from the experience of others. It is also true that in one sense you and I might seem not to need the empty tomb, since we know the Risen Christ and for us that is, understandably, enough. But we would be foolish indeed to jettison belief in the empty tomb because we do not understand how it happened; if it were not empty the history of the Church from its very beginnings would have been quite different. Indeed we might query whether there would have been any history!

Not Understood, but Believed
I do not pretend to understand *how* the Resurrection actually happened, but to me that is unimportant. I am an entirely unscientific person, and I do not understand how my mobile phone works – how I can pick up this instrument which is attached to nothing, press the right buttons, and immediately be able to speak to, and hear, someone in another part of the country. That I do not know *how* it works is irrelevant – it *does* work, I know it works, and I receive the benefit. So with the Resurrection – I do not understand it, but I know I receive the benefit. Like St Paul, I believe partly because others have experienced it, and down the ages things have happened to people

because of it; and partly because of experiences in my own life, which make me certain that Jesus is risen and alive for us today.

Eternal Life
Let me reiterate what St Paul said, writing about the Resurrection to the early Christians in Corinth: 'If it is only for this life that Christ has given us hope, we of all people are most to be pitied. But the truth is, Christ was raised to life – the first fruits of the harvest of the dead' (1 Cor. 15.19,20). And the resurrection of Jesus leads me to the belief that it is not for this life only, that we have hope in Christ, but we have the hope and the promise of everlasting life to come.

D.S.

Resurrection

Lord Jesus Christ, you came to Mary in the garden,
    and turned her tears into joy.
For your love and mercy we give you thanks.
We praise your holy name.

Seventh Sunday after Pentecost *(Trinity 6)*
14th July   **Two Great Commandments**
One of the lawyers came forward and asked him, 'Which commandment is first of all?' Mark 12.28 (ASB Gospel)

The Law of the Kingdom
Our Lord said that the Kingdom of God is within us (Luke 17.21) so a recent commentator was certainly right to describe the Kingdom as 'the world of invisible laws by which God is ruling and blessing his creation'. Christ brought home such truths as this to the minds of his hearers. The Old Testament held this basic thought of the reign of God; even under the kings who reigned in Israel and Judah, there was an inner awareness that it was God himself who was truly the king, and the human sovereign his viceregent. Christ brought home such truths to the minds of the people who heard him, and it is as well to bear in mind that 'originality of thought may be as much apparent in a wise selec-

tion from what is old, as in the creation of what is new. Some of the most striking teaching of the Lord is of this character; Jesus did not repudiate the Old Testament, nor did he despise its truths because his own went further; but he pointed out what was most important in the ancient revelation and rescued it from the oblivion into which it had fallen with over-scrupulous attention to the petty details of external observance. Even his summing-up of the ancient Law of God into two strikingly positive statements, as we hear it today in our text, he is quoting largely from the Book Deuteronomy. (6.5)

The Two Great Commandments
Jesus stated what are the two great oral precepts of the Law. While not explicit in the Decalogue, they are fully implied, and so form the basis of true religion.

'God is to be loved with all our powers and faculties, and nothing is to be preferred to him.
We are to love our fellow human beings as we have regard to ourselves.'

That love is to be something higher than mere animal affection or worldly regard. It must be a love inspired by the highest moral considerations, and therefore holy and lacking self-interest. Our fellow human beings are to be loved because they have been made in God's image, and because they are heirs to the same hopes that we cherish and look for. It is only as we love them, that we can display the reality of our love for God.

The Law of Love
The great disciple of Christian life and conduct is love; so the whole duty of humanity is summed up in love to God and love to our neighbour. The Gospel reveals the love of God, and instils a spirit of love in humanity. No one can be accounted a Christian who is hard-hearted and selfish, no matter how saintly he or she may be in other respects.

Love for God
Nothing in the whole world can take the place of God in our hearts. We are to have no will other than his. We are to exercise our powers, both of mind and body, for his glory and honour. He it is we are to follow, seeking to do his will in thought, word,

and deed. Other things are right and good, but without love they are of no avail. If love is wanting, nothing is fulfilled. So our love of God is to be a reflection of his love for us.

Love for Humanity
Love for our fellow humans is simply the carrying-out of our love for God. It has been well said: 'If thou neglectest thy love to thy neighbour, in vain thou professest thy love to God: for by thy love to God, thy love to thy neighbour is begotten; and by thy love to thy neighbour, thy love to God is nourished.' We cannot separate the second Commandment from the first. ('If anyone says, "I love God," and hates his brother, he is a liar; for he who does not love his brother whom he has seen, cannot love God whom he has not seen.' 1 John 4.20) Neither Commandment can be taken without the other. If it were possible to please God alone, that would not please him. He does not want us to be so enwrapped in heavenly contemplation as to forget our earthly duties.

> Love him, and Love's pure flame
>   The Law in thy heart shall write;
> For Love and law are the same
>   And to serve him for ever is Love's delight.
> For Love is his Name.
>   (W. E. Lutyens: 'The Servant')

Pentecost 7 *Second Sermon* **A Summer Course of Sermons on Belief (5)   Eternal Life Now**
'Now this is life eternal: that they may know you, the only true God, and Jesus Christ whom you have sent' John 17.3

'Everlasting'?
The adjective 'everlasting' – which in fact is not used so much in Church prayers as it used to be – is somewhat misleading, because to the ordinary person it may give the impression of a continuation for ever of the sort of life we are living now. Some of those people living in Bible times seem to have had that impression of the next life; you may remember a certain Sadducee (whose sect did not in fact believe in a resurrection anyway) put

to Jesus the taunting conundrum about who would be the husband in the next life, of the woman whom seven brothers in turn had married. Jesus rebuked the Sadducee by telling him that in the Kingdom of Heaven things are not like that at all! In fact, which of us would want life of the sort we have here to continue everlastingly? Oh yes, indeed for many of us, whatever our outward circumstances life often feels good, life *is* good; certainly, when we are young and fit, and all seems right with the world – and we are confident of our ability to conquer that world – well, then, a continuation of life as it is for ever and ever seems highly desirable – just as it seems so for lovers, who will say, 'Oh, that this moment could last forever'. But even for those who have been blessed with such happiness, sooner or later life seems to have become something of a mirage.

Age comes on . . .
We all get older, our bones begin to creak, we are at the mercy of various fell diseases; we see those we know and love getting older and less capable. We begin to realize that everlasting life as we know it on this earth, would not be so desirable after all.

No. Not in that sense do we want, nor do I believe in, 'everlasting' life. So, what then do I believe 'firmly and truly'?

Frequently we clergy conduct funerals, and in our addresses and in our words to the bereaved, we seek to point to a life after death; we may speak of death as a gateway to new life. However, there is little or nothing in the Bible to refer to, and neither I nor anyone else I actually know, has experienced death and lived – or rather, returned to tell the tale. It is, as Shakespeare wrote, 'that bourne from which no traveller returns'. Am I, are we, justified in holding out the hope of what we should, for the moment being neutral, call a continuation of life?

Evidence
Is there any evidence, here on earth, of a life after death?

Well, we may seek to draw analogies from Nature; we know how trees lose their leaves in winter – and then, lo and behold! in spring they are green with new foliage and new life. But the fact is that trees eventually do die as we well know; and analogies of this sort do not really take us further.

Then there are stories of people who have had near-death experiences; you may have seen programmes on TV on this theme, or some of you may actually have had such – or similar

– experiences. These are examples of people who – humanly speaking – have been nearly dead, and have then returned to life, often with remarkable stories of visions or experiences of what appears to be 'the Other Side'. Fascinating though these experiences may seem – Wordsworth would call them 'intimations of immortality' – yet we cannot really call them evidence – let alone proof – of life after death, because none of those persons in fact died. They have had experiences of dying, we may agree, but not life after death.

Faith not Certainty

The philosopher Bertrand Russell said that he could not believe in life after death, because there is no evidence of it whatever, in this life here on earth. In response, William Temple – then Archbishop of York – agreed that there is little or no evidence of life after death on this earth, and yet he increasingly believed, with increased years and increased experience, that there is such a life.

Yes, it does come down to a matter of faith and not of certainty. As St Paul puts it, 'Hope that is seen is not hope'; similarly; to believe in something that is obviously factual and true is not faith. When we speak of 'life after death' or 'life everlasting' we do not speak of something which we know of a certainty is true, but we speak words of faith.

St John records Jesus as saying these important words (chapter 14., verses 2–6):

'Do not let your hearts be troubled.

Trust in God, and trust in me.

There are many rooms in my father's house; if it were not so, I should have told you. I am going now to prepare a place for you.'

These are words which suggest something other and different from this life. As St Paul said, 'If for this life only we have hope, we are the most miserable of creatures.' Why? Because we preach Christ crucified, and we preach the resurrection – and if there is no resurrection, if there is nothing hereafter, then we are pretty wretched, because we have got it wrong and have been preaching a lie.

Here and Now

Let us not lose sight of the fact that this wonderful thing, which we call sometimes everlasting life, but more properly Eternal Life, does not only have to do with what happens when we 'shuffle off this mortal coil'.

Eternal life is something which is here and now, right here in this present life. You and I are living in two worlds, the material world and the spiritual world. Now we do not forget that the spiritual infuses the material, but to speak of two worlds is the only way I can think of to express the inexpressible – that there is, if you prefer, another dimension to life than what we see and feel and know, when we look around at the world of nature, at the human beings beside us, at the buildings and traffic, at the sky with clouds and stars and moon. 'There are more things in heaven and earth than are dreamt of in your philosophy' says Shakespeare in words he gives to Hamlet.

Every Sunday – and indeed every day there is a Celebration of the Holy Eucharist, the Holy Communion Service, the priest or the assistant who administers the consecrated Bread and the holy wine, will say to the person receiving, 'The Body of Christ keep you in eternal life' and, 'The Blood of Christ keep you in eternal life,' or sometimes, 'bring you to everlasting life.' These words acknowledge eternal – or everlasting – life, as being present right now, and not just sometime in the future.

We can indeed be in contact with eternal life right here and now.

Eighth Sunday after Pentecost *(Trinity 7)*
21 July *St Mary Magdalen* **Compassion**

'Be compassionate as your Father is compassionate. Pass no judgement, and you will not be judged; do not condemn, and you will not be condemned; acquit, and you will be acquitted; give, and gifts will be given you . . . For whatever measure you deal out to others will be dealt to you in return' Luke 6, 36–38 (ASB Gospel)

Saints

You know how it is when you are waiting for a bus in this part of town – the 274 for some of us, the 24 and 31, or that really rare bird, the 168. Absolutely nothing happens for ages, and then

– three of them come along all at once. Saints are rather like that, too. Last week we could only manage one Saint's Day – St Swithun on the 15th, bishop of Winchester away back in the ninth century, when Winchester was the capital of England, and the Saxon kings needed all the support they could get against the Danes. Swithun gave powerful aid in days of peril, and should be remembered with praise and thanks.

You probably know the legend that if it rains on Swithun's Day, it will rain for the next forty days? Well, this year it did; so his festival was not a great success. Then on Saturday we had the feast of St Margaret of Antioch, Virgin and Martyr. Nothing is known for certain about her – just some colourful legends, including a story that she was swallowed by a dragon but miraculously survived. But many mediaeval churches are dedicated to her, and many people are named after her – including the other St Margaret, Queen of Scotland (November 16th). Our other two forthcoming Saints are a different matter – St Mary Magdalen (Monday) and St James the Apostle (Thursday) – contemporaries and friends of Christ himself. Their festivals are 'Red Letter Days' because important enough in the Church's calendar to be printed, traditionally, in red. James was the son of Zebedee, brother of John and partner with Simon (later called Peter) in a fishing business. The three of them – Peter, James and John – formed a kind of inner circle of apostles, named as being with Christ at significant events like the Transfiguration.

Mary Magdalen
But it is the other saint for this week, Mary Magdalen, that I want to concentrate upon now. She is a very important figure in the Gospel story – Matthew, Mark and John all name her, as one of the group of women who followed Christ right to the end of his life upon earth. She witnessed the Crucifixion – either 'beholding afar off' as in Matthew and Mark, or 'standing by the cross', as John says. After the body of the Lord was placed in the tomb, she and the other Mary stayed there in the garden after Joseph of Arimathea had gone, keeping watch for a while. Then, returning on the morning after, they found the stone rolled away, and the tomb empty.

Luke also tells us of a group of women, including Mary Magdalen, who found the tomb empty and encountered two men in 'shining garments', who asked, 'Why seek the living among the dead?'

The women went to tell the apostles that the Lord had risen –
but I am sorry to say that 'their words seemed to them as idle
talk, and they believed them not'.

The Scene in the Garden

But it is in John's Gospel that we find the most vivid and personal
Resurrection story. Mary Magdalen goes to the tomb, finds it
empty, and fetches Peter and 'that other disciple' (presumed to
be John himself) 'who did outrun Peter'. They went into the
tomb and then returned home. But Mary stayed in the garden,
weeping; she meets first the two angels – and then, Jesus himself.
She does not recognize him at first, and thinks he is the gardener,
her eyes blurred with tears. She asks where the body is, and Jesus
speaks her name. 'Mary!' he says, in those well-remembered
tones – and *then* she knows . . .

The moment of their encounter – 'Noli Me Tangere' – 'Touch
me not, for I am not yet ascended to my Father' – has inspired
many artists to very beautiful paintings and stained glass, record-
ing this moment of joy coming through sorrow and despair. Mary
is then entrusted with the message of the Resurrection to be
carried to the Apostles – 'Go to my brethren and say unto them,
that I ascend unto my Father and your Father, and to my God
and your God.'

Who was she?

What sort of person was she, this woman who played such an
important part in the Gospel story – the first witness of the Resurrection, either on her own or with others?

Whenever the evangelists give names of the women who followed Christ, the list varies, but Mary Magdalen is always there.
And in every case but one when she is named, she is first on the
list. For example, here is St Matthew (27.56), 'Mary Magdalen,
Mary the mother of James and Joses, and the (unnamed) mother
of Zebedee's children.'

'Magdalen' simply means 'from Magdala', a town in the Holy
Land. But 'Magdalens' in the 19th century and earlier, were
women who had led sinful lives and repented – named after
Mary Magdalen, who is traditionally supposed to have been a
'fallen' woman, called by Christ to change her ways who then
became one of his most devoted followers. Luke 8.2 and Mark
16.9 both say that Mary was a woman out of whom Christ had

cast 'seven devils'; Luke implies that all Christ's female followers had been healed of evil spirits or infirmities.

Discarded Theories
Gregory the Great, the Pope who sent St Augustine to England, promoted the theory that Mary Magdalen was the same person as Mary of Bethany, *and* was the same as the woman 'who was a sinner' and anointed the feet of Jesus in the house of Simon, wiping them with her hair and weeping (Luke 7, 36–48). Another scene that provided great inspiration for artists: but these identifications are not supported by the scholars of today. However, the idea was a very popular one, not least with those who see the Magdalen as a kind of foil for the purity of the other Mary, the Virgin Mother of the Lord. So on one side of many pictures of the Crucifixion we will see the Virgin Mary demurely veiled, and on the other Mary Magdalen as a passionate and emotional figure, clinging to the cross with her long red hair uncovered, streaming down her back.

The Real Person
Yes, a striking picture, but it may not have much to do with the woman in John's gospel, who is entrusted with Christ's message of his Resurrection – in effect, the apostle ('one sent') to the Apostles. In fact, the Eastern Orthodox Church recognizes the special position of Mary Magdalen by giving her the title 'isapostolos' that is, equal to or the same as, the apostles, as being one sent to proclaim the Gospel. So tomorrow's Saint is described by the Orthodox Church – so much more conservative than any Western Churches – as equal to, or even the same as, the Apostles.

Today
This all has some definite bearing on the Ordination of Women, now a part of the received doctrine of the Church of England, in common with most other parts of the Anglican Communion, as well as other Churches. It is still an unresolved question in the Roman Church, of course, but the signs are that – with the strong pressure in many places that there is – there may well be a move in the not too distant future.

Whether or not we agree with our fellow Christians, we should respect them and their beliefs. To return to our text, we may not be able to become as yet of one mind, but we can heed our Lord's words and his appeal 'to be compassionate; pass no judgement, do not condemn . . .' No insults, no hatred, no back-stairs intrigues – just Christian charity. For 'whatever measure you deal out to others will be dealt you in return.' Like the saints who inspire us this week, we can follow Christ in Christian living, in proclaiming the Gospel, and in bringing people to know the mercy and the love of God our heavenly Father.

JMY

Pentecost 8 *Second Sermon* A Summer Course of Sermons on Belief (6)   Basis for Faith

'Now this is life eternal: that they may know you, the only true God, and Jesus Christ whom you have sent' John 17.3

Eternal Life–Now

'Now this is life eternal,' said Jesus in his prayer, given to us in John 17.3, 'that they may know you, the only true God, and Jesus Christ whom you have sent.' So, by knowing Jesus Christ and the God he revealed, you and I can have – or do have – eternal life right now. Because if we see things through God's eyes, that is through the eyes of Jesus Christ, we find our attitude to life and death changed. We touch the eternal here and now, and we know that – in a way we may have difficulty in expressing, the world and everything that goes on in it, looks completely different from how it looked the moment before we came to *know* Jesus Christ.

Seeing

I mean no offence to anyone who is unfortunately colourblind, when I say that it is, as if, before we knew the only true God and Jesus whom he sent, we were colourblind – but now can see all those wonderful colours which were always there, but which we could never see before.

Or, we were like those Jews of old, of whom St Paul writes: 'But their minds were made dull, for to this day the same veil remains when the old Covenant is read. It has not been removed, because only in Christ is it taken away. Even to this day, when Moses is read, a veil covers their hearts. But whenever anyone turns to the Lord, the veil is taken away.' (2 Cor. 3.14–16)

You see, at that moment we began to see life – and death – as it really is, and not as it has seemed to be; and we find that we are eternally, everlastingly, within the love of God; and that this is something that will not – and cannot – be taken away.

Life after Death

As I have said, I have no idea or explanation of what life will be like after death; and I have no doubt but that St Paul was right to respond to the person who asked, 'How are the dead raised? With what kind of body will they come?' How foolish! What you sow does not come to life unless it dies' and so on (1 Cor. 15,36). It is foolish indeed to speculate; I doubt if a chrysalis is aware that it will become a caterpillar; I doubt too that the caterpillar, any more than the chrysalis is aware that one day it will completely change, that it will no longer be a creature of somewhat doubtful beauty, crawling along the ground or over the twigs of a shrub – but will one day fly with the beauty and freedom of a butterfly – that lovely creature, so often referred to as a symbol of resurrection.

'Rest in Peace'

Sometimes people express concern that we always seem to pray that the departed may 'rest in peace'. We enjoy life and activity too much to find the idea of resting eternally and in peace boring.

I sympathize and understand. In fact, however, that peace of which we speak is, like eternal life, available here and now. Each week whenever we celebrate the Eucharist we exchange the 'Peace' and say to each other, 'The Peace of the Lord be always with you.' That peace, in which we can rest here and now (as well as after death) is not, as I see it, something dull and boring, but vibrant with life and love. The question is not only how vibrant that peace is, in our hearts here and now, but how in the next life that peace will be expressed. We do not know the answer to that question; but may it not be connected to how vibrantly *alive* we have kept that peace in our hearts here on earth. In other words, how far we have sought to know, and get to know, in this life, the true God and Jesus Christ whom he has sent.

There is a wonderful prospect ahead, we may well say; 'there are many rooms in my Father's house.' What things that we have always wanted to do, or share in, to create or to interpret, but the pressures of life and living have prevented us – does it not seem likely that in the life to come, the avenues which were once blocked or unavailable, will now be open and welcoming?

Other Faiths
May it not well be, also, that in their different ways and from their different traditions and perspectives, other human beings who share this tiny fragile space-craft Earth of ours, in the enormous universe, and are able to speak of Eternal Life and of a Loving Faith in their own terms, will also be part of the great Redemptive Process we have been promised. 'Other sheep have I, which are not of this flock,' said the Lord Jesus, 'and there shall be one fold and one Shepherd' – John 10.16. This is beyond our immediate concern, which is to emphasize that I firmly believe and truly in Everlasting Life or Eternal Life, both here and hereafter; and I have this faith because I believe in the Resurrection of Jesus Christ, and that by his death and resurrection he overcame Death and opened to us the way to that Eternal Life now and hereafter.

Ninth Sunday after Pentecost *(Trinity 8)*
28 July   **Steadfast Endurance**
'As God's servants, we try to recommend ourselves in all circumstances by our steadfast endurance' 2 Corinthians 6.4 (ASB NT Reading)

We have to keep trying
In his epistle, from which our New Testament Reading comes today, Paul has taken up a good deal of space and time earlier in demonstrating by argument what a true apostle is not like, what his authority does not depend on, what his success is not to be judged by. 'We are not pedlars of God's Word, like so many, but men of true sincerity; we claim nothing as coming from ourselves, our sufficiency is from God. We need no letters of recommendation – you yourselves are our letters, written on your hearts. We have renounced disgraceful, underhanded ways; we refuse to practise cunning or to tamper with God's word.'

Now, he adds a more positive description of God's true servants – 'Steadfast endurance, beatings, imprisonments; purity, knowledge, the Holy Spirit, genuine love . . .' Yet these marks too are ambiguous – 'We are treated as impostors, and yet are true; as unknown, and yet well known; as punished, and yet not killed; as sorrowful, yet always rejoicing; as having nothing, and yet possessing everything! Everything the Christian does is open to misunderstanding, by its very nature. The paradoxes of Paul's description arise from the very spirit of the Christian life; people of two worlds, poor and yet rich, suffering yet triumphant; enduring all things.

Endurance

A key word in our understanding of the significance of our Old Testament reading, about brave and clever David winning the contest against huge and powerful Goliath; and the strange and terrible healing miracle in our Gospel, is this word 'endurance'.

To 'endure' can mean grimly hanging on in trouble or adversity. We endure pain and refuse to cry out under brutal 'interrogation'; we endure long suffering due to some mistaken illness without giving way; we endure the contempt of others due to some mistaken ideas about us or our lives.

St Paul's word 'endurance' in the Greek has overtones our English translation does not give; for him, it means triumphant endurance – endurance which reaches breaking point and then passes through without breaking. His endurance is able to change or transmute tribulation into triumph.

Consider . . .

Such endurance is not so unusual as we might think. Consider a couple caring for their spastic child – what strains and pressures, yet overcome. Consider a widow or a father, left to bring up a family; the bravery and the endurance that finds a job, carries on with a smile – at least at home, does the best that can be done wins through in the end.

David, the shepherd boy, facing up to giant Goliath. The faith of the father of the epileptic boy in the gospel, his belief in the power of Jesus, even if tinged with doubt.

Steadfast endurance – reaching through endurance to triumph. And its basis? Trust, loyalty, which in themselves come from deep and lasting love; and when that love is centred on God, then endurance, steadfast endurance, will triumph.

Jesus says: 'Everything is possible to one who has faith.' 'I have faith,' the father cries, 'help me when faith falls short!'

Lord, help us when our faith falls short.

Pentecost 9 *Second Sermon* **Strength**

'Finally, be strong in the Lord and in the strength of his might' Ephesians 6.10 (ASB EP)

A Letter from Prison

Paul is 'an ambassador in chains' (6.20) and 'a prisoner for Christ Jesus' (3.1) writing to those who keep the torch of truth and faith burning in Ephesus. He loves that church; he spent three years in the city teaching and preaching. He knows all the dangers the brethren have surrounding them, so he writes this letter, depicting the City of God, in which his converts are 'no longer strangers and mere sojourners, but fellow citizens with the saints, members of the household of God' (Ch. 2, v.19). As often with the early converts, not many were opulent, not many were even earning a good living – but the vision Paul holds out to them is of better things to come. If not in this world, then certainly in the world to come!

Not Discouraged

If anyone had cause to be discouraged, surely it was this prisoner; instead, he is filled with joy and confidence. 'We are not contending against flesh and blood, but against spiritual hosts of wickedness' (v.12) but he is confident that victory will be won. We have an unconquerable Champion, Christ the Victor, and with his might all can be overcome. We need to keep our armour and our weapons ready and burnished, and it is impossible to read Paul's words without thinking that he is looking at the arms and accoutrement of the Roman soldier at his side. Paul is under house arrest; he can move around in the place he is kept in, guard-house rather than prison no doubt, but there is a constant presence of one or more soldiers – on whom, no doubt, he is on friendly enough terms.

'Girded with truth' – the basis of everything must be sincerity and truth; we believe God is true, and the revelation of Jesus is truth in human shape. 'Feet shod with the Gospel of peace' – the Apostle will be led to a martyr's death, and witnessing to the Gospel may lead anywhere that means sacrifice, but Paul never shirked his part, so neither must we. Testimony may have to be given where we should not choose, in our social circle or at our work or in our business. And the phrase must mean also that we should be ready and quick to carry the message of Christ to those who need it.

'Helmet of salvation' – The glinting of the sun upon the polished helmets of the Roman legions struck terror into the hearts of their enemies, before battle had even been joined. We Christians are to 'shine' also, that we display the message of salvation. 'Sword of the Spirit' – constant prayer and supplication is the 'secret weapon' of the good Christian.

Victory

We may not be conspicuous leaders or even soldiers, in the army of Christ, but we will always be on the winning side if we remember that our strength comes from him. 'Keep alert,' he says, 'pray at all times', and praying not only for ourselves, but for all followers of Christ, and especially for those who may be suffering imprisonment, false accusations, special hardship and brutality, as in so many places today.

Yet, we know that in the end, the battle will be won and our Leader and Saviour will lead us to victory and glory. In this hope and trust let us go forward in joy and love, and charity towards all.

Tenth Sunday after Pentecost *(Trinity 9)*
4 August   True Humility

'We have the mind of Christ' 1 Corinthians 2.16

Aspects of Life

'Desert Island Discs' is an enjoyable programme. There is the choice of usually interesting music by the person being interviewed; there is the relaxed approach of the interviewer; and the whole style of the programme seems to draw out aspects of the person's life and thought which we didn't know about before. We may find out, for instance, that someone we thought an aggressive character can reveal an unexpected inner gentleness; another person we had always disagreed with, may give what are actually very good reasons for the convictions which have shaped his or her life. We get inside the exterior, the public image, and learn something about the actual mind of the person being interviewed.

Jesus had the gift of knowing people's minds without the need for an interview. The gospels record how, often, he knew what was in a person's mind without asking questions; and even when he asked a question he knew the answer before it was given. To be able to discern the mind of a person is a gift which comes from a particular sensitivity; a sensitivity which enables us to put ourselves in the other person's shoes, to understand his or her motivations, pleasures and disappointments, as though they were our own.

Examples

So – for instance – when Jesus said to the rich young man 'Go, sell all that you have, give to the poor and come, follow me!' he knew what the answer would be, even as he made the proposition. And when he asked his disciples 'What are you talking about?' he understood at once why they fell silent, shamefaced. He had just told them that he was going to die a violent, brutal death – and they were squabbling about who should get the best places in the coming Kingdom . . . Sometimes we think we can discern other people's minds – sometimes we are right and sometimes, alas, we are quite wrong; but Jesus is the master of discernment. He knows what is inside a mind with accuracy – to him 'all hearts are open, all desires known, and from him no secrets are hidden'. Having revealed to his own disciples their minds, flawed by pride and the desire for power and status, he revealed his own mind.

'Receive a child,' he said, 'and you receive me.' (Luke 9.48)

Why a child?

Because a child sees the world simply; a child has needs but no power; a child is dependent on us. Jesus is saying in effect, 'Don't seek out people you think *you* need – rather, seek those who need *you*!'

Today's collect speaks of Jesus taking upon himself the form of a servant, and of giving himself in obedience to the death upon the cross; and we ask for ourselves something of the same mind that was in him, so that sharing in his humility, we may come to be with him in his glory.

Humility

It is one of the less fortunate attributes of a living language, that a word can lose its meaning while gaining another. We would hesitate in describing someone as 'humble' because 'humility' is in our day, often thought of as servility or submission. True humility is quite the reverse; not denying what we are, it consists more truly in being our real selves. It was equally real for Jesus to proclaim himself Lord and Master as to wash the disciples' feet. David acts in taking a merciful role, sparing the life of King Saul and reaching out for a reconciliation. Paul tells the Galatians, 'Help one another; do not judge others by your own standards.' Jesus draws the comparison with the women of the town, who washed his feet with her tears, kissed them, and anointed them with expensive ointment; while the host stood by, annoyed and disgusted. 'He who is forgiven little, shows little love!' is the Lord's summing-up. Real humility means thinking of ourselves as we really are, seeing the truth and accepting it fully.

Pride
How then are we to apply this humility in our lives, striving to have within us the 'mind of Christ'? First, we must put pride in its place. Remember the man celebrating his 50th wedding anniversary, who said, 'A man is as young as he feels – but seldom as important . . .' Those who seek status and promote their own self-importance have their reward; it is the grim one of being disliked. St Catherine of Sienna wrote:

> True humility makes no pretence of being humble, and scarcely ever utters words of humility.

Put to flight pride, by measuring ourselves against the perfection of Christ, and consider well that the cost of our salvation is no more and no less than anyone else; Christ finds each one of us precious, Christ offers his redeeming sacrifice for each one of us.

Tenth Sunday after Pentecost *Second Sermon*
Light and Glory
'God has shone in our hearts to give the light of the knowledge of his glory in the face of Jesus Christ' 2 Corinthians 4.6

Transfiguration
The feast we keep this week, on Tuesday, August 6th, the Festival of the Transfiguration of Our Lord, is a strange story to our modern ears. The Evangelists were writing, of course, for the

people of their own time. In the ancient world, the world of the old Greeks and Romans, the Egyptians and the Hebrews, visions and voices, miracles and magic, were – in a sense – everyday occurrences. The earthquake or the volcanic eruption showed the anger of Pluto, the Lord and Ruler of the Underworld. Thunder was the voice of Zeus, God speaking in anger from his throne in the skies. All kinds of incidents which we, today, in our clever, scientific, electronic, know-all modern world, know – of course – as perfectly natural, were to our ancient ancestors, the inexplicable acts of Gods or demons, the breaking into *this* world of another – and quite different – world, the spirit-world, the heavenly world, the Other World.

Style and Language
In addition, we have to bear in mind the very concrete and colourful, figurative style of Hebrew thought and writing. Where we would say, 'The powerful protection of God'; they would say, 'God is our high rock, our fortress.' We would say, 'I could feel God's presence'; they would say, 'The sacred shining cloud overshadowed us'. We would say, 'God's will became known'; they would say, 'His voice was heard, his commands were spoken.'

So, considering these differences between them, then – and us, now – just what is the message, what is the meaning, of the story of the Transfiguration for us?

Circumstances
Let us consider the circumstances. Take Simon Peter, for example. Only a very short time before, Simon had made his great declaration of faith. 'You are the Christ, the Son of the Living God' (Matthew 16,16) charged with great emotion and deep conviction. This man Jesus, who went about teaching and preaching and healing, was not just some holy man, was not just a prophet, important though such vocations might be. No, this man was the long-awaited Messiah, the Anointed One of God, the Leader and King of Israel. What a leap of faith this was, and what a commitment – made with this declaration!

Acknowledging Simon's faith and commitment, Jesus re-names him 'Rock-man', Peter; on this faith, on this rock, the Church is to be built. Eagerly, flushed with confidence, Peter awaits the Leader's orders – only to be told that the Messiah of Jesus is *not* the Warrior King.

Eleventh Sunday after Pentecost *(Trinity 10)*
11 August Generosity
'On the Day of Christ you will be flawless and without blame, reaping the full harvest of righteousness that comes through Jesus Christ' Philippians 1.10,11 (ASB NT Reading, RSB)

Rewards
Today we hear a good deal about gifts and rewards, as well as the harvest and reaping the fruits of God's creation and the labours of the workers. St Paul's prayers are always joyful, he says; thanksgiving and joy are emphasized in particular. If we sometimes forget thanks in our prayers, we nearly always miss out on joy – which is a favourite word of St Paul's. It is easy to fill our prayers with our own problems, and the problem and cares of the world about us – sadly in need of our prayers and help as so many causes are today. But let us sometimes at least, like St Paul, take God's help for granted, and tell our Father how glad we are that we have a God to pray to, and a heart ready and eager to pray. 'God loves a joyful giver' we know, but also we can be sure that God loves a joyful interceder!

An Appeal
Gifts and rewards we hear about again in our lesson from the Old Testament, a record of the appeal of King David for the furnishing and finishing of the Temple, and a list of the precious materials and stonework needed and indeed provided from the generosity of the people and their leaders, including the King himself who sets the best example. How often – when the church is in need, or some good cause is appealing – we need to take serious thought, and make a genuine accounting of what we can afford, rather than giving a minimum, or what we happen to have in our pockets or handbags. Then, as St Paul says, we will reap the full harvest of righteousness to the glory and praise of God, on the Day of Christ.

Payments
In the Gospel, Christ tells us about the contrast between the values of our human world, and the values of the Kingdom of God.

The way the landowner carries on is difficult to appreciate, when we are so surrounded by rates of pay, by hours of work and conditions of employment, as laid down by government departments or by the trade unions. The parable is set in a different world; organized labour does not exist, nor does our network of rules. But the landowner has his own sense of justice. The workers need to live, so they all get a living wage. The envy this causes he dismisses, with the comment: 'My friend, I am not being unfair to you. You agreed on the wage for the day, did you not? Take what you have earned and go home. Why be jealous because I am kind?'

The Point of the Parable

Matthew's comment 'The last shall be first and the first last' is clearly not really the point of the parable, but concerns the correct ordering of the Christian Community. Then what is the original point? The scholars tell us that most probably the question which caused Jesus to tell this story was not about priorities in the church, but about his own converse with 'tax collectors and sinners'. According to strict justice and certainly the Pharisee teaching, those who had devoted their whole lives to observing the Law in all its details would deserve a greater reward in the afterlife, than those who responded at the eleventh hour to the teachings of Jesus – however sordid or careless their lives might have been before.

Many of those expecting to be made much of when they arrive at the other side, will have a rude shock; God will be honouring some very unexpected people. God's generosity is the prime factor, not any artificial standard of good or bad behaviour. God is not only just but generous.

Pentecost 11 *Second Sermon* **Mary the Mother**

'A new commandment I give to you, that you love one another; even as I have loved you' John 13.34 (ASB EP), or, 'A great portent appeared in heaven, a woman clothed with the sun, beneath her feet the moon, and on her head a crown of twelve stars' Rev. 12.1

Our Lady

On Thursday, this week, is celebrated the traditional main feast of St Mary, the Mother of our Lord and God, Jesus Christ. The Festival has various names – The Falling-Asleep of Our Lady is the oldest, and used by the Greek Churches still; 'Lady-Day in Harvest' was the old English name; 'Assumption' is the current Roman title, a name originally meaning the 'Heavenly Birthday' of any saint but now confined to St Mary's death and passing to the heavenly world.

It is impossible, for the mortal mind, to understand more than the smallest part of what the Incarnation of Jesus meant, and means.

The joining of divine and human in Christ; omnipotence with the weakness of a child, the Creator of the world with a mere creature, the timeless with the mortal.

Incarnation

Yet, this is what Incarnation involves, and it was Mary whose flesh took the strange and impossible burden of God. God, who is pure spirit, took on flesh. The Second Person of the Holy Trinity made himself small, a child in Mary's womb, in order that he might grow up amidst 'all things made by him', and experience their pressures and the strains and stresses of living a human life among humans. As Mary crouched in the shadows of the stable, a woman suckling her child, she was a familiar figure of this harsh world. Yet she was more; there is here a mystery. Soon, men – rough shepherds, half-frightened, half-joyful – will kneel here. Men will kneel in the shadows of ten thousand caves, grander, cleaner, higher. There will be caves with other names – grottoes, shrines, chapels, churches, basilicas, cathedrals. One and all they will be surrogates of this fetid stable. They will stand more glorious, be graced with precious gifts, symbolize cultures, powers, dynasties, empires. Not all their choirs, psalm chants, hymn singing, will capture the sounds of that night – the voice of Mary murmuring, the fretful protest of the child.

Mother and Child

Holding her child, this peasant girl from Galilee will change and grow. She will hold him in countless attitudes, gaze upon the world in countless faces, be clothed with countless forms of dress. She will become a lady of Byzantium or of Renaissance Italy, a Chinese princess, a woman of the African veldt. Yet, however she is changed, she will forever continue to do what she is doing in this cave. Forever her arms will encompass the child, forever give him birth, forever nourish him. She is more than Demeter the great Earth Mother; Mary is *theotokos*, mother of God, and Jesus her child is first among the Sons of the Morning.

We can understand how a mother's love followed her Son through his life, in good times and in bad times, to the last bitter days of pain and death, when 'there stood by the Cross of Jesus his mother'. Every manifestation of his work, many of his words, his way of life – all these were treasured by his mother, who 'kept all these things in her heart'.

United
Such a union of love and hope and trust could not be broken by death. As Jesus broke through the bonds of the grave, and again greeted and touched and fed and guided his disciples into new life, so also with his beloved mother, we can have no doubt. And that the reunion persisted and was never broken again, we can surely have no doubt also.

With the angel, we may say, 'Hail, highly favoured, the Lord is with you.'

Twelfth Sunday after Pentecost *(Trinity 11)* 18 August   Salt of the World

'Jesus said, "You are the salt of the earth. But if salt becomes tasteless, what can make it salty again? It is good for nothing, and can only be thrown out to be trampled underfoot by men"' Matthew 5.13 (ASB Gospel)

What Value?
A Gallup survey not so long ago asked people which members of society they most valued? Nurses led, followed by Police Officers, Fire Officers, Parents, then Teachers. Church Ministers came last, well after the Armed Forces.

Well, surveys are not all that reliable, we know, and of course much depends on what questions are asked and how they are phrased. But the results mentioned are indicative of the disillusionment felt by many about the Church.

Of course, the Church has regularly found itself in the dock, and debates about 'empty pews' are perennial moans. Yet, with the possible exception of the Oxford Movement, each time the Church has moved towards reform it has compromised to please everyone: and failed. This is because the Church has yet to decide whether it is a hierarchy – in keeping with the concepts of 'God' and 'authority' – or a democracy. Even those who say it is both must accept that without authority in its hierarchy, the democratic element poses problems.

Modernizing?

In 1945, Charles Morgan outlined a scenario familiar to all of us: 'Some have urged that church music should be improved, some that it should be made more singable by the congregation. Others wish the liturgy to be modernized and the whole service to be more "practical", or more in keeping with the needs of the "common man" (and woman). Some givers of counsel, envious of the queues at the cinemas, have implied that the parish priest would do well to learn from the entertainment trade. This suggestion drew from a London priest the memorable saying that 'it is the priest's duty to feed the sheep rather than amuse the goats . . .' In the light of social and global responsibility, that statement is anathema. But it makes pastoral sense. The vital role of the parish priest, as head of a Christian community, is wise stewardship. Such a role has a public and a private domain – where correctness is more spiritual than political. We are a happy church when our stewards are concerned with both the family as a whole, and its individual members. This underlines the fact that the visiting parish priest is as important to the community as the policeman on his beat used to be. The practice must not be allowed to die. Nor can it be replaced by fetes, social functions or parish get-togethers, because the socially skilled and more demanding members collar all the attention. So do the rich and powerful, who – quite properly – need time and skilful handling. The priest who balances the books is a wise steward, and to be commended; but parish visiting links Christian charity towards the work of salvation.

Curators of Body and Soul . . .

Once, doctors, nurses and priests were held in the highest regard because between them they were the curators of body and soul. As for the Church, it is the Body of Christ, representing a healing spirituality which is in all things and above all things. It is not for the Church to seek comfort in popularity or in expediency. Instead, it needs to return to inculcating in society a 'profound and lively religious conviction.' A return to giving Christian rites of passage a sacramental vision; and where a response lacks conviction, a conventional one must be encouraged. After all, is not that often the case with baptisms and marriages today?

There is no hope in apathy; there is some in convention. Like T. S. Eliot we must believe that every attempt to form a civilised but non-Christian mentality will fail, and pray that our efforts should at least make Christian teaching accessible to society.

The Needs of Today
(From Dr Edward Norman's Reith Lectures)
'What Christians most need in our day, is to see that the complicated mixture of the Infinite in the structures of time, is explicable according to the spiritual interpretations of religious tradition . . . But the priest in the sanctuary too often does not speak to them of the evidences of the unseen world, amid the rubble of the present one . . . Around us, however, the materials of eternity lie thick upon the ground, ambiguous in relation to time, lucid as pointers to the celestial forces. For the mysteries of the Kingdom are not the commonplaces of the mere inquirer, but the pearl of great price, which only they possess who dispose of all their other goods.'

Pentecost 12 *Second Sermon*
The Holy Spirit *(First of Autumn Course)*
'All of them were filled with the Holy Spirit' Acts 2.1.

The Holy Ghost
In my childhood, when in stories or cartoons, or on visits to ancient buildings, ghosts were talked about, a picture of a hovering white-sheeted figure was conjured up; and so that is what the word brings to mind for me to this day. Putting the word Holy in front of Ghost does not change the fact – for me – that we are still talking about a ghost!

But the 'Holy Ghost' has an older heritage than my childhood; we find the phrase in the King James Bible as well as the English Liturgies of Cranmer. The English language has always been fluid, both in its forms and its origins. When it came to find a word to translate the biblical words *ruach* (Hebrew) and *pneuma* (Greek) and the credal word *spiritus* (Latin) the English quite naturally used *Ghost*, for it shared – at that time – a meaning which expressed both 'breath' and 'soul'. Ghost is derived from the Anglo-Saxon *gast* which means breath, and its Germanic *geist* we still use in phrases such as *zeitgeist*, the 'spirit of the age'.

Today, with the exception of 17th century liturgy and Scripture – Book of Common Prayer and Authorized Version – the Church always talks about the 'Holy Spirit'. I suspect both to distance it from the mythological world captured by Shakespeare and the Elizabethan dramatists, and to align it with its more historical roots of the inspiring and creative power of God, the Divine Activity which creates and sustains the universe.

Inadequate

But before we get caught up in technicalities of English, we should recognize how inadequate all our words are when we attempt to talk about God. The language we find in the Bible, in Church or wherever should always be approached with caution and with imagination. With caution, because how could we ever possibly claim to speak about God – and yet we must; with imagination, because our simple human words about God need to be liberated from their straight-jackets of meaning in order that they may inspire and enrich our thoughts and prayers and worship.

In our attempts to talk about God, we inevitably use words metaphorically and not literally, for metaphors allow us to talk about the Divine in a meaningful and even creative language, that avoids being exclusive or definitive. Metaphors help us to talk about what we know to be beyond our words, in vivid ways which can capture our imagination. This is certainly what we find in the Bible; and it is the way Jesus preferred to talk, using stories rich in images, rather than bald statements or concepts.

'Abba! Father!' – it is that very Spirit bearing witness with our spirit that we are children of God . . .' (Romans 8.14–17)

It was Jesus who called God *Abba*, and through the Holy Spirit we too can call God our Father. Indeed the great work of the Holy Spirit is to form a Christ-like humanity, a transformation of our human nature into the higher and greater form shown to us in Christ Jesus. Here is God's call and God's yearning for all people, all humanity.

Pentecost

It was the Day of Pentecost that marked not only the beginning of Christian faith, but also the birth of the Church. The Acts of the Apostles records the events of the day:

'When the Day of Pentecost had come, they were all together in one place. And suddenly from heaven there came a sound like the rushing of a violent wind, and it filled the entire house where they were sitting. Divided tongues as of fire, appeared among them, and a tongue rested upon each of them. All were filled with the Holy Spirit and began to speak in other languages, as the Spirit gave them ability.' Acts 2.1–4

These were the dramatic events which were to kick-start the apostles into life-in-the-Spirit brought about by the Resurrection of Jesus. This motley crew who had misunderstood Jesus, who had run away and left him, who had found it hard to accept that he had risen from the dead – on that day of Pentecost were transformed into a bold group of inspired believers with a message for the world. Even Peter, who had denied his Lord three times, was now empowered to harangue the crowd, telling them about the life, the death and the resurrection of Jesus. He had such an impact upon them that:

'They were cut to the heart, and said to Peter and the other apostles, 'Brothers, what should we do?' Peter said to them, 'Repent, and be baptized every one of you, in the Name of Jesus Christ, so that your sins may be forgiven; and you will receive the gift of the Holy Spirit. For the promise is for you, for your children, and for all who are far away; everyone whom the Lord our God calls to him.' – Acts 2.37–40

The Holy Spirit

The 'Holy Spirit' or the 'Holy Ghost' is then a metaphor among many we use in talking of the Divine, and one which has been reliably used by the Christian Church for centuries. 'I believe in the Holy Spirit' is, therefore, not wishful thinking, but a confession of faith that is firmly grounded in the life of the Church and those who follow Christ. Perhaps the Holy Spirit does not receive a fair share of attention, devotion and praise; but we cannot do better than (as a member of the Doctrine Commission put it) 'The Holy Spirit may without exaggerating be called the heart-beat of the Christian, the life-blood of the Christian Church.'

'The law of the Spirit brings us life in Christ,
and sets us free from the law of sin and death.'

Father in heaven
we give you thanks and praise.

Like all who are led by your Spirit,
we are your children.
By your Spirit's power we cry 'Abba, Father.'
Father in heaven
we give you thanks and praise.

The Spirit confirms that we are your children.
And if children, then we are heirs,
fellow heirs with Christ, sharing his suffering now
that we may share his glory.
Father in heaven
we give you thanks and praise.

Thirteenth Sunday after Pentecost *(Trinity 12)*
25 August   Sharing in Sufferings

'Rejoice in so far as you share Christ's sufferings, that you also may
rejoice and be glad when his glory is revealed' 1 Peter 4.13 (ASB Postcom-
munion Sentence)

The Sufferings of the World

Suffering – What do we really know about suffering, personally?
We see on our TV screens and we read in our newspapers, about
the terrible sufferings, persecutions, disastrous wars and cala-
mities, in so many places – Bosnia, Somalia, and in places nearer
home where there is need and trouble, hatred being worked up,
violence being used, brutality coming out into the open in our
midst, the destitute and unemployed still living in Cardboard
Cities with little hope for their future.

   Our prayers and thoughts and practical help should be directed
to the aid and assistance, wherever possible, of these suffering
people, and to the relieving of their needs and conditions. As
members of the wider community of the human race, the troubles

and despair, the sorrows and the needs of so many of our brothers and sisters must be an urgent part of our prayers and our efforts to help.

The Sufferings of the Faithful

Our readings today are all about the Community of Faith, the believers in God and in his Son Jesus Christ, and the sufferings that inevitably have followed, and still follow, faith in and allegiance to, God in Jesus Christ.

Jeremiah, the ancient prophet centuries before Christ, suffered physically, emotionally and spiritually because of his allegiance to God and for his concern for truth. He denounced the false prophets of his own time, who cried 'Peace, peace!' when there was no peace; who courted easy popularity by telling the people what they wanted to hear; who spoke comforting words instead of the challenge of the truth.

He was mocked and derided openly, and whispered against in the circles of power. Isn't that one of the hardest things in life – being laughed at? For many of us, perhaps that is as near as we get to suffering for our faith.

A Farewell Message

St Paul, the great Apostle, suffered many hardships for the sake of Christ and the gospel; and in today's reading, he is very conscious of the troubles and imprisonment and indeed death, that all too certainly await him, when he is taken to Jerusalem and then to Rome for trial. There is great sadness in his words – 'none of you will ever see me again' – 'Remember my tears' – 'Watch over yourselves and the flock.' He warns his flock to be prepared for suffering and persecution – 'Fierce wolves will come among you, and will not spare the flock . . .' Bitter and sad to find your efforts apparently in vain, and what you have built being pulled down; and lies told which lead people astray. Such things have happened down the centuries, and the Church divided – even today, sadly, there are divisions in our own Communion, which only time and truth will eventually resolve.

Warnings

And after St Paul's sorrowful warnings, we hear the Lord Jesus himself in the Gospel warning of sufferings, persecutions and betrayals. Most bitter, perhaps, of all, can be betrayals within families; parents by children, children by parents. Terrible stories from Nazi Germany, Communist Russia, bring such fearful happenings to our minds – and alas, in our own times we know only too well there are far too many regimes of violence and cruelty where basic human rights are disregarded, the innocent are victims, the poor and the weak suffer while the strong and the violent do as they like. Names like Rwanda, Iraq, Tibet . . . The message, therefore, from Jeremiah, from Paul and from the Lord Jesus himself seems to be, that if we are a community of faith – a Christian community – we are also a suffering community.

Can we cope with that idea? How do we separate it from a kind of masochism – 'Suffering is good for the soul' – 'We are not proper Christians unless we suffer' – and so on. There is no obvious and immediate answer, but we can be certain of one thing. Contrary to what Scripture seems to suggest, contrary to what most of us have been taught (I hope this is not heretical) it is not so much that we have to try and identify ourselves as suffering Christ's suffering (though maybe we try to do this, in whatever small way, on Good Friday). No, the important and wonderful thing is that God shares *our* suffering; he is alongside us and with us when *we* are in pain, every agony, every torture is shared by him.

This to me is the truly wonderful, truly mind-blowing fact about the Incarnation; God's taking upon himself our humanity, and entering into our world, with all the possibilities and likelihood of suffering and pain that that entails. Jeremiah knew nothing of the incarnate God; yet already he has a sense of God being with him: 'The Lord is with me as a dread warrior' – beside him closely. Paul commends his followers to the care of God, 'whose grace is able to build you up and give you his blessings'. Suffering will come, but God will be in it with you. Jesus says that when you are hauled into trial, 'the Spirit of God will be speaking in you'. Jesus did not come to our world to explain our suffering, nor to take it away – He came to enter into it with us.

Thirteenth after Pentecost *Second Sermon*
The Call *(Second of Autumn Course)*
'Abba! Father! – it is that very Spirit bearing witness with our spirit that we are children of God' (Romans 8.14–17)

The Call

For some, the calling of the Holy Spirit may indeed mean an experience similar to that of the disciples – an overwhelming infusion of grace that transforms their lives. For others, the Holy Spirit breathes more gently; and this is perhaps where the notion of adoption is helpful, particularly in relationship to baptism. The legal act of adoption is immediate, but that only marks the start of a relationship which needs time to develop and grow. Baptism likewise marks the beginning of our new life as children of God; like any other it is a relationship that is not simply given complete, but one that has to be lived and responded to.

Jesus' Ministry

It was baptism which launched Jesus into his public ministry. Through baptism the Holy Spirit empowered him to proclaim the Kingdom of God. St Luke records the occasion when Jesus returned to Nazareth and went to the synagogue, where he was handed the scroll of the Prophet Isaiah. He read:

> 'The Spirit of the Lord is upon me,
> because he has anointed me to bring good news to the poor.
> He has sent me to proclaim release to the captives
> and recovery of sight to the blind;
> to let the oppressed go free,
> to proclaim the year of the Lord's favour.'
>
> Luke 4.18–19

It is the gift of the Holy Spirit which shaped the life of Jesus; and it is the same Spirit which shapes our lives, and forms Christ in us. It is this which John recalls – when the Risen Lord stood among his disciples and breathed upon them, saying, 'Receive the Holy Spirit' (John 20.22).

Given to the Church

The Holy Spirit, active in Jesus' ministry, was given to the Church at Pentecost, the gift of the Risen Lord. The Holy Spirit identifies us with Christ – his death and resurrection, and the Spirit also binds us into the corporate Body of Christ: 'For in one Spirit we were all baptized into one Body' (1 Cor. 12.13). The Holy Spirit is not only the foundation of the Church, but also that which unites and shapes it, as the Body of Christ, in order that it may bear witness to the gospel in the world. Through baptism we are given the glorious liberty of the children of God, and partake in the life of the Spirit. The words of 'The Grace' point to this: The grace of our Lord Jesus Christ, and the love of God, and the fellowship of the Holy Spirit, be with us all evermore (2 Cor. 13.13). The word 'fellowship' here, however, is a somewhat weak term for the *communion* (koinonia) that is of the Holy Spirit – a communion that we share as disciples one with another, as well as our communion with God.

Communion with God

Communion with God, or the awareness of God's Presence in our lives, is brought about by the movement of the Holy Spirit. John V. Taylor, in his important book *Go-Between God* says that 'the Spirit of God is the power of communion which enables every other reality, and the God who is within and behind all realities, to be present to us.' (p. 19) It is the Holy Spirit – sometimes as the gentle breeze and at other times as the buffeting wind, which causes us to look up from the tiny world of ourselves, and see beyond – beyond, to other realities, whether they are our sisters and brothers, the whole creation, or glimpses of the Divine. To me, one of the most marvellous images of the Holy Spirit is that conceived by John Piper and executed by Patrick Reyntiens, for the Baptistry window in Coventry Cathedral. Its glittering golds and greens, its fiery reds, rich blues and intense purples, draw us up into the great ball of white-hot spiritual fire which fills the whole top of the window. Here is indeed something which expresses that aspect of God-in-Trinity which we name as The Holy Spirit.

A PRAYER

Heavenly Father,
by the power of your Holy Spirit
you give to your faithful people
new life in the water of baptism.
Guide and strengthen us by that same Spirit,
that we who are born again
may serve you in faith and love,
and grow into the full stature of your Son Jesus Christ;

who is alive and reigns with you and the Holy Spirit,
One God, now and for ever. Amen.
                              (Lent, Holy Week & Easter, p. 268)

Fourteenth Sunday after Pentecost *(Trinity 13)*
1 September **Family Life**

'I bow my knees before the Father, from whom every family in heaven
and earth is named, that he may grant you to be strengthened through
the Spirit, and that Christ may dwell in your hearts through faith'
Ephesians 3.14–17 (ASB NT Reading)

The Holy Family
When the Son of Man was born in Bethlehem on that winter night,
centuries ago, a new family came into existence. It was poverty-
stricken, humble, rather unwelcome in the rush of visitors, obey-
ing the irritating tax-laws of the time, filling every room and corner
that could be made remotely habitable. Hence the new arrivals
were shoved out into a stable; not pleasant but at least a shelter.
And yet this family was a complete little society, comprising father,
mother and Child. They seemed to have no earthly possessions;
but they had one spiritual possession in love for God and obedience to him, together with a uniting love for each other. None of
them could possess that treasure alone. The great Christian Family
of God has developed from that lowly and humble first family.

The Human Family
It is indeed a vital part of the Christian message that Jesus was
a loved and loving member of an ordinary human family, and
that in the circle of that home he received his first earthly training
for life on earth among the human race. But if the house at Nazareth speaks of reassurance, of the gentle influence of Mary and
the strength of Joseph, remember that they were scarred by the
massacre of innocent lives which had resulted from Jesus' birth.
They had literally fled away to save his life, to endure years of
uncertainty as refugees in Egypt. Those memories must have
never been far from the surface of life at Nazareth. The Holy
Family knew, from within, the hard, harsh reality of nations
broken and divided, of the fragmentation of family life, of being
strangers and exiles.

Our Time

Each family should be a reflection of that Divine institution which was in the mind of God when he based human life in the background of the human family. God ordained the family as the normal way of life for human beings and for the due continuation of our species, so the family is rooted in the very being of God. We cannot, therefore, look on the family as a social convention, or merely a feature of social life. God wills that we should live together in families; and the foundation of the true family is that fellowship of mutual affection and service, which includes and completes all aspects of human relationships. These inevitably involve responses and obligations one to another; and as we live together as children, sharing in the love and goodness of our heavenly Father, forming one great human family in him, we have a principle which displays for us the ideal plan of human life.

'Man and wife, a king and queen with one or two subjects, and a few square yards of territory of their own – this, really, is marriage. It is true freedom because it is a true fulfilment for man, woman and children . . . making one complete body out of two incomplete ones, and providing for the complex development of the two souls in unison, throughout a lifetime.' (D. H. Lawrence, 'Apropos')

Difficulties

Difficulties there may be, problems there are – we have to try to look at our lives, and – while holding on to the ideals and the directions given to us, treat our all-too-human failings with something of the love and understanding Christ displayed in his life upon earth.

He was well able to understand our human failings and mistakes – witness his discussion with the much-married woman of Samaria (John 4) and his rescue of the unfortunate wife dragged to the Temple to be stoned to death (John 8). We can rejoice in his sense of humour, which most surely he had, even in difficulties – think of his jokes about carpenters and planks, camels and needles, and how he could be amused at a smart reply – remember his response to the riposte of that Canaanite mother (Matthew 15.27):

> *Jesus, born in poverty and soon a refugee*
> *be with families today who suffer through war*

and live in hunger and want and fear . . .
in your mercy hear us

Jesus, who grew up in the family of Joseph and Mary
bring wisdom and the presence of God
into our families today . . .
in your mercy hear us

Jesus, who blessed marriage at Cana
be with those preparing for marriage
and those with difficulties and few resources . . .
in your mercy hear us

Jesus, who on the Cross said, Mother, behold your son
bring healing to those who have lost children
the bereaved and childless, widows and orphans . . .
in your mercy hear us
(Patterns for Worship, 51.13 adapted)

Pentecost 14 *Second Sermon* 'The Holy Trinity' *(Third of Autumn Course)*

'Firmly I believe and truly God is Three and God is One'

The Trinity

So Gerontius begins his profession of faith as he approaches death, in John Henry Newman's famous poem, set to great music by Elgar – 'The Dream of Gerontius' – and included in our hymn books as Number 360 (NEH) and 186 (A & M Revised). It is appropriate that we, while considering not so much death as living and believing in the Christian Life, should consider this doctrine of the Trinity – God as Three and One.

Here is a definition of the doctrine:

'That the One God exists in Three Persons and One Substance . . . This is held to be a mystery . . . in that it can neither be known by unaided human reason apart from Revelation, nor cogently demonstrated by reason after it has been revealed. (Yet though it) is above reason, it is not contrary to it, for it is not incompatible with the principles of rational thought' (Oxford Dictionary of the Christian Church).

The Trinity is not much talked about today, yet it is still one of the central doctrines of the Christian Faith. In the Articles of Faith of the Church of England, the first Article is entitled: 'Of Faith in the Holy Trinity.' In our Canons it becomes the touchstone of those to whom we may offer communion – baptized persons who are communicant members of other churches which subscribe to the doctrine of the Holy Trinity. 'We are ourselves baptized in the Name of that Holy Trinity – 'The Father, the Son and the Holy Spirit.'

Unfashionable?

Yet, despite its central place in our formularies, the doctrine is unfashionable and few of us, when giving testimony to our own faith, would begin with the doctrine of the Trinity. All the same, I have little time for the argument that says, 'Because this is difficult, it has no use today.' Nor am I impressed by those who dismiss the observance of Trinity Sunday as a late mediaeval addition, due to St Thomas à Becket's personal devotion. For as we follow the great sweep of the Church's Calendar of worship, it seems logical and right that as we observe the events of Christ's life from Christmas to Easter, and watch the subsequent events of Ascension and Pentecost, so we should pause to look, as it were, at the whole picture of the God revealed to us, on Trinity Sunday. Thus we may avoid – as it were – not seeing the wood for the trees.

You might think of the post-Easter Festivals being summed up in the doxology to the Lord's Prayer: 'For thine is the Kingdom (Ascension), the Power (Pentecost), and the Glory (Trinity).' So today, the theme is that of glory – the fullness of God himself. How vital it is in most things, to take time to look at the whole rather than the parts – and in faith this is no less important, for it leads us to humility and wonder. For, we cannot begin to understand or comprehend God – so we draw pictures, catch signs, recognize his presence, reach out, yet never entirely grasp him.

The Depth of God

The idea of the Trinity goes on to remind us that we have seen revealed a depth of God which holds that inheritance from Judaism of the One God, over against the many gods of the old polytheistic religions; yet acknowledges more than an austere, single, removed deity. And this reflects our experience of life, does it not? For whilst we may yearn for unity in the fragmented patterns of our lives, yet we value the many complementary facets which make up our varied and colourful human living. And as we try to peer into the essence of God, we find reflections of what we recognize in our human experience, as both the individual and the corporate (though this is, of course, to use human terminology). Perhaps then the Trinity reminds us that although we are made in God's image, we must refrain, on our part, from trying to make him in our image.

Doctrine and Doctrines

Again I welcome the doctrine of the Trinity, for it helps us to remember what 'doctrines' are, and what they are not. They are teachings about God, not God himself. And we are reminded that our Christian faith is not about beliefs which we must hold (though the popular critic will still try to persuade us that it is) but it is about a God *to whom* we must hold. In other words, our faith is a relationship.

So it is that at the heart of the doctrine of the Trinity is the idea of three persons in relationship; yet it remains a unity bound together in love. We know how things can look very odd if viewed back to front or upside down. We often need a clue to help us look at things, and get the right perspective. For example, the clue to understanding the Old Testament lies in geography; without it one would find it very difficult to grasp what is going on. So with doctrine – there is a clue to understanding it. But if we approach doctrine just at face value, and say, 'This is what the Church has taught, therefore it must be what I as a Christian, find in my faith' we shall be hard pressed to match up faith and doctrine in so straightforward a way.

The Clue

The clue we need is to remember that most of the Church's formulas of doctrine grew out of controversy, so, often, to understand a doctrine we have to see what it was trying to prevent. This is true especially of the Trinity. St Augustine wisely pointed out that 'we use this doctrine, not because we think it is good, but because we know that anything else is even worse'.

The Life of Faith

The story of the Early Christian Church is of people who *experienced* something, *examined* it, and tried to *express* it. Hopefully, this is our story too. The life of faith is like a dance, we may say, based upon these three steps, which continue throughout life – our *experience* of God must be reflected upon, seeking greater understanding, so we *examine* it day by day. Then we strive to *express* it, to find a pattern by which we recognize God at work in our lives. Having so expressed it, we bring it back to our experience to see if it rings true. Maybe, then, we find it needs further examination and further expression, leading us back to deeper experience.

And so the Dance of Faith goes on – its music provided by prayer, Bible study, and worship.

The Blessed Virgin Mary *(Pentecost 15, Trinity 14)* 8 September   The Handmaid of the Lord

'Blessed is she who believed there would be a fulfilment of what was spoken to her from the Lord'. Luke 1.45 (ASB Introductory Sentence).

Mary the Mother of Jesus

Today, September 8th, is, in the older calendar, given the title of 'The Nativity of the Blessed Virgin Mary', while in the new Book it becomes a more general title, allowing us to give thanks for not only her birth, but also for her whole life.

And what a life that was! Yet we are not given details as to her birth, nor anything about her gifts of mind and person, in the Scriptures. It is not even stated directly that she was of the royal stock of David, though this may well be so; and we may assume that she was brought up in happy and pious surroundings. Certainly there must have been in her mind – as in the minds of many Hebrew girls – the thought of the tremendous privilege and wonder it would be, to be chosen by God to bear the precious burden of the promised Messiah. When the amazing message came to her, she was able and willing to give her assent, and so enable the plan of God for the redemption of this world to proceed. She had been asked to offer herself to the divine will, and she made her choice. Fully and freely she had said Yes; and nothing would be the same ever again.

Magnificat

When Mary arrived at her cousin Elizabeth's house, Elizabeth greeted her with startling words, in recognition that the Child is to be the son not only of Mary, but of God himself in a special way. Mary's response is to praise God in the words we know well as the Magnificat. Drawn from the ancient song of Hannah (Samuel 1, chapter 2), Mary's words speak of praise and also of quite revolutionary ideas and ideals; words of justice and of care for the poor, and relief for the oppressed. In our world, little of that has come about, but we still pray and work for a fairer society, justice for the oppressed, and for the hungry to be fed. When we use her Son's prayer, 'Thy Kingdom come on earth as it is in heaven', we are joining in Mary's prayer too.

The Sword
The task accepted by Mary involved not only great responsibility, but also a dark and troubled future. 'A sword will pierce your own heart also', said Simeon in the Temple. Yet Mary's sufferings and sorrows did not kill her joy. Always there was a calm and peace in her heart, beyond the fears and sorrows, because of her union with her Son. Even at the foot of the Cross with the terrible tragedy unfolding before her eyes, she was not overcome. She was able to understand how her Son in his last moments, loved her, still committing her to the care of that one disciple who remained beside the Cross.

The Great News
It was with his brethren and his followers that she shared the great – the extraordinary – the amazing news. Her Son was with them again. In a different way, yes; but that it was the same Person they were convinced. They could only say that it was him, alive more vividly than at any moment of encounter they could remember. At the hillside he came among them, and they knew this was not only a meeting but also a beginning, both an ending and a new start, a start to something great.

Tradition tells us that John took Mary to Ephesus, a flourishing city away on the Aegean coast of Asia Minor. The Crusaders followed another belief, and claimed Mary had been buried in the Vale of Jeosaphat, where they marked her empty tomb with loving words.

In Mary we can see a great and loving simplicity, the complete submission of a life to the will of God. Once the angel's message is understood and accepted, God's will is all that matters.

Here for us is Mary's message: love and obedience – God's will always above our human wills; God's love reflected in all that we do.

The Angelus

Hail Mary, full of grace, the Lord is with you.
Blessed are you amongst women, and blessed is
the fruit of your womb, Jesus.
Holy Mary, Mother of God, pray for us sinners
now and in the hour of our death. Amen.

Fifteenth Sunday after Pentecost *Second Sermon* 'The Holy Trinity' – *(Fourth of Autumn Course*

'Firmly I believe and truly God is Three and God is One.'

Problems, Problems

For the Early Church the experience to which they looked was the memory of those first disciples who had walked and talked, lived and laughed, discussed and sorrowed, and had come to feel that they had indeed been in the presence of the Son of God himself. The events of his death and resurrection had confirmed this, and the empowering of them by the Holy Spirit had endorsed it. So they set about examining their memories – How could all these things be? Was Jesus God in human form? Was the Spirit God in their midst? They tried to find expression for their thoughts and reflections, but found that no one picture fully satisfied all they had experienced. If they said 'this' – they also needed to say 'that' – so complex was the subject of their thinking that it could never be tied down to one shape or one size.

They had experienced God's presence in Jesus – was he then just pretending to be a human being? If this were so, how could we say that humanity itself had been redeemed? Or, was Jesus something less than God – somehow a kind of semi-god, as the Arian heresy suggested – and were we then getting into what we call polytheism, and losing sight of the experience of God's presence in his world?

A Picture – that Grew

Gradually a picture began to grow. The Father, the Son, and the Holy Spirit – three separate Persons experienced in different ways, yet nevertheless One God – or one substance (to use the

192

terminology of that period of history). But what was their true relationship? It seems monstrous and impious and altogether crazy, to try and articulate the working of that inner Divine Relationship – but we have to remember that the Faith was being challenged continually by views which seemed *nearly* right, yet not *quite* right – and there is nothing so dangerous as a half-truth, in theology as in the affairs of life. So it was that under the threats from heresies such as Arianism, Monarchism and many other strange tendencies, there grew up the accepted orthodox Faith. It was the fruit of many and various councils of theologians and men of God, sometimes battling with each other and sometimes battling with political pressures, even persecutions.

The Faith
That Faith held the co-equality and co-eternity of the Three Persons of the Holy Trinity – Father, Son and Holy Spirit, each retaining their differing origins and their distinctive personas: The Father ungenerated, the Son generated from the Father, and the Spirit proceeding from the Father (and, in later Western Creeds, 'and the Son').

All this sounds very far from us today, for the language and the thought-forms of those times are not our current use. In that sense, the doctrine is, of course, out-dated.

Yet, as a work of art, a picture in old words and old ideas, that tried to touch the heart of the problems facing the New Faith, in the world of those times, we can surely say that it still has great merit – though it needs and would take far greater understanding and explanation that this sketch being offered to you here and now.

Personal Faith
But for me, in my faith, to be a believer in the Holy Trinity is to be one who recognizes that God is far greater, far more wonderful, far more astonishing, than any of our human words or ideas can contain or present.

This knowledge makes me pause if ever I am tempted to think that I know all about my God, or if I am all too ready to determine his will, for my actions or prayers (for usually, alas, it turns out to be strangely similar to my own). It makes me ready to be surprised by that mystery of life and the world, which strains the boundaries of our normal thinking and expectations.

It makes me ready to value that sense of unity and wholeness beyond all creation, a unity to which we are drawn from our tiny and fragmented lives. And yet, it is also to see hallowed that vital experience of our common human living – our relationships with one another. That is surely the place where so many of us come alive, and feel the presence of God most nearly. And that is rightly so, since relationship is a vital aspect of the nature of the God of Three Persons himself.

The Threefold Name . . .
At our birth we may be baptized in the Name of the Holy Trinity, Father, Son and Holy Spirit. Our commendation at the time of death, when our life here is finished and our soul goes forth into the mysterious and yet wonderful realm beyond this world, is also in that Threefold Name. Let us end then, with another quotation from Newman's 'Gerontius', as the priests and assistants commend the dying man in these words:

> *Go forth upon thy journey, Christian soul!*
> *Go forth from this world! Go, in the Name of God*
> *The omnipotent Father, who created thee!*
> *Go in the name of Jesus Christ, our Lord,*
> *Son of the living God, Who bled for thee!*
> *Go, in the name of the Holy Spirit,*
> *Who hath been poured out on thee!*

Sixteenth Sunday after Pentecost *Trinity 15*
15 September   'Too Late!'

'Anyone who loves God must love his brother also' 1 John 4,21 (ASB NT Reading)

Lavish
The rich man is pictured as living a life of absolute luxury – dressing in purple and fine linen, and feasting magnificently every day. An occasional feast might be expected, but the rich man showed the kind of person he was by feasting every day. And he showed this equally, by the fact that he broke the Commandment which does not only say that you must keep the Sabbath day holy, but also that you must work six days. He did no

work, no goodness, nothing of any value; his life showed the worthless kind of person he was.

Lazarus was in some way crippled; his beggar friends carried him and laid him down at the rich man's gate, hoping that his miserable condition would touch the heart of the rich man. It was so bad that he was unable to keep off the dogs of the street, who came and licked his sores. For food, Lazarus had to be content with 'the scraps that fell from the rich man's table'. There were no knives, forks, or spoons in those days; people ate with their hands, which quickly became soiled. In rich people's houses slices of bread were customarily put beside the guests' places, and on them the company would wipe their hands. They were thrown away, and would make food for such as Lazarus. Day by day Lazarus lay in his plight at the gate; and day by day for the rich man, the wretched beggar was merely part of the scene.

Reversal!

Now the scene is reversed. Both die; Lazarus is in bliss, in Abraham's bosom, but the rich man is in torment. He still thinks of Lazarus as at best a mere convenience: 'Send Lazarus to dip his finger in water to cool my tongue, for I am in agony in these flames!' He is told that he had received his good things, and Lazarus the evil things. Now the situation is reversed. The separation is complete, there can be no crossing of the great gulf. The rich man thinks for once, of someone else – he remembers his relatives, father and five brothers. Surely someone can be sent to warn them? But he is told that they have Moses and the prophets – all that is necessary. If they will not believe them, they will not listen even if someone should rise from the dead.

Identity

In that life, beyond the grave, identity remains. Lazarus remains Lazarus, and the rich man what he is. The Buddhist regards existence as a form of evil and seeks to get rid of it completely; not so the Christian. It is rather to reach its fulfilment in the Father's house, prepared for us. 'Let not your hearts be troubled, believe in God, believe also in me' the Lord said, on the eve of his betrayal. 'In my Father's house are many rooms.' (John 14.1,2)

The fact that we believe that identity remains means, that all we can take with us is ourselves, our character, what we are. Does not this make us understand how important it is, what we do, what we make of our life?

Memory Remains

The rich man was able to look back, and to see the life he had lived, as it really was. When we look back, we see things as God sees them, and the people we have hurt, and the things of which we are ashamed.

In Marlowe's 'Dr Faustus', Mephistopheles is asked by Faust what he is doing, out of Hell. The answer is:

> *'Why, this is hell. Nor am I out of it.*
> *Think'st thou, that I, who saw the face of God*
> *And tasted the eternal joys of heaven,*
> *Am not tormented with ten thousand hells,*
> *In being deprived of everlasting bliss.'*

It was hell to remember what had been lost.

Alas for You who are Rich

We think of our Lord's words: 'Blest are you who are in need; alas for you who are rich!' (Luke 6.21,24) Our Lord spoke bluntly of the danger of riches; a message that some – or many – today in our mercenary City could take to heart. But cannot the rich be saved? The answer of the parable is, that after death it is too late, 'there is a great gulf fixed'. To send a message to warn them is useless; there has been all the teaching they needed, did they but listen. What is necessary is to obey. Even if One should rise from the dead, they will not listen.

Pentecost 16 *Second Sermon*   Our Faith Today
(Fifth of Autumn Course)

'Lord, I believe . . . help thou my unbelief' Mark 9.24 (Part 1)

Our Belief

So we come to the last of our course of autumn sermons under the general title of 'Firmly I believe and Truly'. Over these weeks we have examined certain Christian beliefs, but this evening I want to look at the *manner* of such beliefs. Firmly . . . Truly? is our title – is this how we would describe our own belief as Christians?

Happy – or Reluctant?

Some of us would happily lay claim to those two adjectives – 'Firmly, truly'. Yes, that is how I believe, they might say. Others, no less sincere, would find themselves reluctant to use such a description; they might portray their faith as perhaps more hesitant. Some of us might even be shy of describing what brings them to church as 'faith', since that word seems almost too grand or definitive a title for the inarticulate yearnings that lead them here.

Now it would be fair to say that in the mid-nineteenth century, when Newman's poem had Gerontius claiming 'Firmly I believe and truly', such firmness of faith was considered a virtue. Today, on the other hand, we sometimes consider it to be something of a vice.

To the contemporary ear it smacks of a narrow-minded bigotry; we have seen in history, both ancient and modern, all too clearly how beliefs strongly held can easily become fanatical. Much that we might label as events of evil, in this world's history past and present, may be found to have behind them that warped 'faith' that we call fanaticism.

Distinctions

But, of course, there are vital distinctions to be made when we talk about 'believing' or 'having faith'. First, there is the basic distinction to be made between belief 'about' something, and belief 'in' something. As the old scholars would say, 'fides quae' and 'fides qua'.

This is where there seems to be much confusion, particularly in the popular imagination. So when someone is said to have 'great faith' it can be meaning that they believe a large number of things – from the literal interpretation of the Book of Genesis, through the Assumption of Enoch, via the Immaculate Conception of Our Lady, to the detailed landscapes of Purgatory – and so on. Such belief may have come about after long and reasoned reflection, or just through unquestioning acceptance of 'what the Church says', or is thought to say. But their 'great faith' is only referring to a quantity – it is a great number of things that they believe, in the sense of believing about them, that they did happen or that they do exist. However, all their 'great faith' might make no difference to their lives whatsoever; it is different from saying that their faith is great in a *qualitative* sense, for this would suggest a depth of passion and of commitment, which leads to action, and to a way of living.

Depth of Belief
In this sense we might speak of 'a great faith' when we admire someone whose life has encountered severe hardships, yet somehow it has been accepted, and held within a wider vision of life in God's love. Here it is not the number of things believed, but much more the depth of belief that has withstood so much. For Life is the great tester of Faith; and our firmness in belief can be of two kinds. There is the faith strong as iron, which has a massive apparent strength, but as we know can also become brittle and shatter.

This is sometimes seen, for example, in those who become convinced Christians and seem so sure and solid in their faith . . . until something happens in their lives that appears to wipe away all that they had ever believed. This is, particularly perhaps, a characteristic of faith among the young – one does see it often in students, not only in college but even more after leaving. The world is so much harder than they thought; problems are tougher – it has a good deal, we may think, to do with maturity.

A Supple Faith
But there is the faith that seems less massive, but more supple – like a tree that is able to withstand the high wind, because it can bend and it has its roots deep in the ground. Here is certainly an image of faith, a faith that can cope with the battering of life's experiences, and not only withstand the challenge, but also draw upon the experience. This idea, but with a different image, is expressed by the Psalmist:

'Who, going through the vale of misery, use it for a well: and the pools are filled with water.' Psalm 84.6

Room to Grow and Breath
Faith, however firm and true, needs room to grow and breathe. For the faith by which we truly live is a trusting relationship – and like all relationships, it needs to develop. In a human relationship one needs trust, but not rigidity. Again, we might see in such relationships apparent strength which can mask a deep insecurity. We know that love can turn to hate when betrayed;

we often, of course, betray God – when we fail to live up to his expectations.

But what of when God seemingly 'betrays' us?

When he fails to live up to our expectations of him – does our love then turn to hate – or our faith turn to rejection?

The Ardent Heart

There is also, of course, the manner of believing which is part of our psychological makeup. Look at the example of Malcolm Muggeridge, fierce in his disbelief and a severe critic of the Christian Faith. Then, suddenly, the change; he was converted (to use the technical term) and became as ardent in his belief as he had been against it. The content of his belief, that is the 'fides quae' to be technical, had altered, but not the manner of his belief, not his capacity for faith.

St Paul and St Peter

The most obvious Bible example of such a dramatic conversion has always been Saul of Tarsus, the Pharisee of Pharisees, the persecutor of the Followers of the Way, as the early Christians were known – who went on through a fascinating psychological change, to become St Paul, the greatest missionary figure and the greatest apologist and defender of the Faith ever.

With St Paul of course we place St Peter, another great character and saint of the early days. Peter was a fisherman, but that did not mean he was unlettered nor ignorant; the synagogue schools were for all young folk and without doubt, like Jewish children today, Peter attended and learnt the Faith. But his temper and temperament was very different from that of Paul. 'Peter, the up-and-down-man' he has been called; his faith and love seemed to rise and fall – one moment, 'Blessed are you, Peter,' the next 'Get thee behind me, Satan!' But Peter's faith survived and won through.

Do we have the choice of path to take? Less dramatically acquired than Paul or Peter, most of us received the beginnings of our faith from either our parents or at least the environment we grew up in. What was offered to us was not so much a set of verifiable beliefs, like the chemical formulae we might test in the school laboratory; it was rather that we followed a pattern of beliefs and observances, which informed and guided the lives of those we respected.

Is this enough for the needs of today?

Seventeenth Sunday after Pentecost *(Trinity 16)*
22 September   The Message

'The life I now live in the flesh I live by faith in the Son of God' Galatians 2.20 (ASB NT Reading)

An Undeserved Reputation

Jeremiah the prophet – in our Bible he is placed between Isaiah and Baruch – is generally known as 'The Prophet of Doom'. This is really unfair to him; at heart he was a countryman, a lover of the countryside with a keen eye for the ways of animals and birds, and the memory of all this remained with him when he went up to Jerusalem in troubled times. He was of a priestly family, and the call – or rather, the demand – from God that he should become a prophet, was one that he answered unwillingly and unhappily. The message given him to pronounce to the nation was one of impending disaster, for which the remedy could only be repentance. The national situation was about as bad as it could be – enemy invasions had reduced the former great Kingdom of David and Solomon to a small territory round Jerusalem, which was itself always in danger from the mighty Babylonian Empire, and a good King had been killed in battle and replaced by a weak and wicked man, who cared little for Jeremiah and would not listen to what he had to say.

Disaster – and Faith

The prophesied disaster took place; after a cruel siege, Jerusalem was destroyed and the inhabitants taken away to slavery. The passage we read today shows the indomitable spirit of Jeremiah, and his faith in the future. The business of buying a piece of land, in all legal solemnity and process, is to demonstrate the faith of Jeremiah that in the end things will come right, the capital city will be restored, and normal life return. 'The time will come when houses, fields and vineyards will again be bought and sold in this land' is his prophecy. His message of hope did not come true in the way he expected, except to a limited extent; the history of the Hebrew nation has always been full of trouble; but in the fulfilment of Jeremiah's prophecies of the mercy and love of God, and the redemption of his people through a new covenant brought by 'a branch from the root of David' – Jesus Christ – to restore their fortunes we see a clear vision of the Coming of the Redeemer.

Jews and Gentiles

St Paul, in our New Testament Reading, is doing his best to deal with a tricky situation. The Church was receiving as members, Gentiles – that is, non-Jews, in some numbers. This, of course, was due to the missionary work of St Paul, and his work among the Gentiles had been recognized and agreed by the Church of Jerusalem. In that Church, few members would not be Jews; but in other places the proportions might be very different. How to reconcile a congregation of Jews and non-Jews to take part together in the Lord's Supper? For Jews, it was a serious sin to sit at table with Gentiles. One solution would be for all non-Hebrews to be circumcised; Paul would not consider that, 'it did not square with the truth of the Gospel' (v.14). 'We, Jews by birth, do not put our faith in circumcision (works of the Law) but in Jesus Christ' (v.15) and this has been his own position on the matter, and he is not to be moved. He has died to the law, that he may live to God; crucified with Christ, so no longer he lives, but Christ who lives in him (v.20). The trouble has spread further into the Galatian Church, whose members have actually given way to pressure for circumcision. Paul asks how they received the Spirit – by the Law, or by faith in Christ? Obviously by faith – which conclusion would be blessed by Abraham, the great Jewish leader, who welcomed all 'men of faith' including Gentiles.

'Not even in Israel'

Very appropriately our Gospel reading deals with something of the same kind, in the time of Jesus; that is, the position of non-Jews with regard to the Hebrews. Here the local synagogue had actually been built at the cost of a non-Jew, indeed a Roman centurion. He would have been one of the considerable number of Gentiles who were dissatisfied with the religions in which they had been brought up, and had been drawn to the purer and simpler faith of Judaism. He would attend services with reverence and discretion, and be welcomed as a 'Hearer' though not fully admitted to all Jewish privileges.

His friends in the synagogue have approached Jesus, at the centurion's request, to ask him to heal the soldier's servant. On the way to the centurion's house, Jesus is stopped by a messenger. 'Don't trouble yourself further, sir; it is not for me to have you under my roof.' And he backs this up by explaining he understands from his army experience – 'I myself am under orders, and my soldiers to what I order them to do; so just give the word, and my servant will be cured.'

Jesus is Astonished
To his faith the centurion added humility. Jesus turns to the people, astonished, and says 'Not even in Israel have I found faith like this!' And the servant is found in perfect health when the messenger gets back to the house. We can remember the centurion for his great faith, a reasoned and practical faith; for his generosity towards his Jewish friends; and his compassion and care for his servant. His is a character to take as our example.

Pentecost 17 *Second Sermon*   **'I Believe'** *(6th of Autumn Course)*

I dare say most of us received the beginnings of our faith from our parents, or at least the environment in which we grew up. What was offered to us – and by and large accepted – was not so much a set of verifiable beliefs, like chemical formulae that we might check out on in the school laboratory; but rather, we observed a pattern of beliefs and actions, which informed and guided the lives of those we loved and respected. A solid if rather pedestrian approach, perhaps; but one which made for a quiet Christian life, on the whole.

But such has been the culture change of our society, that it is no longer possible just to take beliefs or codes of behaviour on trust from others; nor are things respected just for their past acceptance. Instead we are keen – in fact we demand – that ideas, beliefs and people themselves, should earn our respect for what they are, not for what they hold or inherit or for their historical background. So, the bias has swung in favour of doubt rather than belief.

Questions
In the area of religious faith, today's feelings are expressed, first, in the way that it is more usual to feel able to question ideas and beliefs, to admit to not understanding, and to admit to doubt. Of course, at one stage this became all too fashionable – unless you doubted, you clearly must have a mere blind faith which (as one hymn puts it) 'is sure to err'.

But at its best, the change means that we recognize the wide canvas of human knowledge of the world and of ourselves and indeed of the vast universe where we are only a tiny scrap in a remote corner; and we see how our religious knowledge is in need of constant re-expression and re-definition.

It also points to a proper humility, as we perceive that God is so far greater than we had ever imagined – because his world strains our comprehension, and he encompasses and transcends that world. So, in the changed atmosphere, we should be glad to see our theological statements as being more hesitant, more reflective of awe and the immensity of life and creation. We reach out to touch meaning rather than declaring that we own it.

Faith

The intellectual atmosphere of today also means that many need to discover faith for themselves – as in fact has always been the case if we think properly over the past – often by leaving and coming back to it afresh. So it is that we find many people discovering the truth of and the need for, an inherited faith, and make it their own later in life – perhaps at marriage, or the birth of a child, or some other significant event in our pilgrimage through the life of joys and sorrows on this tiny earth of ours.

So faith is no longer something just accepted from previous generations; it needs to be tested and tried before acceptance. Yet, faith is tested most of all by the truth of a life expressing it. So, we look to the lives of others, and see in how they live something that attracts us. It is the faith by which they live, the faith which informs all that they do. It is not argument that speaks most powerfully to our world today, but example. Nevertheless, to live a life in faith does involve a belief in the truth of what we declare we do believe in.

> *Firmly I believe and truly*
> *God is Three and God is One;*
> *And I next acknowledge duly*
> *Manhood taken by the Son.*

So Newman's figure, Gerontius, makes his claim of faith. He speaks of the two sorts of belief: for it is the belief about a God seen in the Trinitarian understanding that he lays claim to – but then goes on to express his belief in the saving work of that God:

And I trust and hope most fully
In that Manhood crucified;
  And each thought and deed unruly
Do to death, as he has died.

Faith in Life

My friends, we make our statement of faith day by day, in how we live our lives, how we care – or do not care – for others, for our neighbours, our fellow human beings, near or far. But we also profess that faith in our worship, as we say the Creed. We declare 'I believe in God . . .' for this is the way we are trying to live our lives: in a relationship of trust and belief with God. Our profession of faith, then, is not so much 'I believe *that* . . .' so and so happened a long time ago; instead it is much more 'I believe *in* . . .' a God active *now* in our own time and place, available to us, a source of strength and a giver of joy and peace.

St Michael and All Angels *(Pentecost 18, Trinity 17)* Sunday 29 September **Other Orders**

'The reapers are the angels' Matthew 13.39

Angels in Scripture

The Church has never been particularly definite in her teaching about the angels, simply because neither is Holy Scripture itself. Although angels are indeed mentioned in many parts of the Bible, these references are in very different circumstances and have very different meanings for us. Some occasions are not claimed to be real happenings. Frequently angels appear in visions and dreams, for instance in the Prophet Isaiah's great vision in the Temple (Isaiah 6):

> 'I saw the Lord sitting upon a throne, high and lifted up; and his train filled the Temple. Above him stood the Seraphim, each had six wings: with two he covered his face, and with two he covered his feet, and with two he flew. And one called to another and said, "Holy, holy, holy is the Lord of hosts; the whole earth is full of his glory."

Twice Jesus introduced them into his teaching (Matthew 13.39):

'The harvest is the close of the age, and the reapers are the angels. Just as the weeds are gathered and burned, so it will be at the close of the age . . .'

and Matthew 18,6 from our gospel today:

'Never despise one of these little ones. I tell you, they have their guardian angels in heaven, who look continually on the face of my heavenly Father.'

Not surprisingly, angels occur in legends like the one connected with the pool of Bethesda (John 5,4).

On the other hand, angels appear in several passages in the Gospels and Acts, including the stories of the Annunciation and the Birth of Christ, his temptations in the wilderness, his resurrection appearances, and Peter's escape from prison.

Although these and other diverse references to them in the Scriptures do not enable us to draw definite conclusions about angels, they do suggest a number of reflections for use in our own lives and prayers.

Order and Unity

In the first place, we may say that the concept of angels stands for the unity and order of the whole of creation in the service of God; not merely at the level of cosmic process, but at the level of conscious and free co-operation, God has 'ordained and constituted the service of angels and men in a wonderful order'.

When we look out, as we can nowadays so easily, upon the vast distances of the universe; when we see the photographs of distant galaxies, the depths of space, our earth seen from the moon or from space as just another little planet – we are easily afflicted with a sense of tremendous loneliness. Are we the only 'existants' in the world, are we perhaps just an accident in the vast cosmos? What meaning can there be in our lives, our hopes, our existence?

But if the Christian doctrine of Creation is true, then humanity is no accident, and hence presumably the human race is not alone.

Other Beings

Humanity must be one amongst countless races of beings on which the Creator has conferred existence and life; and some of these races must, like humanity itself, have risen to consciousness, and that freedom whereby they can gladly co-operate with God. Some must have moved higher in the hierarchy of existence, so that they constitute higher orders of creaturely beings.

The doctrine of the angels opens our eyes to this vast, unimaginable co-operative of working and service, as all creation strives to attain fullness of being, as ordered and encouraged by God. Something of this is surely reflected by our reading from the Revelation of St John, which suggests the struggle and indeed battle, in some form or other, of the developing complexity and diversity, as all things seek to be like God and to attain their fullness of being in him. We can see too the significance of the story we heard of Elisha's servant, whose courage was renewed by a vision of supporting angels.

Vastness and Richness

This passage is particularly relevant for our understanding the significance of the angels, in a contemporary formulation of the doctrine of Creation. The doctrine of the angels directs our minds to the vastness and richness of Creation, and every advance of science opens up still more distant horizons. Any humanistic creed that makes humanity the measure of all things, or regards us as the sole author of values, is narrow and parochial.

The panorama of Creation must be far more breathtaking than we can guess at, in our tiny corner of the Cosmos; our hope must be to begin to know and understand something of the many higher orders, whose service is joined with ours, under God.

Pentecost 18 *Second Sermon* 'The Beauty of the Lord'

'Haggai, the messenger of the Lord, spoke to the people with the Lord's message: 'I am with you, says the Lord' Haggai 1,13

A Hopeful Prophet

The appeal of Haggai is not, as might appear at first reading, just an appeal to the self-interest of the people, a sort of bribe – 'Repair the House of God, and things will go better for you' – but rather, a call to recognize that life cannot be properly lived, we cannot enjoy the well-being, which is God's loving purpose for us, unless due honour is given to God, and his primary claim upon us recognized.

The chief motive for rebuilding the Temple is, simply, that the Lord will then come into his own and receive due honour, in the worship which is proper to him. The people look after their own homes – and some at least are living in some style – but the house of God is in ruins.

The picture we get, after the appeal of the prophet, is – like the Middle Ages, when the people of Chartres, for instance, from highest to lowest, turned to and worked, hauled, dragged, carried, built – even yoked themselves like beasts of burden, to rebuild their Holy Place, their Cathedral.

Our Times

There is more attention being given to the parish churches of England today, than at any time since the Ages of Faith. Men like Sir John Betjeman and Professor Nikolaus Pevsner have brought a whole new flood of interest; the Open Churches Trust, founded by Sir Andrew Lloyd Webber, reflects the interest of many who would like to be assured that particular churches will be open at recognized times, is one aspect; another is the strong feelings aroused by the proposal to convert many City Churches to other uses.

It is strange that at the same time, more churches are being declared 'redundant' and destroyed, or turned to other uses, than ever before. Of course we should not strive to keep buildings that are no longer needed, or are in the wrong places, or are unsuitable; the Gospel is about *people*, not about places. But it does seem that too often churches are closed or destroyed, without any recognition that a particular church, in a particular place, is often a symbol to many who would never attend its services. This is shown by the protests that arise when a local building is to be demolished, quite apart from its artistic or historical value,

Vandalism

Sadly, we do hear all too often, of diocesan and other committees which seem out of touch with local, or other, feelings and needs. Sometimes too, the final decisions are taken under pressure from societies or organizations which have become cliques, not always in the general interest; on the other hand, sometimes records are not kept when a church is closed, stained glass and furnishings may disappear or are disposed of to dealers. This is vandalism.

Atmosphere
Finally, how often do we go into a church and find it dull, dreary, even dirty? The atmosphere of prayer is hardly there; instead, a smell of damp and old hassocks, combined with dreary fabrics and depressing ornaments is enough to put the visitor off.

And above all – a church that is prayed in, has an atmosphere of spiritual power – it is 'numinous', there is feeling of awe, for here is a holy place. Making a building welcoming and colourful, with space and dignity, makes it a place people are glad to drop into and pray or rest, as well as attending the regular services.

If we are reflections of, and carriers of God, his light and his influence will penetrate far beyond ourselves.

Nineteenth Sunday after Pentecost *Trinity 18*
6 October   **Two Trees**
'Zaccheus ran on ahead and climbed a sycamore tree in order to see Jesus.' Luke 19,5 (Gospel) 'Nathaniel asked him, "How do you come to know me?" Jesus replied, 'I saw you under the fig-tree' John 1.48

Nathaniel and Zaccheus
Whenever the two men we read about in the Gospels remembered their first meeting with Jesus, they must have said to themselves, 'If it wasn't for the tree it might never have happened.'

The apostle Philip brought his friend Nathaniel to meet Jesus, and Jesus said to Nathaniel, 'I saw you under the fig-tree before Philip spoke to you.' Nathaniel was greatly surprised and impressed, so much so that he made a very astonishing declaration. 'Rabbi,' he said, 'you are the Son of God; you are the King of Israel!' In our gospel today, we hear about the tax-collector Zaccheus, so anxious to see Jesus, who was due to pass through Jericho that day, that he climbed into a sycamore tree to get a good view of the passing Preacher. But Jesus looked up and saw him, and said, 'Come on down quickly, Zaccheus; I must stop with you today.' And indeed Zaccheus climbed down, gladly welcomed Jesus, and took him to his home, with surprising consequences.

Two Stories

It has been suggested that when Jesus saw Nathaniel under the fig-tree, the young man was pondering deeply about God and about his own life, and was trying to make some definite decision. Learned commentators have noted resemblances between this story and that of St Augustine of Hippo. Augustine, before his conversion to the faith of Christ, was thinking deeply under a fig-tree in his garden, when, prompted by the words he heard a child in a neighbouring house call out to another youngster, he took up and opened a Bible. He happened to pick the Epistle of Paul to the Romans, and he read there a passage which led to a great change in his life, and put him on the path towards becoming a great Christian teacher and writer.

Coincidence?

We do not have any real clues as to what Nathaniel was doing or thinking about 'under the fig tree', but there must have been some conflict or problem troubling him. Nor do we have any reason to assume – or deny – miraculous knowledge on our Lord's part. Yet even if everything miraculous is eliminated, was it not providential that the Lord had acquired prior knowledge of a man so soon to be brought to him as a prospective disciple, and adopted as such at once?

Up Aloft!

In the case of Zaccheus, everything was different; he was not anxious to escape notice in a quiet spot, but was very much in full view of a large crowd. And while Nathaniel does not seem to have taken any interest in Jesus until Philip spoke to him, and even then was rather contemptuous, Zaccheus was very anxious indeed to see him. This may be because he had perhaps heard something of the teaching of the new Prophet from his fellow tax-men, for it was to these that Jesus had preached recently some of his most effective and moving sermon-parables – the Lost Sheep, the Lost Coin, the Lost Son – the Prodigal Son, as we call it. All these dealt with the love of God and his anxious searching for, and loving reception of, those who turned to him (Luke 15).

The heart of Zaccheus may have indeed been already turning – he may well have been sickened by the richly rewarding but highly unpleasant trade he was engaged in. 'Farming out' was the system under the Roman occupation for taxing the people;

as long as the Imperial coffers received their appointed tribute, no-one in authority cared what went into the pockets of the publicans, nor how the money was gathered in. Threats, violence, brute force were all in use by Zaccheus; yet the mean, unscrupulous mind behind it all was changing. Suddenly the money, the power, the 'good life' – all are as nothing. He makes his choice openly, in precise Jewish legal terms; he – and his family – are re-instated in the local Jewish community and he can once again take his place in the synagogue. The words of Jesus confirm all this, and more, they restore him to the Kingdom of God.

Our Relationship with God
We can learn about our own relationship with God from two men who each had good reason to remember a tree. Sometimes, as with Nathaniel, Jesus looks at what we are doing or thinking, and his voice speaks to us and calls us. Sometimes we seek him out, as Zaccheus did, and he meets us halfway perhaps quietly and alone, perhaps publicly and in view of the whole community.

Let us remember that there are many ways we may come to God, and many ways in which he comes to us and calls us. Let us be ready to make the most of his approaches and his invitations.

Pentecost 19 *Second Sermon* 'Let there be Light . . .'
'Your word is a lantern to my feet, and a light to my path' Ps 119,105 (Cloud of Witnesses, Introductory Sentence)

William Tyndale
Translator of the Bible, Tyndale was a Gloucestershire lad, entered at Magdalen Hall in 1510 and soon noted for his knowledge of languages, and of the Scriptures. Moving to Cambridge, to his house 'there resorted many abbots, deans, archdeacons with divers doctors and great beneficed men; who did use to enter communication and talk of learned men, as of Luther and Erasmus; also of controversies and questions upon the Scriptures.' In Bristol, before long, in a dispute, he announced his intention of translating the Bible. 'If God spared his life, ere many

years he would cause a boy that driveth the plough to know more of the Scripture than he did.'

His vision was not shared by the Church hierarchy of the time, partly no doubt on the grounds that too close a knowledge of the Scriptures could stir people's awareness that there might be something rotten in Church or State, but also because there were few scholars who were actually capable of judging whether Tyndale's translations – going back to the original Greek in the case of the New Testament, and later the Hebrew in the case of the Old Testament – were accurate and above suspicion of Protestant bias.

Influence

One of the finest linguists and humanists of his day, Tyndale is claimed by a recent biographer to have had a greater influence on our regular idioms of speech than even Shakespeare. The reason is simply that much of his work was lifted unchanged into the 'King James' Bible, the Authorized Version of 1611. To mark the 500th anniversary of his birth, Yale University published Tyndale's translations of both the Old and the New Testaments (1995). The British Library has the sole surviving complete copy of the 1526 edition of Tyndale's New Testament, printed in Cologne since he had been forced to flee into exile. The Archbishop of Canterbury (Warham) ordered all who had copies to surrender them on pain of excommunication; he himself is said to have bought up two complete editions – much to the profit of the translators, who lived on the proceeds while issuing further editions. In 1528 Tyndale produced 'The Obedience of a Christian Man', defending the Reformers, and laying down the doctrine of passive obedience to temporal rulers. Henry VIII was delighted with it, 'for, saith he, this book is for me and all kings to read'. However, the next work 'The Practyse of Prelates' was not so acceptable, as it denounced the King's divorce!

Caught

Eventually he was caught in Antwerp, imprisoned, and tried as a heretic. Great efforts were made for his release; the English merchants petitioned Henry VIII, and Thomas Cromwell wrote to the Netherland authorities asking them to use their influence in Tyndale's favour. However, he was tried as a heretic, strangled, and his body burnt at the stake. His last words are said to have been 'Lord, open the King of England's eyes.' A tragedy by no means untypical of the times, but for all that a sad sacrifice of one of the most able scholars and wordsmiths England has ever produced.

> *Most Gracious God,*
> *grant that as we give thanks (this day)*
> *for the translating of the Scriptures*
> *by thy servant William Tyndale,*
> *so we may ever find within them*
> *a lantern unto our feet*
> *and a light unto our paths;*
> *through Jesus Christ our Lord.*

(Collect used in St Paul's Cathedral at a Commemoration of William Tyndale held on the 500th Anniversary of his birth, October 6th 1494)

Twentieth Sunday after Pentecost *Trinity 19*
13 October   **Perseverance**

Every athlete in training submits to strict discipline, in order to be crowned with a wreath that will not last; but we do it for one that will last for ever. 1 Corinthians 9.25 (ASB NT Reading)

Action!

Our readings today are full of action; Jacob with his wrestling match, St Paul with his running and boxing – he was trained and educated at what we would call today a university, the famous school of the great teacher Gamaliel. No doubt there would have been opportunities for sport, to enable Paul to use such expressions of athleticism as he does today. Our Lord's own teaching is concerned with walking through the small gate and along the narrow road, which suggests, at the least, a certain amount of needful exercise.

Going back to Jacob – in this passage from the very first book of the Bible, we are in a world where every stream has its own local divinity, every valley its patron spirit; each has to be propitiated in some way or other so that the traveller may pass in safety. Whether the 'man' who wrestled with Jacob is the local spirit or god, or is an apparition of Yaweh, Jehovah in his early appearances, is not entirely clear. Jacob, in spite of a severe injury, was not overcome; indeed it is the 'man' who wants to call halt as the day begins to break. (Supernatural creatures do seem to have a dislike of the daylight; we all know that vampires, for instance, must return to their graves before dawn, otherwise the films made about their exploits would lose much of their tension and scary-ness!)

God and Jacob
All Jacob's encounters with God have something of the character of the struggle which reaches its climax at the ford of the Jabbok stream. Jacob's will is at work all through; he is determined to get the birthright and his father's blessing, and does so by cheating Isaac with very questionable morality. He is determined to get Rachel, the wife of his choice, but is compelled to take Leah, whom he did not choose.

All through the Jacob story we have the sense of God's strong hand firmly shaping hard and refractory material, reaching through all adventures to their 'duel' with the struggle at the brook, when Jacob acknowledged the fact that through all his trials and wanderings God's hand has been over him to guide him towards the desired end, and crowned with the divine blessing.

Paul and God
Paul also has his struggles – if not with God, at least with the observances of the Mosaic Laws among the Jews, and with the inconsistency to that Law needed to cope with the Gentiles, and bring them to Christ. He justifies all this on the grounds, first, of being a free man – as a Christian, not subject to Jewish laws and ordinances; and also that whatever freedoms he has been exercising have been for the sake of the Gospel, and to aid in spreading its blessings.

The main thing is, to aim for the prize, to run straight for the finish, to avoid wasting effort and energy on punches that do not reach the target. If athletes are prepared to go into strict training for the award of mere fading wreaths, how much more should we be ready to prepare and to act for the wreath that never fades – the heavenly reward.

Jesus teaches us
Our Gospel reading is part of the Sermon on the Mount, that compilation of his teaching through which we may still hear the very voice of Jesus. First, like the moralists of old, Jesus uses the

metaphor of 'two ways' between virtue and its opposite, but combines the image of the roads with that of the two gates, one small and narrow, one wide and easy. The gate that leads to life is that of Christian discipleship, and it has been true enough that since the beginning of Christianity, those who find it are few.

He warns further against 'false prophets' who can be identified by the results of their teaching; and against our relying upon praise and prayers, rather than actually doing the will of God.

Finally the reading ends with the parable of the two houses, representing men's lives; both looking good outwardly, but when the moment of testing comes, all the pretensions of the one will collapse into ruin.

The Lesson
The lesson for us is surely that we should not slacken our Christian life of prayer and good deeds, rather make sure that we always keep in the forefront of our minds the need to keep close to God and to be careful to obey his laws and to follow our Christian precepts.

Perseverance

God of compassion,
you have willed that the gate of mercy
should always stand open for your people.

Look upon us with compassion,
that we who would follow the path of your will
may continue in it to the end of our lives;
through Jesus Christ our Lord.

(PHG, 104)

Pentecost 20 *Second Sermon* **Beloved Physician**
'Surrounded by so great a cloud of witnesses, let us lay aside every weight, and sin which clings so closely, and let us run with perseverance the race that is set before us, looking to Jesus the pioneer and perfecter of our faith' Hebrews 12.1 (ASB EP)

St Luke

Amongst the cloud of witnesses, we will be remembering St Luke, whose festival is on Friday next. St Luke's particular ministry included the ministry of healing; as a doctor he attached himself to St Paul and travelled with him on his missionary journeys. Not only did he look after the physical health of the Apostle, Luke also kept the fascinating diaries we know as 'The Acts of the Apostles'. The section that is most interesting and striking is from chapter 16, verse 10, where Luke breaks into the use of 'we' and 'us', giving a wonderfully personal style and atmosphere which carries on until the end of the book. Such incidents as the shipwreck on Malta (27, verse 13–44) with the story of Paul's adventures on the island (28, 1–10) are very immediate and obviously from an eye-witness. The book ends with Paul under arrest in Rome, writing and preaching, but the final events of trial and execution do not appear.

His Gospel

The Gospel of St Luke is his greatest work, full of pictures of the events of the Lord's life, with much information, it seems certain, from Mary the Mother of the Lord. Traditionally he spent much time with her after the Ascension, and she provided the familiar stories of the Annunciation, of her visit to Elizabeth, of the Child in the manger, the angelic host appearing to the shepherds, and the account of the Presentation in the Temple, as well as the story of the Finding of the boy Jesus in the Temple. Luke includes in his work six miracles and eighteen parables not recorded in the other Gospels; and he is particularly noted for his mention of the women who travelled with the Lord and his disciples, supplying their needs, and also for the account of the additional seventy disciples sent to spread the Gospel (10.1–20) in addition to the sending of the Twelve (9.1–2).

With Paul

Luke was with Paul apparently until the Apostle's martyrdom in Rome; but what happened after this is unknown. Tradition has it that Luke wrote his gospel in Greece, and that he died at the age of eighty-four in Boeotia.

Patron

St Luke is patron of physicians, and as has been said, 'Health is one and indivisible', consisting of the wholeness of the personality – body, mind and spirit. This truth is today taken more and more into practice, and it is recognized that treatment needs to take account of physical, mental and spiritual aspects.

The Last Sunday after Pentecost *(Trinity 20)*
20 October   Being Ready

'Keep awake, then; for you never know the day or the hour' Matthew 25.13 *(ASB Gospel)*

A Warning and an Encouragement

Our Gospel today is all about being ready, ready for the Great Day, the Day when the Lord will return, and the Kingdom will be established.

The parable that Jesus tells us, to give us an inkling, a foretaste, as it were, of what to expect, is all about being ready; and ready for a great event, which in the parable is the arrival of a Bridegroom.

Incidentally, an expert on Eastern life and customs tells us that every detail of the story of the arrival of the Bridegroom has been and still is very much the ordinary Hebrew countryside wedding programme; the lamps, the dancing, the excitement at the call 'The Bridegroom is here!' – and the sad refusal of admission to those who come too late.

'The door was shut . . .'

It is a warning and an encouragement, both, for us in the story. An encouragement for us to get on with our lives, living as close to God as we can, using all the gifts God has given us – including prayer and sacrament. We are to love and serve one another as the Lord has commanded, we are to help to make this world a better place for everyone to live in, to enjoy, to find happiness in. And taking care of the resources of the world, minerals, oil, the land and the sea, as well as the living creatures, the animals, the plants, the forests we share on this tiny planet Earth we call our home. For the peoples of this earth: fairness for the poor and neglected, freedom for the falsely imprisoned, in so many places, the end of war and cruelty; a fairer distribution of God's gifts together with care for the old and the sick, and hope for the unemployed, imprisoned, the old and the sick. We are all brothers and sisters, let us remember; whatever our colour, our nationality, our history, our place upon the surface of this earth.

Our Relationship

Our relationship to one another is one aspect of our relationship to the human Jesus Christ, since all human beings are related in this earthly existence of time and space. But that, of necessity, brings the question of our relationship to Jesus as the incarnate Son and Word of God.

There is no limit to the theoretical possibilities for good in humanity. That is the reason – or, shall we say, excuse – for all the man-made Utopias, philosophical or political, that have come, or will come, all leaving or trying to leave, God out. Only one Man has in the conditions of earthly life, already achieved the total victory of love, faith and hope over malice, self-righteousness and despair. That one Man was able to take humanity to the limit of perfection, because he was divine. Through him we are related not only to all humankind but to all the saints in the heavenly Kingdom. We have the hope of entering that new kind of existence that was inaugurated by the resurrection of Jesus, his triumph over sin and death. St John tells us what it is to be truly human, as we look forward in hope and faith:

'Beloved, we are God's children now. It does not yet appear what we shall be, but we know that when He appears, we shall be like Him, for we shall see Him as He is.'

(1 John 3.2.)

Last Sunday after Pentecost *Second Sermon*
Citizens of Heaven

'For us, our homeland is in heaven, and from heaven comes the Saviour we are waiting for' Philippians 3.20 (ASB EP)

Citizens of Heaven

Of whom do we think, when we hear that surprising phrase, 'Citizens of Heaven'? Do we, perhaps, think first of our loved ones who have 'gone ahead' of us? Do we think of the Saints in glory – those in our Calendar and those whom we would like to add to the Calendar, those whose lives and examples we revere? Do we – dare we – even think of ourselves as citizens of Heaven? I can almost hear one or two of you thinking, 'What, me? A citizen of heaven?'

But that is what I think we are.

Sadly, there is – or has been – a tendency in the Church to separate completely the earthly from the heavenly; to make a dichotomy between the sacred and the secular. In a way, this is all very natural; we are always hoping to get to a place where things are better, and indeed, that is a quite legitimate hope. In fact, our readings tonight reflect just this hope – the first, the ideal of a free land of Israel, a free and joyful Jerusalem; and the second, an idealized glimpse of heaven where all is joy and happiness, and sin and sorrow are banished.

Focus on the Future?

We do tend to focus too much on the future, and thereby we miss out so much. We are failing to get on with our co-operating with God in building his kingdom here, on this earth. We tend to separate the material from the spiritual, too easily. It is all part of the same syndrome which we may call 'Dualism'; and it is strange because we know that Christianity is the most material-istic of all the world faiths – as well, of course, as the most sub-limely spiritual, for the Word became flesh, and dwelt among us!

From next Sunday we shall be looking forward to celebrating the Incarnation – the taking of human flesh by God himself. That is not about separating the heavenly and the earthly dimensions; no – it is about the coming together of the two in perfect harmony. And we pray – most of us every day – the prayer our Lord taught us, including the vital phrase 'Thy kingdom come; thy will be done; on earth as it is in heaven.' So we are praying for just that precisely – God's kingdom to come on earth; and we are already citizens of that Kingdom as well as being citizens of this town, this country and this world.

The Second Coming

We can get very preoccupied with the 'Second Coming' of Christ. Of course there is scriptural warrant for this, but personally I feel we have enough to do getting on with things in the 'here and now', working for God's Kingdom of peace and justice here on earth. We can safely leave the celestial sphere in the mighty hands of God; but this world, this fragile space-ship Earth, he has entrusted to us. This is surely the best way to prepare ourselves for the future, whenever and whatever that may be.

It is very true, of course, that we are taught that there will be a final consummation and a Day of Judgement – though precisely in what terms we do not know; but it is surely foolish to wait idly for 'The Day' – instead, let us be learning *from* God how to work *with* God in the here and now, the busy and troubled and eager world as we have it.

On Earth

Surely the best way of exercising our 'Citizenship of Heaven' is by being concerned with events upon earth, especially such issues as are close at hand, concern our fellow citizens, and can be influenced by us (in however small a way). Rights and duties, local affairs and local government, local housing, fair treatment and justice for local people, the care of the sick and the elderly, the local schools and the provision of help and care for the young, especially those unemployed.

All this is surely a part we can play in making ready, being ready, for the Day of the Lord.

A PRAYER

> *Almighty God,*
> *you sent your Son to redeem the world,*
> *and will send him again to be our judge.*
> *May we so imitate him*
> *in the humility and purity of his first coming,*
> *that, when he comes again,*
> *we may be ready to greet him*
> *with joyful love and firm faith;*
> *through the same Christ our Lord. Amen.*
> *(PHG: Collect 32)*

Ninth Sunday before Christmas *(Trinity 21)* 27 October Paradise Lost *(The ASB Readings now change to Year 1)*

'He was in the world, and the world was made through him, yet the world knew him not. He came to his own home, and his own people received him not' John 1,10–11 (ASB Gospel)

Questions, questions . . .

A friend, a vicar in London, tells us he was invited to address the Sixth Form at a local school. 'To my surprise,' he says, 'the students actually wanted me to talk about theology! In their English Literature class they were studying Milton's *Paradise Lost* and found that it raised many questions about the nature of God and about religion. It was very good for me to sit down with a group of perhaps thirty young people in a situation where the initiative to talk about religion came from them rather than from me. The issues we discussed were not simply abstract or theoretical; for the students the questions had arisen out of their English studies and were absolutely genuine for them.

Why did God create mankind?
Why did God give us a capacity for evil?
Why do we give way to temptation?
Is God himself the creator of evil?
If there is a God, does there have to be a Devil also?

You can see how quickly we got into deep theological waters. Inevitably the questions came up: *Is the Bible true? Is all of it true? What about the claims of other religions?*

These questions enabled me to talk about an idea that is very important to me – the evolution of religious ideas. I was also able to introduce the students to the development of a science of biblical criticism over the last one hundred and fifty years. We grappled with the meaning of the word 'myth'. Oddly enough, while there are many people today who believe in the literal truth of the stories in the early chapters of Genesis, I do not think that the scribes who took these Babylonian stories into the Jewish tradition, would themselves have believed the stories in any literal sense. The stories were there to make a point – rather like the parables of Jesus. We grasp the point of the parables without believing that a story such as 'The Prodigal Son' or 'The Good Samaritan' is literally or historically true.

Milton

Milton wrote before the development of biblical criticism, so probably did believe in the historical veracity of the Scriptures. But he weaves a long and marvellous tale which has little foundation in the Bible, painting his vast canvas of the drama of humanity's fall from innocence, and looking forward to the work of redemption through the incarnation of the Son of God. One student asked why the Creator should make humanity go through its long years of suffering if the final result – *Paradise Regained* – was really just where we began before Paradise was lost in the first place. That's a good question, and if we did end up where we began, we would indeed be justified in asking if all the pain and sorrow of the human story was really justified. But the end is not exactly like the beginning. In the *Four Quartets*, T. S. Eliot says that we arrive where we began – but we know the place for the first time. The human drama does find its conclusion with men and women living in harmony with God. If the drama began in Paradise with humanity in harmony with God, that harmony is described as innocence; whereas the final harmony with which the drama concludes is not innocence but maturity. The long story of human sorrow is the path whereby we grow from an innocence which might be characteristic of childhood, to what St Paul calls 'mature manhood', the measure of the stature of the fullness of Christ, no longer children but growing up in every way into Christ.

The Search

I am sure that the dominant religious question in the 20th century, is the search for an assurance that our existence has meaning. We want to be assured not only that our achievements are significant, but also that our pains and sorrows themselves make their contribution to the completeness of the human drama. It simply would not be good enough for God to say that we shall forget what happens in this human life, in order that we might share again in the harmony of Paradise. Mature human beings do not ask to go back to the childhood world of innocence. We want to go forward with all that we have learnt in this life, to discover a deeper and more adult relationship with the God who made us. We can do this because our human experience is not alien to him, but something in which he has himself also shared.

J.S.

Lord God Almighty
you have given us the vision of your holiness,
and thereby of our unworthiness to be your witnesses.
Touch, we pray, our lips with your cleansing fire;
that so cleansed and hallowed, we may go out into the world
with the authority of your commission;
for Jesus Christ's sake.

Eric Milner White (Daily Prayer)
for Bible Sunday (The Promise of His Glory)

Ninth Sunday before Christmas
Second Sermon   **The Kingdom**
'Jesus answered, "In truth, in very truth, I tell you, unless a man is born anew, he cannot see the kingdom of God"' John 3.5 (ASB EP)

A Conversation at Night
Nicodemus was deeply interested in this much-talked-about preacher, who was being looked upon by many as very possibly the Messiah, so long promised and so long hoped for. But Nicodemus was not yet prepared to commit himself. The opening of the conversation was diplomatic enough, but Jesus swept away everything, to confront his visitor with the real process of entering into the Kingdom of God. Nicolas was aware of cleansing from sin by baptism, as was preached by John, and indeed as a long-standing sign of penitence, by Jews, and acceptance into the Hebrew faith, by converts. He had ideas of God's Kingdom, too. Yet birth of water and the Spirit was new to him, it seems; this birth is alone able to give the grace of entrance into the Kingdom. It is not enough to know of the Kingdom; it is more important to know it from within by personal experience.

A Spiritual Reality
After all, the Kingdom of God is a spiritual reality, experienced within the soul, but demonstrating itself outwardly in the life that is lived. The Kingdom is the world of invisible laws by which God is ruling and blessing his creatures; the laws are 'a world', inasmuch as they have a connection and coherence of their own; they form a system, a cosmos within the cosmos, and they come direct from heaven, that is to say from God.

It is worth noting that the idea of the Kingdom of God is rooted in Holy Scripture. We find it in both the Old and the New Testament. Another point should be noted – Scripture never argues about or seeks to prove, the being of God, who is over the Kingdom. His existence and his authority are taken for granted. The basis and foundation of the Kingdom are unchangeably right, just as God himself is unchangeable. In all things his law is holy, just and good; its moral perfection is seen supremely in the atoning life and work of our Lord. And, God's kingdom will know no end.

Our Response

God has a right to expect our obedience to his will and his way; so to know God's will should be to obey: 'Blessed are they that keep his commandments.' There can be no truer Gospel than that of the Kingdom which Christ came to establish: 'God sent the Son into the world, not to condemn the world, but that the world might be saved through him' (John 3.17). Because we are in Christ through baptism, we are members of the Kingdom of Heaven (Catechism). Our present possession of this spiritual Kingdom in the soul is assured to us by the indwelling presence of the Holy Spirit, who is also the pledge that we shall reach the fullness of the Kingdom in the life of the world to come.

Eighth Sunday before Christmas *(Trinity 22)*
3 November   The Journey of Life

'We know that we have left death and come over into life; we know it because we love our brothers' 1 John 3.14 (ASB NT Reading)

Penitence

In these words, St John speaks to us of a journey which every Christian must have made during his spiritual life. Journeys, we all know, can be happy occasions, pleasant to contemplate and to plan. Or, they can be things to dread which we put off as long as possible.

The journey of life for the Christian differs from one to another in many ways, but certain stages must mark the route of every believer. We all have to pass through the gate of penitence to reach the pastures of Christ's peace. We have to leave the dark kingdom of death and pass into the light of life which is in our Lord. This blessed change is within the realm of our consciousness; we must know that we have made that journey, and the evidence of it must be sufficient and ample. What is the evidence? It can be stated quite simply: Do we love our brethren? If we do, we are over our first stage, for we know that the person who does not love is still prisoner in the realm of death. To quote the Apostle: 'Anyone who does not do what is right or does not love his brother, that person is no child of God.'

It is also clear that St John does not allow the existence of a 'no man's land' between the two realms. It is either death or life, either hatred or love. Love is the sign of a change from death to life. Terrible as Cain's history is, it is still all too easily realized in ourselves – in essence if not in actuality. Love among Christians is the sign of a new life.

Travelling
This journey from death to life is one that we all have to undertake; we have to pass into a new sphere of living. J. B. Phillips translates our text: 'We know that we have crossed the frontier from death to life, because we do love our brothers. We have entered upon a new life; we now first truly live. The passage has been made; the new sphere of being has been gained. Life is not future, but present!' This spiritual journey takes place in the inner realm of our mind and our spirit, not in the outer tangible world in which we live and move and have our being. We can start upon our journey in this place or that, without the end product being postponed. And every Christian – or would-be Christian – has to face the occasion for travel, and must act upon the call.

Arriving
Death and life are regarded as the two spheres in which we humans live and move – 'the death which is truly death' and 'the life which is truly life'. St John makes it clear that anyone who does not love is living in the old country of death – the country of the selfish, the self-centred, the self-confined. Take the step, put yourself at the point of departure, from which you are to travel towards what the Apostle calls 'life'. St Paul puts it in similar words: 'If any man be in Christ, there is a new creation.' Our spiritual journey has as its point of arrival, a life that is centred upon God; and the rate of our progress towards this rich and amazing goal is estimated by the love we have for our brothers and sisters. Love among Christians is the sign of a new life. Consequently, hatred among Christians is the sign of not only the absence of life, but of the destruction of life. 'Whoever hates his brother is a murderer . . .' The apostle is very blunt, very clear – so too is our Lord Jesus himself. Take his words to heart, from the Gospel today, 'It is what comes out of a man that defiles him. For from inside, out of a man's heart, come evil thoughts, acts of fornication, of theft, murder, adultery, ruthless greed and malice; fraud, indecency, envy, slander, arrogance and folly; these evil things all come from inside, and they defile the man.' What a list! and how true it all is.

Let us look at another place in the Gospel which throws a more cheerful light upon the journey of our human life. 'God sent his Son into the world, not to condemn the world, but that the world might be saved through him . . . The light has come into the world, and men loved darkness rather than light . . . But he who does what is true comes to the light, that it may be clearly seen that his deeds have been wrought in God.' (John 3.17–21)

8th before Christmas *Second Sermon*
A Reformer: St Charles Borromeo, 1538–1584

'I will raise up for myself a faithful priest: he will do what is in my heart and in my mind,' says the Lord 1 Samuel 2.35 (RM)

The Care and Education of the People of God

St Charles has a good claim to be the Patron Saint of parish clergy, of liturgists and sacristans, of church furnishers and of church musicians. Indeed, he has been compared to the great St Ambrose – also of Milan – and like St Ambrose his concerns were the Liturgy, together with 'the ornaments of the church, and of the Ministers thereof, at all times of their ministration', and the care and education of the people of God. So important did he believe education to be, that he established Sunday Schools in his diocese two hundred years before Robert Raikes began his work in our own country.

St Charles came from an aristocratic family with strong Church connections – his father was a Count and his mother a Medici, while his uncle was Pope Pius IV – so it is hardly surprising that the Church became his career. That career began somewhat early, since while a mere child he was appointed titular Abbot of a rich monastery in N. Italy; then, at 22, he was made a Cardinal and shortly afterwards Archbishop of Milan, although he was not actually ordained priest and bishop until 1563 at the age of 27.

An Influential Adviser

He was probably the most important and influential of the advisers at the Council of Trent, and his hand can be traced in many of the documents and decisions. It is interesting to notice how similar in some important respects were the principles of our own Archbishop Thomas Cranmer and those of St Charles. First, the many and varied liturgies in use were to be edited, revised and simplified, resulting in the Tridentine Mass (for the Continental Church) and the Communion Service of the Book of Common Prayer (for the Church of England). As Cranmer put it, 'Whereas there hath been great diversity in saying and singing in churches . . . now from henceforth all the whole Realm shall have but one Use . . . commodious for shortness and plainness' which would most certainly have been the ideal of St Charles. Secondly, the liturgical authority which had been earlier vested in the diocesan bishop, was now transferred to one central figure only – in the case of the Church of England to the Sovereign as Supreme Governor, and in the Roman Church to the Pope. In other words, the principles that the reviewers, in both the Anglican Church and the Church of Rome, adopted, were – in these areas – practically identical. Getting rid of much interesting and in many respects devotional material, accumulated over many centuries, and returning to simpler forms and more meaningful language, made it possible for the people in general to take a more genuine part in the services, as in the early days.

Percy Dearmer

It is interesting to note the similarity of St Charles' rules on ceremonial, on the design and style of vestments, and on church planning and ornament, with the teaching of our own great Anglican figure in the domain of liturgy, ceremonial and music – Percy Dearmer, sometime Vicar of St Mary-the-Virgin Primrose Hill, and author of the immensely influential 'Parson's Handbook', first published in 1901 and still selling in a revised and modern version.

Indeed Dearmer and St Charles were both forerunners of the Liturgical Movement of today, with its emphasis on simplicity combined with the best possible artistic contributions, and its desire for the fullest recognition of the part to be played by the laity.

St Charles' decrees on such things as the size and shape of the chasuble, the length and style of the surplice – it ought to be, he says, half-way between the knee and the feet, with wide full sleeves – and many, many other practical and artistic details read exactly like extracts from Dearmer's 'Handbook'. (Incidentally Dearmer was himself of aristocratic lineage, as was his notable disciple, Conrad Noel of Thaxted, later known as the 'Red Priest' for his left-wing and pacifist views.)

An Early Death
Sadly, St Charles died in 1584, at the age of only 46. He was worn out with his work among his people, especially during the great plague of a few years previously.

May his example and his outlook guide us, and his prayers aid us.

PRAYER

Father, keep in your people
the spirit which filled St Charles.
Let your Church be continually renewed
and show the image of Christ to the world
by being conformed to his likeness,
who lives and reigns with you
and the Holy Spirit, for ever and ever. Amen.
(R.M.)

Seventh Sunday before Christmas *(Trinity 23)*
10 November   Abraham

'The Promise of His Glory' suggests the Third Sunday before Advent as 'The First Sunday of the Kingdom', and gives readings and collects (page 383); also for Remembrance Sunday (p. 384)
The Lord said to Abraham: 'Through you I will bless all the nations' Genesis 12.3 (ASB OT Reading)

Faith
It almost seems as though a new element entered into religion with Abraham, for the importance of his example lies in his faith in God. It was in faith that he obeyed God's call to him to leave Haran for Palestine. It was in faith that he trusted God in the birth of his son, and in his willingness to offer him in sacrifice to God. It was in faith that he looked down the ages, believing the promises of God as if already fulfilled. Because of his faith he did indeed become the father of many nations. Above all, he was the father of Israel, and the ancestor of the Messiah, Jesus, who was the promised Seed. In our reading from St Paul's Letter to the

Romans, it is stressed that Abraham is the ancestor of all the faithful, inasmuch as he is the outstanding example of the virtue of faith, which Christ required of all who would follow him.

Trust
Our Divine Lord is the true object of human faith, so when he has declared his will, it is for us to follow in complete trust. Abraham showed that his faith and trust in God was in control of his whole life. 'He drew strength from his faith and gave glory to God, convinced that God had power to do what he had promised' (Romans 4.21). He was not one who would give the assent of his mind, or the words of his lips, while holding back the service and devotion of his life. He lived, too, as though all God's promises were already fulfilled, even though their full completion could be realized only in his descendants.

Abraham had faith, and it was a faith which not only believed, but actually issued in practical works. 'Faith without works is dead', wrote St James; Abraham's faith was a living and active faith.

Our Calling
As Christians, we are not only called upon to believe, but also to live by our belief. We are to show our belief in and through our actions and our lives. If we believe in God's promises, if we acknowledge our acceptance of Jesus Christ as Lord and Leader, our faith will always condition our thoughts, our words, and our actions.

Our religion and faith is to be not only of inward dispositions, but also of outward actions and deeds. Both the inward and spiritual, with the outward and visible, are alike of importance, but always the outward is to be inspired and controlled by the inward. Our actions and our whole life, therefore, must be the expression of the living faith in Jesus Christ that is held in our minds and in our souls.

Seventh Sunday before Christmas
Second Sermon **'What do you think?'**
'Jesus said, "Which of the two did the will of his father?"' Matthew 21.31 (ASB EP)

Publicity

When some politicians, or TV or film star, visits some town – perhaps for the first time – a routine procedure is to send ahead the publicity people; their job is to stir up interest in the person coming, and get people talking about the visit beforehand.

Jesus was the very opposite of this; he usually avoided publicity as much as possible, though rather like Gandhi in India he tended to be accompanied by crowds who flocked to see and hear him. In his last visit to Jerusalem, however, he seems to have specially wanted the attention of the people, for this was the time when they must either accept him or reject him. He even arranged beforehand for an ass and a colt to be ready, and gave a password to the disciples so that the owner would understand and let them take the animals at once (21, vv. 1,2 and 3) for the Lord to ride upon at his entry into the Holy City.

Helpers and Haters

In seeking attention Jesus was also helped by the country people from Galilee who had come up for the Passover feast, and who knew him through his preaching and miracles in their towns and villages. They gave him a noisy welcome (vv. 9, 10 and 11). The priests and elders were naturally furious; the next day they were demanding to know what authority Jesus claimed? (v.23). Jesus replies with the two parables, the 'Man with Two Sons' (28–31) and the 'Murder of the Heir' (33–39). These two stories completely demolish the claims of the priests and elders, and show them up as hypocrites who should have all authority taken away from them for their betrayal of their faith and their refusal to accept Christ.

Today

There are plenty of people today, who, like the scribes and Pharisees, are enemies of Jesus, or at least enemies of the Christian faith. They misinterpret what he taught and did; seek to bring down the Church which Jesus founded; pick on those weak followers who may have given way to temptations of various sorts; and eagerly push their own theories and brand new ideas (usually recognized by those who know, as old heresies or errors long past their 'sell-by' dates). Yet Jesus continues to love all men and women, in spite of the enmity of some and failure of others. Like the apostles of old, they fail to live up to the faith they profess to hold. But Jesus still loves his opponents and all whose love is growing cold, all who forget him or ignore him.

Unfailing Love
Too often, when we are sadly disappointed by somebody who loved us, our love turns into despair or even hatred. Christ's love will never do this, because it is stronger than ours, being not only the human love of the Man Jesus, but the divine love of Christ the Son of God.

Sixth Sunday before Christmas *(Trinity 24)*
17 November   Moses

'Who am I, that I should go to Pharaoh, and bring the sons of Israel out of Egypt?' Exodus 3.11 (ASB OT Reading)

The Call of Moses
Moses, leading the flock of his father-in-law, Jethro, sees the surprising sight – a bush apparently blazing and burning, yet it is not being consumed. He is conscious of the Presence of God. The place is holy ground, and he knows it. Then comes the divine call: 'I will send you to Pharaoh.' Moses feels that he is unfit and quite unqualified, for such a tremendous task; but he receives the assurance: 'I am with you.'

   Moses learns that this God is the great 'I AM'. He is the Living God, in whom we live and move and have our being. As we say in the General Thanksgiving, we thank him 'for our creation, preservation, and all the blessings of this life'. As the poet expresses it:

   'Every bush aflame with God, yet only he who sees takes off his shoes.'

A Remarkable Man
What a remarkable man Moses was! What a strange and adventurous life he led! How full of ups and downs that life was. And what a great triumph he accomplished for his own nation, and indeed for the world, in that life. It is not surprising that the Jews look upon him as one of their two great national heroes, King David being the other. Three thousand years ago he was buried

'in a valley in the land of Moab', yet his influence is still strong. Not only are his words religious and moral law to his own people, the Hebrews, but they echo and re-echo down the centuries.

Christianity and Islam are outgrowths of the Judaism which Moses founded, and are still rooted in his ethical system. Mohammed hailed Moses and Jesus as the greatest prophets of old. Jesus said, 'I have come not to destroy the Law (of Moses) but to fulfil it.'

The Covenant
Moses was inspired to represent the moral life as part of a Covenant with the One God, the Voice that spoke from the flaming bush, revealing himself as a moral, personal God and making a contract of mutual promises. 'I promise to be your heavenly and supernatural guide and protector: you in your turn promise to obey my orders and keep my commandments.'

Are we too ready to take all this for granted, or to say that it is simply superceded? Now, we have gone beyond the concept of 'Divine Law' to a philosophy of a vague attitude of benevolence. We rally round a sentimental and self-indulgent distortion of the teachings of Jesus Christ and St Paul – certainly both spoke in terms of abolishing Moses' edicts, but claimed to be building new thinking and new theology upon his foundations.

Promises, Promises . . .
We seem well on the way towards losing sight of the importance of seeing promise-keeping and binding contracts as things rooted in the Covenant of God – they are not simply matters of social convenience, indeed necessity, but sacred. God himself is the great promise-keeper, the great keeper of contracts.

A disturbing feature of our modern life is the common 'standing up' in the sense of abandoning arrangements or promises, the frequency of industrial disputes, going back on agreements, shifty dealing where once our word was our bond. Can anyone have confidence in the City, in industrial arrangements over pay and rewards, today? Ask a Lloyds 'name', or a person who had an account with BCCI, or a parson whose living depends on the Church Commissioners . . . And above all, marriage, where solemn promises and vows are today set far too often, for frivolous or blatantly selfish motives.

The New Covenant
Reconciliation, mutual trust and concern, mutual sympathy and love, all find their perfect expression in the New Law of Christ; the New Covenant between God and Man, instituted at the Last Supper with the words 'This is my blood of the New Covenant.' A fundamental revelation of covenant-making, promise-keeping, renewed and brought to perfection and triumph at Calvary. 'God so loved the world that he gave his only-begotten Son . . . for God sent not the Son into the world to judge the world, but that the world should be saved through him.'

A PRAYER

O Lord Christ
before whose judgement seat we must all appear,
keep us steadfast and faithful in your service,
and enable us so to judge ourselves in this life,
that we may not be condemned
    on the day of your appearing;
for your tender mercy's sake.

(PHG p. 347)

6 before Christmas *Second Sermon*
The Wind of the Spirit

'The wind blows where it wills, and you hear the sound of it, but you do not know whence it comes or whither it goes; so it is with everyone who is born of the Spirit' John 3.8 (ASB EP)

The Vision
Mysticism has been described as 'religion in its most concentrated and exclusive form', as 'that attitude in which all other relations are swallowed up in the relation of the soul to God'. The mystic quest begins in every case with an inward call, felt in a moment of vision. In such moments there is a consciousness of being in direct communication with a world of spiritual reality, which at other times seems closed to our understanding or reaching. In such moments the individual feels himself or herself most truly alive and most fully a self, complete, united.

In our ordinary Christian life we are vouchsafed more vision than we take note of, for when we feel ourselves lifted up to God in prayer and worship, or when in the presence of beauty, or in the awareness of nobility of character, or in moments of insights, service, love and peace, we find ourselves transcending the discords from within and without, and we feel ourselves identified with the 'real thing' – then we are having experiences that are common to mystical intention.

The Presence

Upon a lucky night
In secrecy, inscrutable to sight,
I went without discerning
And with no other light
Except for that which in my heart was burning.

It lit and led me through
More certain than the light of noonday clear
To where One waited near
Whose presence well I knew
There where no other presence might appear.
St John of the Cross

Fifth Sunday before Christmas *(Sunday next before Advent)* 24 November   Responsibilities

'Restore us again, O Lord of hosts; show us the light of your countenance, and we shall be saved' Psalm 80.3 (ASB Yr.1)

Relief . . .
With the announcement of a 'cessation of military operations' to quote the precise wording of the IRA, there was a general expression of thanksgiving that twenty-five years of violence seemed, at last, to be at an end. One commentator reacted to the euphoria by saying that if it were right to give thanks to God for the ending of violence, was it not equally right to blame him for allowing that violence to continue for twenty-five years?

The point is well made and not at all frivolous, because it draws attention to the dividing line between human responsibility and the responsibility of God. For what can we blame ourselves, and for what can we blame God? It also raises the issue of the activity of God; does God actively intervene in the affairs of the world? If not, why not? And if he does intervene, why is his behaviour so unintelligible?

It would be unwise to attempt to answer these questions until we have faced the issue of responsibility.

Memories . . .

Those of us who are of a certain age and above, can remember the growing civil rights movement in Northern Ireland, which began public demonstrations towards the end of 1968. It began mostly as a protest at the way the minority community in the Province had been treated by the majority since Partition in 1922. The initially peaceful protests gradually began to end in violence, and by the summer of 1969 the police were no longer able to maintain law and order, and in came the Army to maintain the peace.

The sad irony of August 1969 is the memory we have of the way in which the troops were welcomed as protectors by the Nationalist community; the TV pictures of a Roman Catholic housewife bringing out a cup of tea for a soldier on patrol was a moving sight, and it has remained a poignant memory. Consequent developments have all but obliterated the remembrance of such open-hearted action, and the problems of religion, politics and economics are now so closely interwoven that it is very difficult to separate them. We can only wish the parties now meeting eventual success.

Pointless

When the tragedy does seem to be pointless, it is very tempting to point the finger. Someone must be responsible, and as always, the person at the top has to carry the can. We know that God does not condone violence, but we cannot understand why he did not act to prevent it or intervene to stop it – and it is always satisfying to attribute blame to someone who cannot or will not, answer back.

Perhaps before we blame God, we should take a good look at ourselves and our own behaviour. Until we have faced up to the fact of our own responsibility for much if not all, of the world's suffering, as well as our own personal misfortunes, there will be little chance of alleviating that unhappiness. Too many people refuse to accept responsibility for what they have said and done, and the blame always lies somewhere else.

> *'Set your heart right and be steadfast,*
> *and do not be hasty in time of calamity.*
> *Accept whatever is brought upon you,*
> *and in changes that humbles you be patient.*
>
> *For gold is tested in the fire,*
> *and acceptable men in the furnace of humiliation.*
>
> *Trust in God, and he will help you;*
> *make your ways straight, and hope in him.*
> (Ecclesiasticus 2.2, 4.6)

5th Sunday before Christmas *Second Sermon* Crusade

'At Salem is God's tabernacle, and his dwelling is in Zion. There he broke in pieces the flashing arrows, the shields, the swords, and the weapons of battle' Ps 76 (ASB EP)

900 Years Ago . . .

An event of considerable importance to the world happened almost exactly 900 years ago; an event having a telling influence on the histories of the Christian West, of Islam, and of the Jewish people to this day. What was this event?

On November 27 in the year 1095, in the fairly insignificant town of Clermont in southern France, a particularly energetic Pope – Urban II – began to preach the First Crusade. Four years later, and after countless barbarities and much slaughter which accompanies the passage of the crusading armies across Europe and the Levant, Jerusalem was conquered on July 15th 1099. The Crusader Kingdom of Jerusalem, which came into being shortly thereafter, lasted through turbulent vicissitudes of fortune for nearly a century. Jerusalem fell on October 2 1187, following the crushing defeat Saladin inflicted on the Kingdom's armies on the parched plateau of Hattin, in Galilee, four months before.

Shock

The fall of Jerusalem hit the Christian world with an emotional and spiritual shock not dissimilar to the one experienced by Islam, when the Crusaders conquered the city a year before the end of the previous century. Jerusalem was never regained for Christianity, except for a brief period during the first half of the 13th century, when, through a curious diplomatic coup, the Holy Roman Emperor of the time, Frederick II, 'Stupor Mundi' – excommunicated at the time – became the nominal ruler. The remaining physical vestiges of Crusader rule in Palestine are few, but highly charged with historical reverberation. There is a cluster of ruined fortresses, in particular Krak des Chevaliers – built largely by Richard Lionheart – and a number of churches. Chief amongst these latter are the Holy Sepulchre in Jerusalem and the Church of the Nativity in Bethlehem, where diverse Christian denominations squabble over their rights of tenure. And there is the mosque of Al-Aqsa – the third holiest Moslem shrine – once the headquarters of the most notorious and illustrious of Christian military Orders – the Templars. These religious sites are still today something like dormant volcanoes, potential focal points of disturbance and violence – as we have witnessed.

Just why Pope Urban II's call elicited such a powerful response is an enigma. No doubt it will continue to preoccupy scholars in future, as it has done in the past. However, the concept of a 'Crusade' took root and has survived through various mutations to this day.

Irony

For me personally, the fascination with the whole business of Crusades is twofold. First, the irony inherent in the word through its entire evolution. What followed Urban II's appeal to redeem Christ's sepulchre from the infidel, exposed the Church at its most venal. The cross-bearing warriors contradicted every Christian tenet while crying 'God wills it!' The kingdom established in Jerusalem in the name of divine spirituality proved to be one of the most corrupt and worldly feudal regimes that ever existed. And for nearly four centuries thereafter, the crusading ideal was periodically implemented to settle scores against 'heretics' and political opponents.

Secondly, there has always been an ominous dark cloud of Millenarianism hovering about the evangelical zeal which propelled the Crusades; and this has produced a number of bizarre

236

events both in the distant and recent past. Like the Children's Crusade in 1212, the Klu Klux Klan in the USA and, more recently in the news, the mass killings of 'Doomsday' cults in the USA, Canada and Switzerland.

I do not share the view of those pessimists who declare that uncertainty over faith in the world today, is promoting fundamentalist evangelism. Besides, life is far more certain than ever before, in most parts of the world.

But I do wince inwardly when I hear some senior cleric call for a 'moral and spiritual crusade' against this or that, just as a reflexive tremor passes through me at the mention of a fatwa against some writer or politician, by an Islamic leader, or the threat of a holy 'war' or Jihad, or the shocking case of the Pakistani Christian boy accused of blasphemy – dropped, thank God, by the judiciary of the country.

(Adapted from an article by Elon Salmon, novelist & journalist)

Church of the Holy Sepulchre

The guide said, 'The earth is sensitive here;
Often we have earthquakes. The rocks are soft.'
Miss Lacy crossed herself. 'He came down',
She whispered. 'He came down, and that
Is all we have.' She wiped away a tear,
And we all crept out of the gold-encrusted Sepulchre.

Black Mount Ararat bobbed above a beard;
Wax from his crooked candle soaked his book.
Those glowing Armenian eyes were as indifferent
To us, as the bold stare of a leopard in the zoo.

'To save us' is 'To save us' in any tongue.
I hear peasant harmonies in chapels, choirs
In unheated churches. I see dawn
Breaking out over the Powys frost.

And a boy dressed as a king, carries Christmas
In a heavy censer as he sings
His wounded sound. His lips are curved
Like a Coptic pharaoh's: is it a sneer or a smile?

'Here,' said the guide, pointing to a post-hole.
His voice too shot up and flattened on the roof,
'Is the middle of the world.' And so it was.

He had no need to smile and bow. Halfway
Between the manger and the Cross.

Emyr Hymphreys

Sermons for Saints' Days
and for Special Occasions
1995

Wednesday 29 November *Eve of St Andrew*
Day of Prayer for the Missionary Work of the
Church
'Their voice has gone out to all the earth, and their words to the ends of world' Romans 10,18

On this day we are asked to pray for the missionary work of the Church, that is, the spreading of the Gospel throughout the world. Many well-known societies and causes are devoted to the mission of the Church, and our first duty is to interest ourselves in their work and support them financially. Regular giving and constant prayer, and getting to know what the needs are, should be very definite parts of our religious life.

> *Eternal Giver of love and life,*
> *your Son Jesus Christ has sent us into all the world,*
> *to preach the gospel of his kingdom.*
> *Strengthen us in this mission,*
> *and help us to live the good news we proclaim,*
> *through Jesus Christ our Lord.*
> *(Patterns for Worship)*

Thursday 30 November *St Andrew the Apostle*
The Call
'Andrew said to Simon, "We have found the Messiah" (which means, The Christ). And he brought him to Jesus' John 1.41,42

The Church in the World

Today we remember St Andrew as a symbol of the Mission of the Church in the whole world – the task of spreading the Good News, the Gospel, to all nations, as the Lord Jesus commissioned his disciples; and on the Eve and today we pray for the work of the Church overseas, that Christ may be known and loved in every country and by every nation.

The striking example of Andrew is simply the urgent way in which he – having heard John the Baptist refer to Jesus as 'The Lamb of God!', followed Jesus to where he was staying and remained – doubtless discussing the things of the Kingdom – then brought his brother, Simon, having excitedly told him that here was the Messiah! Jesus at once sees something special about Simon; was it his strength of character or his powerful will that appealed to Christ? Whatever it was at that very first meeting, the nickname Christ gave him – Peter, 'The Rock' – implies a solid foundation, a conviction that would not easily be put aside.

Fishermen

Simple fisherfolk, we might say, of that little group on the shore of the Sea of Galilee. Yet they must have heard about the new Teacher, the healer of the sick and the scourge of the conventionally religious. His doings must have been eagerly discussed, his teachings mulled over, and a spark struck – so that at the moment of destiny, they were ready and willing to leave all and 'follow him'. And their immediate action, after that decision, is to bring others – Andrew brings Simon Peter, Philip brings Nathanael, and so on. The Gospel, the Good News, is something to be shared, to be spread about; this is the message of the early days, and it is the message still in our own time.

We are All Called

Our calling is to do all we can to help the spreading of the truths of the Gospel of Christ to all people everywhere. This may mean for us that we are to be missionaries in the small and perhaps humdrum circles in which we live and move and have our daily lives. Our simple and straightforward human care and concern, sympathy and interest, can be the best way of bringing others to the Faith we know and love; an opportunity to talk over a cup of tea for someone lonely, in distress, unhappy, in trouble of some kind. So many of us are shut off, sad, and missing out on human contacts, that the simplest approach can be of great help.

As Christians we have ourselves a divine calling; since we have been given so much in Christ, our life and outlook is so changed, we simply *have* to pass on what we know to be true. All we have is given to us liberally, not to hug close to ourselves, but to share and pass on.

Bringing Others
Let us remember St Andrew and his eagerness to bring others to Jesus – Simon, who became the leader of the apostles; the boy with the loaves and fishes; and with Philip, Andrew brought the Greek visitors who wanted to meet Jesus, but were hampered by lack of an introduction, and probably by difficulties with language. These events are recorded in the Gospels, but we may be sure that there were many other examples not noted down at the time. Always be ready to help, like Andrew.

Friday 8 December *The Conception of Our Lady*
Hail Mary
We know that in everything God works for good with those who love him, who are called according to his purpose; for those whom he foreknew he also predestined. Romans 8.28,29 (PHG)

History
The doctrine that the Blessed Virgin Mary was preserved from any stain of original sin was widely accepted from early days, in both East and West. This does not mean that Mary was conceived without the sexual union of her parents; rather, it is perhaps most simply stated as the belief that Mary received, at the moment when her soul was infused into her body, the graces that Christians normally receive in Baptism. Since 1854 (the date of the definition by the Roman Church of the Immaculate Conception) Orthodox theologians have generally rejected the doctrine; before then, many accepted it in some form. The Anglican Bishop Ken taught it in his stanza:

> *The Holy Ghost his temple in her built,*
> *Cleansed from congenial, kept from mortal guilt;*
> *And from the moment that her blood was fired*
> *Into her heart celestial love inspired.*

Present Usage
The feast appears without the adjective in the BCP Calendar, but is omitted from the ASB, which gives prominence to the Birthday (September 8th) as the principal feast of Mary. However, *The Promise of His Glory* gives proper readings and the following collect, and notes that the festival 'is appropriate to the Season of Advent.'

Almighty and eternal God,
who prepared the blessed Virgin Mary to be the mother of your Son:
Grant that, as with her we look for his First Coming as our Saviour,
so we may be ready to greet him when he comes again as our Judge;
for he is alive and reigns with you and the Holy Spirit,
one God, now and forever.

Readings:
Gen. 3.9–15, 20; Ps. 98 1–5; Eph. 1. 3–6, 11–12; Luke 1.26–38
Additional Psalms and Readings are indicated in PHG, p. 401.

Tuesday 26 December *St Stephen the First Martyr* Rejection

'O Jerusalem, Jerusalem! The city that murders the prophets and stones the messengers sent to her!' Matthew 23.27 (BCP & ASB Gospel)

'Full of faith and of the Holy Spirit'
Stephen, 'a man full of faith and of the Holy Spirit', was one of the seven assistants or deacons appointed by the Apostles to relieve the pressures of 'serving tables'; that is, assisting with the Lord's Supper and the 'Agape' or Love Feast (see 'Lent, Holy Week and Easter' pp. 97, 98 for suggestions for our own times) and other duties and administration.

Incidentally, we make an error if we think of the early deacons as mere 'learners' or 'junior assistants'; the deacon was a person of importance and had considerable responsibilities. In a local church, he would be the chair of the PCC, churchwarden, and treasurer all combined, in our terms of today. It was not until the early Middle Ages that his important status was gradually reduced to that of a junior, and even then the Archdeacon,

though ordained a priest, was a figure of power and responsibility
– as in our own times.

'Grace and Power'

We are told that Stephen was 'full of grace and power' (Acts
6.8). Some members of the early Church wanted to remain in
Jerusalem, hugging to themselves their faith. Stephen, on the
contrary, realized the importance of a literal obedience to Christ's
command 'Go and make disciples of all nations!' (Matt. 28, 19)
The Council was enraged; they stirred up the people and produced false witnesses; but Stephen put up a magnificent defence.
Infuriated by his words, they became more and more threatening;
but Stephen was sustained by his sense of the presence of Christ
– 'I can see the Son of Man standing at the right hand of God!'
They rushed him outside and stoned him. Stephen followed the
example of his Master, praying for those who were murdering
him – 'Lord, do not hold this sin against them.' And so he 'fell
asleep' in the spirit and the love of Christ.

The Example of Christ

Jesus made it quite clear to his disciples that they must be prepared to face persecution and even death. Jesus was hounded to
the death of the Cross; this is the kind of world we live in, and
the toll of violence and death goes on in front of our eyes on our
TV screens as the news brings war and brutality, crime and disaster and accident. Think of Archbishop Luwum, and all the clergy
and nuns killed in Africa; think of the martyrs in the Sudan, some
actually crucified; persecution in Iran, repression in some Islamic
states; violence in Ireland may have stopped, but it seems
endemic in parts of Europe, in Japan and in America.

Loss for Christ's sake

To follow Christ, and to do what we believe to be right, may lead
to rejection, suffering, loss, even death.

Bishop George Bell, the distinguished Bishop of Chichester,
disapproved of saturation bombing in the last war, and expressed
his disapproval in many speeches. Some people think that Bishop
Bell would have been Archbishop of Canterbury, if he had not
been so vocal in expressing his strong feelings that it was wrong
to use such bombing.

Dietrich Bonhoeffer felt that Hitler was so evil that it was right
for him to take part in a plot to assassinate the dictator.

Bonhoeffer's courage resulted in his imprisonment and death by hanging. But his example lives on.

Wednesday 27 December
St John the Evangelist **The Vision**
'The darkness is passing away and the true light is already shining'
1 John 2.8

A Close Friend
Being a member of one of the most prominent fishing businesses at the Sea of Galilee, with connections in many other places, including Jerusalem itself, it seems very possible that John, son of Zebedee, knew Jesus and probably was a close friend. The designation given John in the New Testament as 'the disciple Jesus loved' indicates a special friendship; and certainly John, with his brother James, and Peter, was on terms of intimacy which ripened into a close bond with the Lord. These three were chosen to be with Jesus on a number of occasions when they were able to share special experiences – the Transfiguration, for example, and that fateful night of the arrest in the Garden of Gethsemane.

Tradition
Again, tradition tells us that John exercised an apostolic care over the infant church in Asia Minor from the great city of Ephesus, a cosmopolitan centre of trade and culture. Another tradition tells that Mary came to Ephesus, and eventually died there; this tradition begins with the words of Jesus on the Cross giving his mother into the care of his friend, as noted in St John's gospel. In fact, since the first century, a strong connection has existed between John and the whole area around Ephesus.

Patmos
Later it is traditionally reported that John was exiled – or perhaps retired? – to the island of Patmos. He continued there, and formed the centre of a group who pondered and prayed much on the deep things of the Faith. The scholars tell us that John himself wrote the letters that appear in our Bibles under his name, but that his Gospel may well have been put together by his followers

from his own reminiscences and under his direction and influence. On the other hand the 'Apocalypse' or 'Revelations', the last book of our New Testament, is generally thought today to have been composed by disciples in times of great distress, but incorporating visions and teachings from John.

A Precious Legacy
In John's gospel, what wonderful and elevated thinking and vision there is; and what help and comfort its words have been to many, with their emphasis on 'love', on 'hope', and perhaps most of all, 'light'. John is indeed the apostle of light, and the collect prays that we may 'walk by the light' and 'finally know Jesus as the light of everlasting life'.

Thursday 28 December *The Holy Innocents*
The Children
'They have been ransomed as the first fruits of mankind' Revelation 14.4.

Protection
It is clear that the young life of the Infant Jesus was under divine guidance; the Father's protecting hand was over him. Joseph's dream, the visit of the Magi, the search for 'a new-born King', to say nothing of the knowledge of Herod's brutal and cruel character, must have all had a part in the way events turned out.

Egypt would be a natural place of refuge. It was not far away, and many Jews had settled there. There would be a welcome, no doubt, to a refugee family; and indeed there may already have been some relatives – near or distant – with whom the refugees could stay. In the same way, the return to Palestine would be natural after Herod's death.

Cruelty
'Absolute power corrupts' is a historian's verdict on the lives of many rulers and kings of very different periods. Those in positions of authority were and are all too easily able to take their own decisions, whatever the cost to others. Specially was this true of the Middle East – as indeed it seems, sadly, much the same today. Unscrupulous and cruel, Herod's action in having the children murdered was no isolated act. History tells us that

he did many brutalities of this kind, often involving his own kith and kin; and usually with just the same reason behind them – the safety of his throne.

Our Times
Horrible though the story seems, it must be remembered that far worse butchery has been done in our own times. In Africa, the dreadful slaughter of refugees in Rwanda and Burundi; the Cambodian massacres, the Chechen war; the killing in Bosnia and so many other places. The United Nations shows little ability to control or halt what goes on; brutality, killing, destruction goes on and on. We are appalled by events in countries abroad, yet in our own land the murder of children by careless driving on our roads, by those who are perverted or ignorant and callous goes on in a dreadful litany of pain and hatred. As we remember the children murdered at Bethlehem, let us remember and mourn for all innocent victims down the ages and in every place. As we pray for them, pray too for ourselves, that God in his mercy will not bring down upon us his justifiable and justified wrath and judgment.

1996

Thursday 18 January *The Confession of St Peter* The Rock

'Simon Peter replied, "You are the Christ, the Son of the living God"'
Matthew 16.16

'Who do they say I am?'
The people had reached the stage of a certain expectancy in relation to Jesus; his constant talk about the 'Coming of the Kingdom' led many to take it that he was one of the Old Testament figures whose reappearance was prophesied as herald of the Promised Kingdom – or even a reincarnation of John Baptist. But when Simon Bar-Jona confessed, 'You are the Christ', Jesus responded, 'You are Peter, and on this rock I will build my Church.' This rough fisherman and his brother Andrew were the first disciples called by Jesus.

It was Peter who attempted to walk on the sea, and began to

sink; it was Peter who, amazed and astonished, wanted to build three tabernacles on the Mount of the Transfiguration; it was Peter, having boldly stated his faith at the Last Supper, then three times denied his Lord. But it was also Peter who, after Pentecost, risked his life to speak boldly and publicly of his faith in Jesus; it was Peter who with courage helped the young Church to go beyond the Jewish community and out into the Gentile world; true, Paul had to rebuke him for giving way too easily to the separatist demands of Jewish Christians, but there is no doubt of his position as a leading figure (or indeed, *the* leading figure) in the Early Church, nor of his martyrdom finally, at Rome. 'I am not worthy to be crucified as my Lord was,' he is supposed to have said, and died on a cross, head downwards.

As we watch Peter struggle with himself, often stumbling, often 'foot-in-mouth', loving his Lord, acting impetuously and rashly, we are reminded that Jesus came not to save the godly and strong, but the sinful and weak. Simon, an ordinary human being, was transformed by the Spirit into the 'Rock', to become the leader of the Church.

The Promise of His Glory gives proper readings and the following collect, and notes that this festival 'is observed in the Episcopal Church of the USA as a celebration parallel to that of the Conversion of St Paul. The two Apostles thus begin and close the week.'

> *Almighty God,*
> *who inspired your apostle Saint Peter*
> *to confess Jesus as Christ and Son of the Living God:*
> *build up your Church upon this rock,*
> *that in unity and peace*
> *it may proclaim one truth and follow one Lord,*
> *your Son our Saviour Jesus Christ,*
> *who is alive and reigns with you and the Holy Spirit,*
> *one God, now and for ever.*
>
> *(p. 363)*

Readings:
Ezek. 3.4–11 or Acts 4.8–13; Ps. 23; 1 Pet. 5.1–4; Matt. 16.13–19
Additional Psalms and Readings are indicated in PHG, p. 402; also for 18–25 Jan., Week of Prayer for Christian Unity, and Sunday in the Week.

Thursday 25 January *The Conversion of St Paul*
See sermon on p. 37 (Third Sunday of
Epiphany)

Friday 2 February *The Presentation of Christ in
the Temple* (Candlemass)
The Light of the World
*'When the day came, as laid down by the Law of Moses, the parents of
Jesus took him up to Jerusalem, to present him to the Lord' Luke 2.22
(ASB & BCP Gospel)*

Three Titles
In both our Prayer-Books (1662 and 1980) today is entitled 'The
Presentation of Christ in the Temple', reminding us how Joseph
and Mary brought the baby Jesus to the huge and magnificent
Temple – as the Gospel reading tells us – in accord with the Law
(Exodus 13,2,22 and 29) that every first-born son had to be offered
to God. The child could be 'redeemed' by the offering of an animal
for sacrifice – for the very poor, this meant the minimum, a pair
of pigeons or turtle-doves. Joseph and Mary came into this cate-
gory, and made their simple offering.

'Purification'
In the old Prayer-Book there is an alternative title – 'The Purification of St Mary the Virgin', thus making this day one of the
Festivals associated with our Lord's Mother, and also echoing the
name of a little-used Service (in our time) – Thanksgiving after
Child-birth. The mother would come to church and offer a lighted
candle as a token of her thanks, and also as a sign of restoration
into the community. This reminds us of the custom of setting-up
candles in the church and the carrying of them in procession, a
sign of rejoicing with Mary at the birth of her Son, and her coming
to the Temple of God to give thanks.

'Candlemass'
Our remembering this event, as we carry our candles round the
darkened church, should be a sign of our Christian profession;
we have passed from darkness to light, and we are to 'shine as

a light in the world to the glory of God the Father' as the Baptism Service tells us. Certainly Candlemass was a very popular service in mediaeval times, and the custom of putting up lighted candles in churches and homes long survived; remember that by early February everyone was very tired of the long cold nights and short bleak days of winter. Candlemass cheered people up, and brought to mind the promise of longer days and summer sunlight. And what a wonderful symbol of our Christian faith, when we 'pass on' the light of the candle-flame which can be 'given away' yet without ourselves losing anything of the light and warmth.

The Climax of Christmas
Today we have considerable attention focused on Candlemass in 'The Promise of His Glory', our Church's official book for the Season. It is seen as the climax of the Christmas cycle, and as pointing forward to Lent and Easter. It is as if we say, 'One last look back to Christmas, and now, turn toward the Cross!' Let this be the lesson we take away from the festival today.

Tuesday 19 March *St Joseph, husband of Our Lady* **A Good Man**
'Joseph, son of David, do not fear to take Mary your wife, for that which is conceived in her is of the Holy Spirit' Matthew 1,20 (ASB Gospel)

Known and Unknown
Many of the saints of God whose names are in the Church Calendar, have many facts about their lives well known, but with Joseph there is little – a surprise when we consider the important place he had as guardian of Mary and of Jesus, at least in the earlier years. The Gospels tell us that he received God's clear message and did as directed, but we do not know of the pain he had to carry, nor the fears that must have confronted him. The future must have loomed dark with almost incomprehensible choices ahead; it was not easy for Joseph to face the fact that an event had emerged from prophecy into his own everyday life. Pain and love must have merged with faith to carry the Mother and himself through the difficult months ahead.

A Refuge in Egypt

After the birth of Jesus, it required courage to set out with the young mother and the Babe, to the foreign country of Egypt. There were numerous Hebrew settlements and help would doubtless have been forthcoming; the Jewish people are all too well-trained in coping with dispossession, exile, threats and violence. On the family's return Joseph showed good sense in leaving Judaea and making a new home in Galilee, where Jesus could grow up in safety, and where a carpenter could make a decent living. No doubt he made a reasonable income; the estates and small farms that covered most of Galilee always needed farm implements, new or to be repaired; furniture of various sorts for better-off homes. No doubt Joseph worked from time to time for the army of occupation – axles, wheels, cages for prisoners, perhaps sometimes crosses.

The Son

No doubt Joseph was helped by another set of hands, beginning with half-play, half-work in the carpenter's shop, the pieces of wood – so handy for bricks to play with or build; the twists of strips from the plane; the tools and nails (overlooked without doubt by Joseph's sharp eye, to avoid scratches or wounds). A carpenter in those days required skill and patience. He does so today, but in the past the limited number of tools available, their simplicity, and the absence of electric power and other helps, made special demands. Often men reproduce the special qualities of their trade or profession in the other activities of their lives. Joseph would be a calm man, a careful worker, ready to listen to the demands or ideas of the customers, always concerned with the quality and strength of the materials available. Jesus doubtless took note of all these things, and many of his parables and stories reflect the days in the carpenter's shop and the meetings with stewards, farmers, local notabilities and others. Above all, perhaps, it was from Joseph that Jesus the child learnt what it means to call God 'father'.

Farewell . . .

The evangelists do not tell us the full story; Joseph drops quietly out of the picture. Tradition has it that he was an older man when he married, and that he died peacefully in the home at Nazareth some time before the final events in Jesus' life. His motto and epitaph may well be: 'A man of principle, obedient to God's call';

and we may fairly see him mirrored in the descriptions of the loving Father that Jesus gives – getting up at night to provide for the hungry stranger, hard-working and upright, but fair, like the owner of the vineyard in the parable.

Monday 25 March *The Annunciation of Our Lord to St Mary* **Grace**

'We beseech you, O Lord, to pour your grace into our hearts . . .' Collect, ASB

Full of Grace

Today we commemorate how God made known to a young Jewish girl that she was to be the mother of his Son; and how that girl accepted this tremendous and daunting task. 'Blessed' indeed we may call Mary; 'full of grace' or 'highly favoured' as the angel declared her – for if she had refused her agreement and co-operation, the plan of God for the redemption of this world of ours would never have gone ahead. No doubt, the Lord would have found some other way in which his purposes would have been accomplished – but for us, it is enough to know that Mary's 'Yes!' meant that the Incarnation could take place, and that the whole story of Christ and his saving life and work could be unfolded. What a wonderful event! and how precious and lovely is that obedience and self-dedication that Mary showed.

The Presence

We speak so casually of the presence of God. We assume things of it – that it is nice, that it is soothing, that it is encouraging and affirmative. Indeed, there are times when the presence of God is like this. But to describe the presence of God in this way, is like describing the ocean as calm, the wind as a whisper, the fire as warming. There can be terror in the presence of God. The fact that we may sometimes feel this terror, its demand, its vocation, its cost – is precisely how clear is the measure of our understanding of God.

For Mary, the Presence came: she was suddenly aware of it, aware of being encountered from an incalculable distance. Yet, it stood so near that she felt occupied by its gentle yet terrible energy.

The Response

But Mary knew that the reality around her, solid though it seemed, had been penetrated by a greater. She had felt the divine visitation, which in some way comes to us all. What had been asked of her was unique, and yet an echo of it reaches all of us, if only we have ears to hear. She had been asked to offer herself to the divine will, to become a servant of that will. She had said freely and fully, Yes. And nothing is ever the same again.

Thursday 25 April *St Mark the Evangelist*
See 'The Writer' for Easter 2 (Second Sermon) p. 105

Wednesday 1 May *SS Philip & James the Apostles* **Steadfast**

'I will guide you in the paths of wisdom, and lead you in upright ways'
Proverbs 4.11

Philip

Of the two saints commemorated today, St Philip was one of our Lord's earliest disciples. He showed something of the missionary spirit from the start, since he brought Nathanael to Christ. It would appear too, that he was of some importance amongst the apostles, since it was to him that Christ turned for help in the task of feeding the five thousand – 'Where are we to buy bread, so that these may eat?' (John 6.5) This seems to have been intended as some sort of test, though Philip's response is rather pointless, as there is certainly no bakery up there in the hills. At least Andrew does come forward with the lad and his fishes and loaves! Similarly, the question in today's gospel brings a gentle rebuke from Jesus, suggesting that Philip is slow in reaching useful conclusions.

Solid and Slow

Philip shows himself faithful, but slow in his practical responses; and perhaps also slow in heart and spiritual understanding. Many of us are like this – drawn to Christ, attracted to goodness and truth, yet living just on the verge of that knowledge which brings life eternal. God asks us to reflect and inquire, so that we may arrive at our conclusions, rather than simply accept all things as they come. If we are simply receptacles, we are not using God's gifts of choice and selection, nor in fact, are we stirring up the brains and thinking powers which the Lord has given us. No task should daunt us, nor should we allow the sheer magnitude of a problem to make us give up. We need both thought and action, to live fully useful lives.

A Relative of Jesus

The James who is commemorated today is the author of the 'Letter of James', which is printed immediately after the 'Letter to the Hebrews' in our New Testaments. James is referred to in Scripture as 'the Lord's brother' (Matt. 13.55, Galatians 1.19 etc). Who were our Lord's brothers? for others as well as James are mentioned (Matt. 12.46, Mark 3.31, Luke 8.19).

A theory popular in the past was that the word 'brother' really means 'cousin'; but this seems rather far-fetched in our time, and indeed St Jerome, who first suggested it, himself admitted it to be 'doubtful'.

Another suggestion is that the 'brothers' were children of Joseph and Mary, born after Jesus; but this is of course unacceptable to all who wish to believe in the perpetual virginity of the Mother of the Lord.

A view which would satisfy some is that the 'brothers' were sons of Joseph by an earlier marriage. This would explain why on the Cross Jesus commended his Mother to St John, and not to them.

It seems that our Lord's family were not entirely in favour of his preaching, and perhaps definitely opposed to him (St Mark 3.21, 31–35). It seems to have been after the Resurrection that James became a follower; tradition has it that he was killed at Jerusalem while Philip was martyred in Hierapolis in Asia Minor. The two saints appear in the Church Calendars on the same day, due to the historical accident of a church in Rome being dedicated on this day in the sixth century, with relics of both saints being presented to the treasury of the new building.

The Epistle of St James

What will strike the reader most about this work, is surely its simplicity. It has no theology, as do St Paul's letters, St John's

First Letter and even the First Letter of St Peter. James tells us simply what we must do and not do, to be a Christian; practical help, not just words; no snobbery. In other words, live out our faith in our daily lives, avoiding temptation and giving help and comfort wherever we can.

Tuesday 14 May *St Matthias the Apostle*
(BCP: 24 Feb.) Selection

'You have not chosen me; I have chosen you' John 15,16

The Young Church

We are given a fascinating picture of the young – indeed, infant – Church in the Book of the Acts of the Apostles (1,12–14)

First, in a room upstairs – perhaps the very room of the Last Supper – are met together the leaders, the Apostles, the original 'Twelve' (though now reduced to eleven by the defection and death of Judas). There is the group of women, including Mary the mother of Jesus. These are no doubt the same women who ministered to the Lord and to the disciples on their preaching missions, as we read in St Luke 8,2–3. Next there is the 'brotherhood' of about one hundred and twenty people, assembled outside.

Peter addresses them. He reminds them of the defection and death of Judas, and points out that they are now faced with a vacancy. He proposes that one of the men who had been with the apostolic band all the time, should now fill the empty place, and become with them a witness to the Resurrection (Acts 1,21–22).

So, already, we are presented with a considerable 'church' with its 'congregation' and its 'ministers' – already beginning to take a shape which looks familiar.

Casting Lots

The method of choosing by casting lots may seem strange to us, primitive and somewhat dubious; but it has its roots in the ancient Jewish system of 'Urim and Thummin' as we find in the Old Testament, e.g. 1 Samuel 14,14–42.

The High Priest carried about with him in a pouch on his breast, what the scholars tell us were probably black and white stones or counters – perhaps black on one side and white on the other. When ceremonially 'thrown', the results (presumably white for 'Yes' and black for 'No') were taken as the will of God for whatever problem or course of action had been suggested.

It seems strange to us in our day, but let us not forget that this part-election part-lottery had been preceded and accompanied by earnest prayer, and also that both candidates had known Jesus well, and had been close to him for some considerable time.

Faithful

Nothing further appears to be known about Matthias after his selection, and how he lived up to the great trust that the infant Church placed in him. He was indeed faced with a great responsibility and on the threshold of a great opportunity. He must stand as an example to us of those who – perhaps very unexpectedly – find themselves in positions of great responsibility, and proceed to give a good account of themselves.

Unknown and unsung – except to God – their faithful work has built up the Church and added a glory to the whole Body, even if the individual is lost in the general. We too, seeking the Holy Spirit's guidance and strength, will be enabled to do our duty in service and in sacrifice.

Sunday 19 May *The Wesleys – Saintly Brothers*
p. 120

Saturday 29 June *St Peter the Apostle (ASB – and St Paul)* **The Rock**

Jesus said to his disciples, Who do you say that I am? and Peter answered, You are the Christ of God. Luke 9.20 (ASB Introductory Sentence)

Failure . . .

In one way Peter is the easiest of all the saints of God to talk about; easy since of all the characters in the Bible, he seems to be the one with which most of us can easily identify. Oh, we all know the problems of failure; we all have failed our Lord Jesus in some way or another. We have all kept quiet when we might have spoken up; we have all tended to look the other way when things were difficult. Yes, we can all see – all too clearly – those characteristics we share with Peter; the ducking-out, the inability to stand up and be counted.

The Rock
Anyone less rock-like it would be hard to imagine; yet Simon son of Jonah – Jesus uses a pun for a nickname – Petros in Greek, Cephas in Aramaic; Peter in our English version of the Greek, 'The Rock'. Jesus is, as it were, commissioning Peter for a new look, a new life, in the future. But to call him the Rock seems extraordinary. Anyone less rock-like it would be hard to imagine. Peter the up-and-down man, more like it! We think of the times recorded in the Gospels when Peter just did not understand what Jesus was saying, or took it the wrong way. He could be so right – 'You are the Christ, the Son of the Living God!' yet next moment, 'Get thee behind me, Satan!'

Trust
Jesus trusted Peter, loved him and saw what was in him, perceived his potential. Trusted him even though he was untrustworthy; unable to stick with his promise made so vehemently – 'Lord, I am ready to go with you to prison and death!' but so soon to protest vehemently 'I do not know the man!' Yet later, on the beach beside the lake, we read how grieved Peter was, and to his Risen Lord he said, 'You know everything, you know that I love you!' And Jesus said to him, 'Feed my sheep.' It was to Peter that the other apostles clung, as to a standard on a battle-field; it was Peter who organize the little body of men and women into the Church; it was to Peter in Jerusalem that Paul, the great new figure who was to spread the Gospel message through the Roman Empire, came for advice and recognition (Galatians 1.18,19) before beginning his mission.

Triumph
Peter still had his ups and downs, but he was rock-like in his adherence to God and Christ Jesus the Son; he made mistakes and must often have been afraid. Yet God was able to use him to build the Kingdom, weaknesses and all – and he can do the same with us.

The Builder

*Paul and Cephas, the world, life and death, the present and the future,
all of them belong to you – yet you belong to Christ, and Christ to God.
(1 Corinthians 3,23)*

Contrast

How very different is Paul to Peter. His background, unlike Peter
who was a working man, a member of the fishing firm of
Zebedee, was that of a son of a well-to-do Pharisee family in the
prosperous city of Tarsus; educated, as we would say, to university level. As a Roman citizen, very conscious of the power and
culture of the Empire; his friends, no doubt, were among the
wealthy and influential of the land. As a promising man, to him
was entrusted the persecution of Christians, no doubt the first
eager step in rising to an important post in the Church of the
Hebrews.

All this he deliberately relinquished. To embrace the faith of
Christ meant to give up all hope of sympathy from family, friends
and faith; and in fact, as he said, to 'suffer the loss of all things'.
But so far from regretting this, he 'counted it as mere refuse',
that he might win Christ; he parted with evil – and in thus acting
set forth a proof of his unquestionable sincerity.

Not without difficulty, Paul was accepted by the infant Church
– St Barnabas played a prominent part in this (Acts 9.26 ff) – and
in due course Peter and James realized the immense worth of the
new figure. They agreed to a sharing of the work of spreading
the Gospel – Peter to continue working amongst the Hebrews
while Paul was to take the Gospel into Asia Minor, Europe and
the islands of the Mediterranean Sea.

Paul's word to all was, that in Christ Jesus God had not only
visited and redeemed his people, but had brought salvation to
all humanity, to every race and to every nation.

Paul's Message

Almost all the early converts to the Faith were from the Jews.
Yet in the providence of God all peoples have been swept into
the scheme of salvation, and we honour Paul and praise the God
who raised him up. 'He is a chosen instrument of mine, to carry
my Name before Gentiles and kings, and the children of Israel.'
(Acts 9.15)

Lord, you have founded your Church
on the strength of Peter and the wisdom
of Paul; taught by their examples, may
we combat error and unbelief, and from
them learn the fullness of the truths
of the gospel, as we praise you for
both, as lights of the world and founders
of the Church. Amen.

(from the Orthodox)

Wednesday 3 July *St Thomas the Apostle (BCP: 21 December)* **Loyalty**

'Thomas, called the Twin, said to his fellow disciples, 'Let us also go, that we may die with him' John 11,16

Loyalty
In St John's gospel we read the story of the shock and fear that overcame the disciples, when Jesus announced that he was intending to go to see Lazarus, the brother of Martha and Mary, at Bethany, where he lay ill.

Why the shock and fear?

Bethany was 'enemy territory' – the clergy and Pharisees, whose hatred and distrust of Jesus had risen to boiling point, would surely seize the opportunity to waylay 'The Preacher' and kill him off – for the sake of the Nation and the Faith, of course.

The disciples, fearing the worst, try to deter Jesus; but when it is obvious that whatever they say, he is going to go, Thomas comes out with his desperate loyalty 'Let us also go, that we may die with him!'

His loyalty, however, seems to have faded somewhat, since the awful events of Holy Week and Good Friday. Can we blame Thomas, again the practical man, thinking perhaps along the lines of 'It's all over now; the trumpets have been silenced, the great idea and the ideals have died away – why bother to meet?' So he misses the astonishing event, the appearance of the Risen Lord; and he, with his practical style, is not going to accept what the others tell him. 'No, I must see for myself, and touch his wounded hands, see the nail-holes, and see and touch his wounded side. If I can do that – well, I would believe indeed. But – not else.' And of course as we know, the Lord did appear, and Thomas did touch and did believe – with his great cry, which echoes down the centuries, 'My Lord – and my God!'

His loyalty was there. Let us follow his example, not swept away by the words of others, but in adoring love making his decision and voicing his thought, his belief and his faith.

Thomas' honest questioning and doubts, and the assuring response of Jesus to him, have given many Christians the courage to persist in faith, even when surrounded by questions and filled with doubts.

Tradition has it that Thomas went to India to preach the Gospel; and Francis Xavier in his journeys found on the Malabar Coast, a group of Christians who claimed that their Church had been founded by St Thomas, who had been speared to death near Madras.

Thursday 25 July *St James the Apostle* **The Martyr**

'About that time, Herod the king laid violent hands upon some who belonged to the Church. He killed James the brother of John with the sword' (Acts 12.1,2)

The Brother of John
From the family business of Zebedee, fishermen at the Sea of Galilee, Christ called two brothers, John and James. They left their homes and their trade at once, in obedience to the words of the Lord.

Apparently, James shared John's rather hot-headed disposition; and Jesus nicknamed the brothers 'Boanerges' (Sons of Thunder). But however blunt or even over anxious about who would get what positions of authority 'when the Day came' (Mark 10.35–45) they were, Jesus made them part of the 'inner circle', a specially privileged group picked by the Lord to be with him on particular occasions such as the rising of Jairus' daughter, the Transfiguration on the hill-top, and at the Garden of Gethsemane before the Lord's arrest.

Witnesses
The group comprised John, 'the disciple whom Jesus loved', James his brother, and Peter, the sometimes blustering and over-bearing apostle who could so easily become the heart-broken

betrayer of his Lord. Like us all, in our own particular ways, exuberant one moment, depressed and down in the doldrums the next. 'Can you drink of my cup? Can you be baptized with my baptism?' Easy to answer 'Yes!' when all seems to be going well – but a different story when the dark clouds threaten. How far would we – do we – really share the suffering, the strains, the difficulties, the pain that following Christ brings? It is no primrose path being a follower of Christ; as indeed James first, followed by Peter, found, as martyrs for the Faith.

The Shrine
According to Spanish tradition, the body of James was taken to Compostela, where his shrine in the magnificent cathedral has attracted pilgrims for centuries and is still a great centre of devotion. Under the name of Santiago de Compostela, the aid of St James was involved against the Moors in the Middle Ages; he was depicted as a warrior upon a white horse, beating down the enemy.

Saturday 21 September *St Matthew the Evangelist* **The Summons**
'Jesus saw Matthew at his seat in the custom-house; and he said to him, "Follow me." And Matthew rose and followed him' Matthew 9.9

The Call
In the Gospels we see how Christ called men to himself, and how, as they responded, he appointed them to their sphere of work for the Kingdom. He knew best how they could serve; he knew their characters and their circumstances, and appointed them where they could be most useful. One man was called to leave everything behind and go out to 'announce the kingdom of God' (Luke 9.60). The healed man with the name 'Legion' was told, 'Return to your home, and tell them how much God has done for you' (Luke 8.39). Matthew, or Levi as he is also called (Mark 2.14 and Luke 5.27) was called to entirely leave his past life and employment, and follow the Master.

The Answer
It seems likely that Matthew had heard Christ preach and teach; and in his own heart there must have been a revulsion against the business of doing the 'dirty work' of the Roman government by getting in – often with threats or bribery – the taxes imposed on the conquered people of Palestine. Lucrative the tax-gathering may have been, but it was a soul-destroying game. What is striking is not so much the change in his outward circumstances as the change in his inner life; and he is not afraid to witness to that change before his old friends and associates. He prepared a great feast in his house, with a large company of his old mates; and so in his own home and among his associates he bore witness to his changed life, due to his contact with the Lord. They knew what had been his life: yet he was renouncing all his shady tricks and underhand subterfuges. He wanted his friends to see and understand what the Lord had done for his soul.

The Life
We may feel that it would be better for us if we were not employed or working as we are. We may think that a different environment would help, or that a real change of employment would make all the difference. Outward things are important, but inward things are more important, as we see from Matthew's experience. If we want change, we have to make the change first in our hearts, our minds, and our wills.

Matthew repented of the past; he changed his mind on just about everything. And he acted on his mental decisions. If we will to make a change, in true discipleship, Christ will be at hand and the Spirit will give us strength and courage. If we are ready to follow his call, he will point the way, and indicate the life to which he intends us, and give us his strength to carry it through.

Friday 4 October *St Francis of Assisi*
'God has chosen the foolish things to confound the wise' 1 Corinthians 1.27, or, 'The wisdom of this world is foolishness with God!' 1 Corinthians 3.19, 'We are fools for Christ's sake' 1 Cor. 4.10

Fools for Christ's Sake
What does it mean to be a fool for Christ's sake?
I was struck by a headline in *The Times* last year:
'I Believe in God, not in Getting On!'

It was a summary of the line taken by a rather unpopular cleric at the time, the Archdeacon of York, who had just written a book *Affairs of State; Leadership, Religion and Society*. I have not read it, but judging by the publicity it must have made him even more unpopular.

Risking unpopularity, rejecting worldly values and ambition, making oneself vulnerable to ridicule, criticism and rejection – all these are things which are foolish in the eyes of the world. I do not usually agree with what the Archdeacon of York says, but I must respect him for having a go.

Popular . . .

Turning to somebody who is popular now, but rejected popularity in his lifetime – if you were asked who was the most popular saint today, across the whole spectrum of Christianity – admired too by non-Christians – your answers would probably be Francis of Assisi, whom we commemorate today. He was certainly a fool for Christ's sake: the son of a wealthy merchant, he gave up everything, abandoning and rejecting his inheritance and even his clothes. For, when Francis renounced his father's wealth, he actually removed all his clothes and stood naked in the market-place, until the bishop came forward, covered him with a cloak, and led him away to begin his life of holy poverty.

Identification

It is not surprising that Francis was one of the saints and mystics who were believed to bear on their hands and feet the 'Stigmata', the marks of the nails of crucifixion. He identified himself so closely with the one who – as St Paul writes to the Corinthians – 'Though he was rich, yet for your sakes he became poor, that ye through his poverty might become rich.'

That self-sacrifice – of one who could have been invulnerable, making himself vulnerable – is something we should meditate upon today. How can we embrace the foolishness of God in Christ?

Clowns

There are people who take it literally and call themselves 'Holy Fools' – priests who are clowns deliberately – and lay people too. They see this as a part of their Christian ministry, to dress up as clowns and perform, too. They help their fellow-Christians not to take themselves too seriously (a very valuable service) and they illustrate, in themselves, the wisdom of foolishness. That is not the way for all of us, but we can make the effort sometimes to remember that where the values of this world conflict with the values of the Gospel, the values of the Gospel are the ones for us to live by.

Risks
We can remember and demonstrate that, though it's difficult for those of us who are conformist by nature and upbringing, but vulnerable. Let us not be afraid of controversy, even becoming unpopular if necessary, risking criticism and ridicule if we have to.

'For we preach Christ crucified, unto the Jews a stumbling block and unto the Greeks foolishness, but unto them which are called, both Jews and Greeks, Christ the power of God, and the wisdom of God.' (1 Cor. 1.23,24)

'Because the foolishness of God is wiser than men; and the weakness of God is stronger than men.' (1 Cor. 1.25)

J.M.Y.

> Most high, omnipotent, good Lord,
> Grant your people grace to renounce gladly
> the vanities of this world;
> that, following the way of Blessed Francis,
> we may for love of you
> delight in your whole creation
> with perfectness of joy;
> through Jesus Christ our Lord,
> who lives and reigns with you
> and the Holy Spirit,
> one God, for ever and ever. Amen.
> (Lesser Feasts & Fasts, ECUSA)

Monday 28 October *SS Simon & Jude the Apostles* **Two Disciples**
'Keep yourselves in the love of God, looking for the mercy of our Lord Jesus Christ unto eternal life' The Letter of Jude, v.21

Apostles

The Gospels only tell us that Simon was one of the apostles, and that he was called 'The Zealot' (or perhaps nicknamed – Jesus was fond of giving his friends nicknames, like 'The Rock' for Peter, or 'Sons of Thunder' for the brothers James and John). It is also possible that Simon had been a member of the Jewish extremist group, the 'Zelotes', who might well be compared with the IRA for their brutal murders and cruelty. If this were so, it is a tribute to the remarkable powers of Jesus, and his love, that he could retain men of such differing beliefs and actions as Matthew, the one-time collaborator and taxman for the Romans, and Simon, the bitter opponent. Jude is mentioned by John in his gospel, as putting a question to Jesus at the Last Supper – 'Lord, how is that you will manifest yourself to us, and not to the world?' Jesus replies to the effect that whoever loves him will keep his word, 'and my Father will love him, and we will come to him and make our home with him' (John 14.22). Luke mentions Jude as the son of James the Greater (6.16). Tradition supposes that Simon and Jude took the Gospel to Persia. In the Western Church, it is thought that they were both martyred; in the East, however, Simon is thought to have died peacefully at Edessa, and Jude either at Beirut or Edessa.

The Message of Jude

St Jude writes as 'the servant of Jesus Christ' and 'Christ's bond-slave, bought with a price. He appeals' to those who are called, beloved in God the Father and kept for Jesus Christ' to 'contend for the faith one for all delivered to the saints.' He condemns certain 'ungodly persons' who 'are blemishes on your love-feasts, as they boldly carouse together' – presumably they misbehaved at the agapes or fellowship meals, which in the early Church often occurred in association with the Eucharist. St Paul comments on the difficulties that could occur (1 Cor. 11, 17–22) and makes a clear distinction between the agape and the Lord's Supper. Jude makes a call to the people he is writing to, 'to build yourselves up on your most holy faith; pray in the Holy Spirit; keep yourselves in the love of God; wait for the mercy of our Lord Jesus Christ unto eternal life.'If the Church of Christ is to be holy and acceptable to God it will not be because it is the home of a lifeless orthodoxy, but because the Faith so earnestly cherished is displayed in lives of beauty and holiness.

He ends with a lovely blessing and commendation:

Now to him who is able to keep you from falling,
and to present you without blemish
before the presence of his Glory, with rejoicing,
to the only God,
Our Saviour through Jesus Christ our Lord,
be glory, majesty, dominion and power,
before all time, and now, and for ever.
Amen.

Friday 1 November *All Saints' Day*
The Communion of Saints

I began to praise those who had stood valiantly for the Name of the Lord;
then the angel said to me, 'Go, tell my people how great and many are
the wonders of the Lord.' 2 Esdras 2.47,48 (ASB Reading)

The Cloud of Witnesses

'While many of us think of the Saints as examples of 'virtuous
and godly living' this hardly does justice to the Biblical insight,
that in our pilgrimage through this world we are surrounded by
'so great a cloud of witnesses'. Sanctity is not so much about
hero-worship, as about accessibility. The Saints are the men and
women of every age in whose lives we can glimpse heaven in
our midst. They are our partners in prayer.'

That is an extract from the Introduction to *The Promise of His
Glory*, an excellent and authorized book of services for our Church
of England, first published in 1991.

It is followed by a short poem by Richard Baxter, the evangelical
pastor (1615–91)

Before the throne we daily meet
As joint petitioners to thee;
In spirit each the other greet,
And shall again each other see.

The Communion of Saints

These two passages well sum up what is meant in the Apostles'
Creed, by the phrase 'The Communion of Saints'. That clause,
which is included in both the Creeds we use at Morning and

Evening Prayer, is one which we can surely all say joyfully and whole-heartedly and fervently. The Communion of Saints consists of all the people down the ages, and including our own times, who have loved and served God, who have tried to follow and obey the commandments of God, and have tried to love and serve their neighbours, whoever those neighbours might be.

For some this has been at great cost, at the cost of life itself in many cases. These we call the martyrs – we are not all called to be martyrs, but we are all called to love and to serve. So it is, indeed, that the Communion of Saints consists – dare we say? of us also, of you and of me. We are all pilgrims, on our way to the Kingdom, we hope and pray and strive; a great company of people of all races and all types and all ages surrounded by a great cloud of witnesses (Hebrews 12,1) that is, the saints in heaven who look down and cheer us on, like a crowd at a great athletic contest, encouraging the competitors. We are surrounded by an unseen host of people, on our pilgrimage; all are partners in prayer and supplication, anxiously supporting us by their callings at the Throne of Grace. Known or unknown, they are our helpers and inspirers in whatever troubles and trepidations come upon us.

The Beatitudes
Jesus, in his Sermon on the Mount, tells us that the people most greatly blessed are often those who are deprived of many of the things we enjoy. Those without resources, without money, without decent or plentiful food, in poor living conditions, slums, 'Cardboard Cities', unpopular because of race or religion, depressed and degraded. Jesus turns worldly values upside down; most of us find this 'a hard saying' – hard to understand and hard to live by.

Not right . . .
What Jesus is saying in these 'Beatitudes' is not that it is right for people to be hungry or poor or persecuted – far from it – but rather that those in such kinds of situations are less cluttered than those who have plenty. He is saying that we all need to keep ourselves uncluttered by over-dependence on material things, or on other people's opinions of us; that we need to take a firm stand against wanting power for ourselves, and the tendency to think ourselves superior to the rest of creation.

The Saints we are celebrating today are people who have been able to become uncluttered, to keep themselves 'unspotted by the world', so that in this way God's love and grace have been able to reach them at a deep level; that God's light is able to shine through them and enlighten those about them.

They did not all start uncluttered – think of St Peter, who so often put his foot in it, and indeed even denied Our Lord in the hour of greatest need; think of St John and St James, over-ambitious for glory at the very moment Jesus tells them he is soon to die; St Mary Magdalen and her life of sin; St Francis, lover of animals and nature, who threw aside his very clothes so as to start life anew; and so one could go on.

To Define a Saint . . .

A small child was asked to give a definition of 'A Saint' in Sunday School. She looked up at a stained glass window – it must have been a window by Comper, or else Martin Travers, both artists who could use colour well, and avoid clutter and congestion – and the child said: 'A Saint is someone who lets the light through.'

That seems a very good definition, a very good way of putting it. A Saint is someone who is completely him- or herself, with the gifts, or talents, or just the personality that God designed them to be; certainly an individual with all the character and the quirks that make an individual, yet at the same time transparent to God, letting the light of the Eternal One shine through.

Let us pray that we too may become transparent to God, people who let the light shine through; beacons and witnesses for God's kingdom of love and truth, of hope and of righteousness.

Saturday November 2nd *Commemoration of the Faithful Departed (All Souls' Day)*
Life for the World

Jesus said, 'I am the resurrection and I am life' John 11.25

Sadness and Mourning . . .

The death of someone we have known and loved is bound to bring sadness and grief.

Jesus was a frequent visitor to the house at Bethany, where lived the two sisters, Martha and Mary, and their brother Laza-rus. It must have been a peaceful oasis in the midst of the busy life the Lord followed, the teaching and preaching, the constant arguments and discussions – sometimes carefully faked up by his opponents, sometimes the sheer inability of good honest people to see any further than the hidebound arguments parrotted from the local rabbi. Above all, perhaps, the constant crowds, the importunate people in need, in sickness, with problems, with questions – hardly a moment's peace. At the house of the sisters and the brother, Jesus found quietness, companionship, consideration, release from pressure.

When Lazarus became sick, then died, Jesus did not come at once; it was some days, we are told, before he made the effort and arrived. He was 'deeply moved and troubled'. When someone we love dies, the shared companionship, the voice, the laughter, the personal quirks and foibles, the special character have gone; an emptiness of spirit is left and a deep sadness. Now the loved one can only be a memory preserved in our minds, aided perhaps today by photographs and videos; a recorded voice, souvenirs and tokens.

Consolation and Hope

Mary and Martha knew the sorrow and desolation of the death of their brother, and it was to them that some of the most beautiful and comforting words in the whole of the New Testament were spoken by Christ.

'I am the resurrection and the life. If a man has faith in me, even though he die, he shall come to life; and none who is alive and has faith shall ever die.'

As Christians, we have the supreme consolation of Christ's words. We know from them that death is not an end, only a beginning. It is the opening of a door, the tearing down of a partition. Those who mourn are sad; the loved one is not. If death were complete extinction, we might well feel near to despair. But this is not what death is; and we know that Christ is waiting for those whom we love.

There is every reason to mingle with our sadness, the consolation of our faith.

Christ is All

Christ is all and is in all, says St Paul. (Col. 3,11)

Let us then have faith and trust. We must all die, but Christ is there before us. As he said to his disciples, 'I go to prepare a place for you.' He rose from the dead that we might rise with him; the Easter story teaches us that death is the beginning of a wonderful happiness, which nothing can take away from us, for we too can rise with Christ.

> *'And now we give you thanks because through him*
> *you have given us the hope of a glorious resurrection;*
> *so that, although death comes to us all,*
> *yet we rejoice in the promise of eternal life;*
> *for to your faithful people, life is changed,*
> *not taken away;*
> *and when our mortal flesh is laid aside,*
> *an everlasting dwelling-place is made ready for us in heaven.'*
> *(ASB, p. 333)*

The Lover of Souls

O God, the God of the spirits of all flesh, in whose embrace all creatures live, in whatsoever world or condition they be, we beseech Thee for those whose names and dwelling-place and every need Thou knowest. Lord, grant them light and rest, peace and refreshment, joy and consolation in Paradise, in the companionship of Saints, in the presence of Christ, in the ample folds of thy great love.

Grant that their lives may unfold in thy sight and find a sweet employment in the spacious fields of eternity. If they have ever been harmed by any unhappy deed or word of ours, we pray Thee of thy great pity to heal and restore them, that they may serve Thee without hindrance.

If in any way we can minister to their peace, be pleased of thy love to let this be; and mercifully keep us from every act which may deprive us of the sight of them as soon as our trial time is over, or mar the fullness of our joy when the end of the day has come.

Pardon, O gracious Lord and Father, whatever is amiss in these our prayers, and let thy will be done; for our wills are blind and erring, but thine is able to do exceeding abundantly above all that we ask or think; through Jesus Christ our Lord.

Remembrance Sunday (10 November 1996)
'The Healing of the Nations'

'Down the middle of the city's street is the river of the water of life; on either side of the river stood a tree of life. The leaves of the trees are for the healing of the nations.' Rev. 22,1–2

An Act of Love

To remember the departed is in itself an act of love; just as to forget them is a failure of love. To remember in prayer – especially in the setting of the Eucharist – is to bring our act of love into union with God's love for them. Secondly, it is an affirmation of our recognition that we are still in communion with them, an inevitable but true and real communion.

Understandable

This is understandable, in more or less degree, to us, according to our beliefs and hopes in life, in its possibilities and in its very nature. Those who have departed this life in the faith of Christ, who we know by their affirmations and their faith, to have been members of that sacred Body when on earth, we are surely confident that we and they share in a mystical fellowship which death does not, and cannot, destroy.

Again, those with whom we have had an intimate bond of love or affection, must also be sharers in that fellowship, and with them we too know that the spiritual Christ encloses and holds them, with us, in one communion and bond that cannot be broken.

All Souls are in the Hand of God

But this Remembrance Sunday, by its very name and import, forbids us to put any limit to the all-embracing love and mercy of God. It is merely that we – poor limited human minds that we are, unable to comprehend the mercy and love of the Creator towards his creation – have greater grounds of confidence in the eternal destiny of some rather than others.

But it is in the true and ancient principle of standing against evil, that we honour our dead today, commend their souls to God's loving care and mercy. Those we remember on Remembrance Sunday have a special claim on our remembrance, because they died for us; all in the common cause against dictatorship, against the imposition of fearful penalties and cruelties, against brutality and against injustice and repression of all kinds.

Whether we are of their generation or of the younger one, it is in no way false to describe their sufferings, their wounds and their deaths as truly sacrificial.

Instruments of Freedom
Above all, we remember them bearing in our minds the fact that their deaths and sufferings were instrumental in permitting us to live in freedom, free to say and to do what we wish – within civilized limits – and above all free to worship and to follow the Christ, who by his sacrifice and death on the cruel scaffold of the Cross, won for the whole world redemption and the hope of God's kingdom of peace and joy, love and happiness.

In that suffering, obedience and sacrifice, all human pains and hopes, ideals and noble strivings are summed up. As far as we can place our hope, our confidence and trust in God, we gain inward peace; if all nations of humanity would do the same, there could be not only outward peace on this tiny, spinning Earth, this little speck in the vastness of space, but a sharing of inward peace also.

An Act of Commitment

Lord God our Father,
we pledge ourselves
to serve you and all humanity,
in the cause of peace,
for the relief of want and suffering,
and for the praise of your name.

Guide us by your Spirit;
give us wisdom;
give us courage;
give us hope;
and keep us faithful
now and always. Amen.

(The Promise of His Glory, p. 87)

Harvest Thanksgiving
Realities and Illusions

'Life means more than food, and the body more than clothing' Luke 12.23
(An ASB Gospel)

Three-D Pictures

Waiting my turn at the barbers, I flicked through a Sunday magazine and stopped at a page densely covered with curious markings, a bit like a concentrated Paisley design in black and white. At the foot of the page it said that if it was looked at in a rather complex, almost cross-eyed way, a three-dimensional object would appear. Not for me it won't, I thought. But to my astonishment it did. From within the design there appeared, first gradually and then firmly, the distinct shape of a motor car with windows, bumper bars and everything else, so 3D that it looked as though it was driving out of the page towards me. Optical illusion, I thought. But then I pondered: which was the illusion and which was the reality; the innocuous patterned page or the 3D picture. I am tempted towards the 3D picture as the reality because the car did undoubtedly appear to my eyes. But – can I trust what I seem to see . . .

Trying to discover which is real and what is illusion is an age old problem which I will put into biblical terms. (You can read the story in the Second Book of Kings, chapter 6.)

Elisha, the prophet, was being hunted down by the King of Syria and decided to rest overnight in the safety of the little town of Dothan. The next morning, his young servant got up first and went outside. He looked and was terrified because the little town was surrounded by the Syrian army – horsemen, chariots, siege equipment: the lot. He rushed to Elisha in panic and cried out 'Master, what shall we do?' And Elisha's answer must have seemed silly and unreal. 'Don't be afraid,' he said, 'we have more on our side than they have on theirs.'

The Eyes of Faith

Then Elisha prayed that the boy's eyes would be opened; his prayer was answered and the young man saw what Elisha had seen all the time. The Syrian army was still there, strong and menacing; but around and beyond and above was the vast army of the living God, with horses and chariots of fire, all around Elisha. Now, the young man saw differently because he looked through the eyes of faith.

The obvious question is: which of them saw things as they really were? Elisha, or the young man before the prayer? Was it that the boy had been seeing the situation as it really was, whereas Elisha had been dreaming and his vision was only wishful thinking: or was it that the boy had only seen things as they seemed to be, whereas Elisha had seen things the way they really were? Which was the illusion? Which was the reality?

There is no doubt that the story was told to answer that very question and to answer it emphatically; that the real world is not the world as it appears to be. It demonstrates that faith sees the world differently, but sees it correctly. Before his eyes were opened, the lad saw things only as they appeared to be.

The same question confronts us. Which is the real world; the one which we see in the same way as everyone sees, or the one we see through the eyes of faith? When we see the Church surrounded by powerful forces of unbelief and indifference, the question cannot be avoided.

The Answer

The Bible's answer, time and time again, is that the real world is the one like that which Elisha saw, the one which is visible to the eye of faith.

And it is a serious question because only a minority of us now believe, or behave as though we believe, that God provides the food we eat and all else that sustains body and soul. The evolution of farming methods and the ingenuity used in production, packaging and transport lead people to believe in man and the supermarket; and not unreasonably so, because that is the way it seems. We can become so accustomed to accepting things at face value that we lose the perception to see the mystery that lies behind the obvious.

The world as it appears to be to us, is one in which we are rich even though we may not care to admit it. We are one of the seven richest nations on earth. We have our problems! Some of our people have hardly enough money to buy the food they need. Some seem grossly overpaid. Many of us resent out taxes. We produce food so efficiently that the European Commission is paying farmers to leave some of their land idle. We have problems of distribution, of fair shares. Overall, we are still very rich. Sadly, there are far too many in our world who are very poor; many afflicted by famine and disease, much of it caused by a lust for power and civil wars of shocking barbarity. We are very rich and there are these disturbing problems, and we wish the food mountains could be given to the poor in this and every land where there is need. But we know, because it is so obvious in the world as it appears to be, that *we* can't do anything about it; only governments can, and given the right governments the problems ought to go away, but don't seem to.

That is just a glimpse of what appears to be.

What happens if we look at our world picture with the eyes of faith?

Eyes of Faith

Seen through the eyes of faith the world is just the same; it doesn't change, the facts remain. Riches, famine and war are still there, undeniably. But it is we who change. Through the eyes of faith we see it all in a new perspective. Through the eyes of faith we see that despite human failings it is a beautiful world, full of colour and light, revolving on its axis, precariously, audaciously, in the nothingness of space without any apparent means of support, but secure in the hand of its Creator.

We will see the wonder of growth in little simple things; the one superbly formed flower, and the little weed that thrusts up through a town pavement, as well as in the loaf of bread and the stacked shelves of the supermarket.

We will know that it is not a grey world of dismal expectation, but a beautiful world. We will see in the fields of grain that the Lord does indeed multiply bread in the miracle of life and growth.

And we will see that life is stronger than death: that beauty surpasses ugliness and that kindness and grace are more powerful than evil.

Joy, Hope and Certainty

Amongst the real perplexity and the real sorrow, we will find also the beat of joy and hope and certainty; and all because we comprehend the greatest of all harvest hopes, that Christ is the first fruits of 'those who slept', and that he embraces our world with the power of his love, his wonder and his grace. We will see a world which is fallen – but redeemed.

Which is the real world and which is the illusion?

If we think that through the eyes of faith we see the world correctly, then no doubt the gratitude so evident in our lives will help others to see the same.

P.R.

Dedication Festival (which may be observed on the first Sunday in October if the actual date is unknown)

'My house shall be called a house of prayer' Matthew 21.13 (ASB)

Inspiration

We live in an enchanted world. It is full of beauty and wonder, fascinating in its vastness, its variety, and its promise, and all that it means to us. Perhaps we find it almost impossible to see it that way, when we are confronted with the terror and ugliness of so many of the things that happen in our tormented world; when all that is evil and wrong seems so formidable and mammoth and beyond our control.

Yet we all enjoy the best in our experience of living; we all sense something of the faith and hope and love which lead us on. The poets, the creative artists and the saints of all ages, have helped us more than anyone else to know that this is not a blind instinct. The psalm writer of long ago was able to see that 'The heavens declare the glory of God; and the firmament shows his handiwork.' For him, as for the saints, the enchantment of the world comes from the conviction that our world is a sphere of God's creative activity.

Meaning

Even with the poets and the artists, who may be less confident to trace their vision to its source, or explicitly to name it, there appears the same sense of the eternal and perfect order which gives meaning to this world of time. Blake was able to describe the poet's vision as one which makes it possible:

> *'To see a world in a grain of sand*
> *And heaven in a wild flower;*
> *Hold infinity in the palm of your hand*
> *And eternity in an hour.'*

There is a good deal to support the claim that those who have so penetrated beyond the world of sense, beyond the scope of reason and intellect, are the ones who have most fully lived; for they are the inspired people, the people of vision and of faith.

Moreover, those who have done most to alleviate the world's

needs and to heal its pains are not the 'tycoons, the captains of industry, the demagogues, the conquerors, but the starveling poets, the derided geniuses, the quiet lovers of wisdom, the humble saints and hidden mystics.'

Dedication

So I ask you to remember with me, on this our Dedication Festival, not only great leaders whose names we revere, but also the many unrecorded worshippers whose faith and prayer and love has gone to hallow this place, and to declare in their lives that the world is the sphere of God's creative work.

In our collect today we give God humble thanks for the fellowship of all who have used this church in its past years (since its Dedication in . . .) Then we go on to pray that those who seek God here, may find him. This is not only a prayer for ourselves, but for all who will come to worship here in the days ahead of us. It is a prayer which should also suggest the obligation which is ours, to make this fellowship one in which God is truly known; a fellowship which encourages and supports.

Future

So may we worship together, so may we pray and so may we live, that God's way may be more clearly known and seen – creating, restoring, leading and loving in this world which is so truly His.

H.H.

God our Father,
we thank you for this house of prayer
in which you bless your family on our pilgrimage.
So quicken our consciences by your holiness,
nourish our minds by your truth,
purify our imaginations by your beauty,
and open our hearts to your love,
that, surrendering our wills to your purpose,
the world may be renewed in Christ Jesus our Lord.

Prayers for Use at the Alternative Services
David Silk

Reflections from Bosnia *Alison Butcher*

'O my God, enlarge our hearts and facilitate the task we face. Take the stammer from our speech, that the people may understand what we tell them.' A prayer from the Koran, the petition of Moses before the great task of leading the people out of captivity and misery, to a new life; I have been learning a little of the Muslim way of life and of prayer, during my time in Bosnia.

Trust
Back here, in church at Pentecost we heard of the trust we must have if we are to risk a new journey, a new growth in ourselves, and of the gifts which will help us all along the way. We echo St Peter's words from the New Testament Reading: 'God gave them no less a gift than he gave us when we put our trust in the Lord Jesus Christ; then how could I possibly stand in God's way' (Acts 11.17).

While you were celebrating here, we were joining you in worship in Bosnia, through the medium of a Muslim call to prayer. Here is what happened.

After a long day in the front line of the war, working in the refugee camps, Annabel – another nurse – and I were returning to Tuzla with Niera our translator. The stresses of the day – the desperate overcrowding, the abject poverty, the loss and fear in the eyes of the women; also our constant alert for snipers, mines and bandits – despite our flak jackets and helmets – wore us down. Yet, that evening, the balance was redressed by an invitation to a party. There was food and drink, good company and music. We danced as never before – out there you know you may not be alive to dance again – and in the meantime, it was good to thank the Lord for the gift of life.

The Call
Later, Annabel and I walked home in quiet companionship. As we climbed up the steep deeply rutted stony track leading from town, the night of Pentecost was perfectly and beautifully still, except for the chirping of the crickets in the balmy, scented air. Suddenly, the silence was pierced by the chant of a *muezzin* calling to prayer from the mosque. I have rarely heard anything so beautiful – or felt so close in companionship and prayer to all that lay around, both near and far. Then, the chant was echoed further down the valley on the other side of town, by another

muezzin calling from another mosque. We stood in humble silence and prayed – while our spirits soared.

We knew all too well that within an hour, when dusk had fallen, the peace would be shattered by the piercing screams of shells, by artillery fire, by the puncturing rattle of machine guns, the wailing of air raid sirens – and of children. Predictably it was so . . .

And God?
So where is God in all this? Is he in the prayer – or in the place? We know he lives within each one of us, and is in each situation; he is there in all that happens, but how can we recognize him? I believe he comes to us through the gifts of faithfulness and trust that we receive, so freely offered. For instance, each day we set out on our journey of aid, from the house of the lady we stayed with in Tuzla, never knowing what the day would bring. Every night when we returned, hungry and exhausted, always we found a small offering of food for each of us laid out on the kitchen table. Every night our beds were ready, covers turned down, to receive our tired bodies. Each morning this lady would pray – and each night we would return; what a gift of friendship, and trust, and faith. So our days continued, sharing in the lives of the Muslim, Orthodox and Catholic peoples of Bosnia. For we are told 'God gave *them* no less a gift than he gave to us, when we put our trust in him.'

Prayer
I prayed more in Bosnia than I've ever prayed before. Only afterwards did I realize that I never felt angry about the death and destruction there, but in my head I found myself singing as we passed the bombed-out houses and villages –

> *'Dear Lord and Father of Mankind*
> *Forgive our foolish ways.'*

In those two lines lies the future of Bosnia – and of us all: the need for forgiveness. There will be no other solution. The arming of men and the division of nation from nation will never resolve the conflict. The next generation of fighters are already on their way – in the games the children play daily, as soldiers with their toy guns. I never knew what pacifism meant until I held a bullet in my hand! Now I know it is about bringing up our children in the spirit, and with the gifts, of God. How many of us have given children gifts of guns and weapons of destruction at Christmas and at birthdays? My prayer continuously is – If we love the world, then don't give the children violence as a gift!

Help

Give as the Lord giveth. I saw him daily there in Bosnia – as I was privileged to see in my work the agony and suffering, I saw the true Cross of Christ at Mejugore sharing in the pain of his people. But I also saw the gifts of hope and joy – and a future. Three and a half years ago we 'travelled barefoot' to Romania; and through that act of faith Romania is growing. Now Bosnia is occupying a part of my life – and Albania hopefully is to follow. We shall be setting up a new charity, to do the work we have been doing, but with a remit more firmly based on teaching and training in health needs. We shall be working in places you have heard of already – Ionaseni and Podriga – our hospitals in Romania, and then Bosnia and Albania. It is all possible with your gifts. In Jesus' hands, small gifts were used to work miracles; will you help with yours?

Support for this work is needed, and will be much appreciated. Contact Alison Butcher at 20 Salisbury Mansions, St Ann's Road, Harringay, London N15 3JP Tel: 0181-809-7134.

(Based on a sermon given in St Mary's Church, Primrose Hill, London NW3)

INDEX OF SUBJECTS

HYMNS & VERSES

Simply Preaching
A Programme for Clergy and Readers
Lewis G. Higdon

Foreword by Archbishop George Carey

Covers sermon preparation, delivery, and afterwards, together
with suggestions for preaching on special occasions.

ISBN 1-85311-106-6   £7.95

Like a Two-Edged Sword
– The Word of God in Liturgy and History
Martin Dudley (Editor)

Essays in Honour of Canon Donald Gray. Contributions by
twelve distinguished liturgical scholars concerning the word
of God.

ISBN 1-85311-115-5   £9.95

Encounters for Unity
G. R. Evans, Lorelei F. Fuchs, Diane C. Kessler (Editors)

Contributions drawn from all over the world help record the
excitement in the period after the Second Vatican Council.
Includes prayers as starters for discussion groups and ecumenical
meetings.

ISBN 1-85311-096-5   £11.95

(plus 10% p&p. in UK: overseas postage on request)

The Canterbury Press Norwich
The book publishing imprint of Hymns Ancient and Modern Limited
ST MARY'S PLAIN, NORWICH, NORFOLK, NR3 3BH
Telephone: (01603) 616563 and 612914   Fax: (01603) 624483

Approaching Light
Paul Iles

A collection of readings and prayers for use in Advent and throughout the Christmas season, which will help to develop and strengthen our openness to God and our knowledge of his presence with us in Christ.

ISBN 1-85311-100-7   **£4.95**

Intercessions at the Eucharist
Raymond Chapman

Part One suggests prayers for Festivals and Church Seasons, and Part Two for Sundays, following the ASB themes of The Church, The World, The Community, The Suffering, The Departed. Many who are asked to lead the intercessions at the Eucharist will find this a helpful booklet.

ISBN 1-85311-108-2 (New Edition)   **£3.50**

Daily with God
John Pitchford

Foreword by Bishop Mark Santer. 'A wealth of new prayers . . . combines practicality and spirituality admirably in this lovely book.'   *– The Reader*

ISBN 1-85311-028-0 boards, 2 ribbon markers   **£8.50**

The Joy of Jesus – Humour in the Gospels
Richard Buckner

Illustrated by Phil Densham

The author, who was chaplain at four famous schools, shows us how Jesus used various types of humour, ranging from pure absurdity to subtle irony, from riddles to amusing parables. He brings us a smile that radiates good humour, compassion, fellowship, serenity and love.

ISBN 1-85311-067-1   **£3.50**

(plus 10% p&p. in UK: overseas postage on request)

The Canterbury Press Norwich
The book publishing imprint of Hymns Ancient and Modern Limited
ST MARY'S PLAIN, NORWICH, NORFOLK, NR3 3BH
Telephone: (01603) 616563 and 612914   Fax: (01603) 624483